Human Rights around the World

Recent Titles in the
CONTEMPORARY WORLD ISSUES
Series

Advertising in America
Danielle Sarver Coombs

Cyber Warfare
Paul J. Springer

Extremism in the Police
Carla Lewandowski and Jeff Bumgarner

The U.S. Criminal Justice System
Sarah Koon-Magnin and Ryan J. Williams

Women and Girls in STEM Fields
Heather Burns Page

Remote Learning and Distance Education
William H. Pruden III

Religious Belief and Science
Glenn H. Utter

Child Welfare in America
Yvonne Vissing

Water in the West
Jacqueline Vaughn

Teen Runaways in America
Michele Wakin

Electronic Waste
Josh Lepawsky

Youth Activism
Hava Rachel Gordon

Extreme Weather and Climate Change
Mariangelica Groves

Black Lives Matter
Shaonta' Allen, Simone N. Durham, and Angela Jones

Human Rights around the World

A Reference Handbook

Yvonne Vissing

BLOOMSBURY ACADEMIC
NEW YORK • LONDON • OXFORD • NEW DELHI • SYDNEY

BLOOMSBURY ACADEMIC
Bloomsbury Publishing Inc, 1359 Broadway, New York, NY 10018, USA
Bloomsbury Publishing Plc, 50 Bedford Square, London, WC1B 3DP, UK
Bloomsbury Publishing Ireland, 29 Earlsfort Terrace, Dublin 2, D02 AY28, Ireland

BLOOMSBURY, BLOOMSBURY ACADEMIC and the Diana logo are trademarks of Bloomsbury Publishing Plc

First published in the United States of America 2026

Cover image: Supporters of China's Muslim Uighur minority hold torches and placards of people allegedly killed in China's 're-education camps' on December 20, 2019 during a demostration at Fatih in Istanbul. Photo by OZAN KOSE/AFP via Getty Images.

A catalog record for this book is available from the Library of Congress.

ISBN: HB: 979-8-7651-2003-3
ePDF: 979-8-7651-2006-4
eBook: 979-8-7651-2005-7

Series: Contemporary World Issues

Typeset by Integra Software Services Pvt. Ltd.
Printed and bound in the United States of America

For product safety related questions contact productsafety@bloomsbury.com.

Contents

Preface

Human rights have been a guiding force in the establishment of a humane world. What are human rights, and why are they important? These questions frame this book and provide readers with detailed information about what human rights are and how they have evolved from the past to today. Human rights have the potential for creating justice, peace, and harmony between individuals and among nations. However, in many ways throughout the world, human rights are under attack. At the macro or system level, wars, conflicts, terrorism, torture, and inequality fester and jeopardize the future of nations and the world. At the micro or individual level, interpersonal violence and discrimination oppress certain groups of people more than others. Hunger, poverty, homelessness, and obstacles to receiving equal education, access to healthcare, and justice within police and legal systems prevail. Demographic characteristics, such as one's gender, race, ethnicity, religion, age, and social class, limit people's health, wellbeing, and opportunities.

Chapter 1 provides a background of what human rights are and how the field has evolved over time. Chapter 2 discusses some of the main issues in the field, focusing on key problems and controversies and discussing some solutions to address them. In Chapter 3, five experts in the field share their perspectives about what is going on around the world with respect to human rights—and what they think needs to happen. Chapter 4 provides profiles of key people who have contributed to the development of human rights around the world and across time. It also profiles major human rights organizations, which readers may find helpful in guiding them toward further research. Primary documents are showcased in Chapter 5, including human rights treaties, such as the Universal Declaration of Human Rights, and testimonies from people warning of threats to human rights in various places around the world. Chapter 6 contains even more resources, while Chapter 7 gives a historical chronology of human rights events. A Glossary and Index round out the book.

This book provides readers with a historical framework for understanding what has happened in the past to promote, or inhibit, the integration of human rights into our governments and social systems. It seeks to address the issue that many people do not actually know what human rights are, why they are important, or how to use them. It is our hope that this book will give the concepts, resources, and skills necessary to embed a human rights framework into our minds, our work, and our social institutions.

Appreciation is given to Kevin Hillstrom at Bloomsbury Publishing, and to Taylor Autiello and Eric Knudsen, my graduate students, who helped me craft this book. To all those human rights defenders, past, present, and future, I thank you for using your life, gifts, time, and talents to make the world a better place. How we think, how we speak to and about others, and even the little things we do have a big impact. Let us remember that wisdom and loving kindness are more powerful than violent words and self-interested actions.

1

Background and History

Human rights are an important concept for organizing social interactions and the functioning of social systems. They are an ancient idea and found throughout the world in a variety of forms. As a practice, social institutions, like government, courts, schools, or healthcare, have often been structured to protect people's rights. Human rights have been foundational to the creation and maintenance of global and national social orders. The United Nations and other organizations have been instrumental in codifying what human rights are and how they should be implemented for the betterment of both individuals and societies. This is why human rights education is vital—people cannot be rights-respecting if they do not know what human rights are, why they are important, or how to use them. The goal of this book is to provide the reader with a history of human rights, a description of what rights are, and an overview of key leaders and organizations that have fought to support human rights. Through understanding what human rights are and why they are important, readers may develop a greater appreciation for their fundamental role in society.

While the idea that people are entitled to human rights is ancient and global, how these rights have been embedded into the social order has changed over time. Like drops of water that have come to fill a pitcher, a variety of individuals, actions, events, and organizations have created human rights as we know them today. Human rights and the organizations that support them advanced significantly after the devastation of World War II. War destroys not just lives and buildings but also the social fabric that binds us together. The emphasis of the post-WWII human rights movement was to better educate people and to help them to be healthy and safe, to be free from oppression, and to develop their best selves in a world that was safe, just, equal, and peaceful.

Top of a pillar containing the law code of Hammurabi, King of Babylon, at the Musée du Louvre. The code established fundamental laws to protect human dignity and freedom. (Fred Romero via Flickr, Creative Commons license CC-BY-2.0)

Human rights treaties have emerged to safeguard people's rights to basic necessities, such as food, water, and shelter, as well as other markers of wellbeing, including healthcare, education, jobs, and freedom of speech. Treaties have also endeavored to protect rights related to more complicated concepts, such as a sustainable environment, equality, justice, and peace. Human rights, by definition, apply to all human beings. Major steps have been made toward ensuring that all people's rights are protected and defended, regardless of differences in factors such as race, gender, and religion. Protections are intended to influence how people are treated in their everyday lives, both as individuals and as collectivities.

As beneficial as human rights protections have been, they have and continue to be under attack. Many are in grave danger of being eliminated by opponents around the world and by political agendas, especially from populist and authoritarian movements. As British lawyer, parliamentarian, and human rights defender Shami Chakrabarti states, human rights are essential for our future, the future of nations, and the future of the planet:

> We have seen increased inequality and economic turmoil, accelerating threats from artificial intelligence … we face the biggest refugee crisis since just after World War II, and the biggest displacement of people in our history. Hard men dominate too many nations and corporations. Fundamental rights and freedoms seem to be in retreat everywhere, just when we need them the most. (Chakrabarti 2024: 203)

Terrorism, the rise of autocracy, oppression of women, a global environmental crisis of unprecedented magnitude, increasing economic inequality, attacks on education, corruption by leaders, and the pervasive spread of misinformation as "truth" are all realities that put human rights at terrible risk. This book is an examination of what human rights are, some of the major challenges that face the planet, who some of the premiere rights defenders have been, and why human rights education and activism is desperately needed now.

What Are Human Rights?

Social Norms and Natural Law

In order to understand what human rights are, it is useful to consider how they relate to other central norms, including ethics, morals, values, politics, laws, and justice. Ethics are a system of personal judgments about how to behave and the principles that guide those decisions. In other words, ethics inform personal choices. Morals are often thought to be the same as ethics, but morals suggest judgments or how people respond to others. Morals may convey a sense of obligations about how we treat each other. Politics is the way communities and societies organize themselves and make decisions. Influencers have competing views about how things should run and different theories about what ought to be. Laws are systems or ways of enforcing those choices, obligations, or rights. Values are broad ideas about how people believe they should live their best lives. Values inform ethics, morals, politics, and laws.

An underlying value in human rights is that of dignity. Dignity is a concept that is considered as a philosophical basis for human rights. Rights are regarded as mirrors of obligations. There are many different types of rights, as discussed in this chapter. Justice is a commonly used term in relation to rights, but one that is highly subjective. People talk about things like equity and inclusion in conjunction with justice, but these terms are abstract in nature, in part to avoid talking about specific disputes in highly political or controversial terms. Therefore, when people talk about justice, scholars consider that it is often meaningless because of its masked lack of specificity (Chakrabarti 2024; Dworkin 2011).

One way to think about determining what constitutes a human right is a positive–negative rights framework. Positive rights could be considered life- or peace-affirming. Examples of positive rights might be access to healthcare and free education, the right to work, the right to have a clean environment, the right to socialize with others, or the right to vote. A negative right might be something that, if supported, would cause harm to others. Societies, therefore, usually do not support negative rights. For example, we do not have the right to shoot up a store because we don't like the prices they charge or the way they do business; we do not have the right to have sex with someone who does not want to be with us; and we do not have the right to drink and drive. The challenge here is that what one person thinks is positive, another may perceive to be negative. For example, economic systems that allow for enormous wealth disparities in a society may be considered positive and supported by some but derided as negative by others. Using a positive–negative, good–bad dichotomy to resolve disagreements is fraught with challenges. A human rights standard of fairness for all people everywhere provides a framework to allow for resolution that is to the benefit of all, not just some people.

According to the United Nations, human rights apply to everyone, individually and collectively, because everyone is a human being and member of the human family. The basic rights of humankind include the right to peace, safety, and security. They also include civil rights, political rights, economic rights, social rights, cultural rights, and environmental rights. These are rights that are inherent to all human beings, regardless of their sex, race, nationality, religion, ethnicity, language, ability, social class, or other factors.

On the surface, what constitutes human rights seems straightforward and simple. One can argue that The Golden Rule provides one of the first codifications of a human rights framework, holding that we are all responsible for treating one another with the justice and kindness that we would like to be given to us. This "do unto others as you would have done to yourself" perspective can be found in religions such as Buddhism, Christianity, Confucianism, Hinduism, Islam, Judaism, Taoism, and Zoroastrianism (Gensler 2013).

But human rights are more than just being nice to each other. The concept is associated with what is called natural law, which assumes that human rights are universal, inalienable, and indivisible. By natural law, human rights are universal, in that everyone is entitled to them. It does not matter where you live, what your gender or race are, how old you are, or whether you have ability challenges. Everyone has the same basic rights. Human rights are indivisible, in that one right directly and indirectly impacts another. For instance, if a person cannot obtain their right to clean water and good food, their right to good health will be compromised. When a person is not healthy, it will be difficult for them to learn, which violates their right to obtain information and education. If someone is poorly educated and sick, this prevents them from seeking meaningful employment, earning money, and taking care of their family. Their ability to participate in society is, therefore, compromised. Having rights makes one stronger, but, like a game of dominos, the violation of one right may have direct and latent negative consequences on other rights. Human rights are also considered inalienable by natural law, meaning that no one can take these rights away. Even if a government or set of laws fails to recognize that people have certain rights, this does not negate the innate existence of human rights by natural law or the position that rights *should* be protected.

Throughout history, people have not been allowed to access their human rights in the face of discriminatory opinions, actions, and laws that deny rights based on factors such as sex, gender, race, and religion. The concept of human rights as inalienable under natural law comes into conflict with societal ideas, where what constitutes a right, as well as whose rights are the most important and how rights should be integrated into a society, can be points of contention and debate. The idea of human rights does not necessarily resolve the tension between competing interests and various visions of how people think the world should be, but it does provide a vocabulary for people to debate about which interests should prevail and how to create conditions for constraining attacks on liberty (Kundal 2023). Legal institutions and governments have stepped in to make decisions about human rights, but the resulting laws and actions do not necessarily reflect the universal premises underlying human rights. Groups of people have had to fight for their rights to be recognized. What to do when rights are violated is also a point of dispute.

The recognition and protection of human rights, or lack thereof, has huge implications in today's global, interconnected world. Population and demographic changes worldwide have altered the composition of human societies. Technological and societal changes pose significant challenges, as does the rise of immigration, terrorism, climate change, and economic inequality. Many human rights transgressors exist and need to be held accountable, but whether they will or not is questionable. Social changes beg for the enduring global peace, stability, and human dignity that the protection of human rights can bring (Kundal 2023).

Types of Human Rights

Human rights consist of many different types. Basic categories of rights typically include the following:

- Economic rights
- Social rights
- Political rights
- Civil rights
- Cultural rights
- Constitutional rights
- Legal rights

Economic, social, and cultural rights (ESCRs), as described by the United Nations, include the rights to adequate food and housing, to education, to health, to social security, to take part in cultural life, to water and sanitation, and to work. The United Nations has declared that governments have a duty to respect, protect, and preserve people's economic, social, and cultural rights. Governments must ensure that the policies and measures they implement do not undermine access to healthcare or social security benefits. They are required to help individuals to realize their rights and are prohibited from discrimination. That is, they must protect the rights of all persons, including those in marginalized populations. Violations of human rights by governments can include forcibly evicting people from their homes, failure to ensure wages that will allow people to live a decent life, failure to provide healthcare services, segregating children with disabilities from mainstream schools, allowing exposure to toxins and contaminates, or not ensuring sufficient food to keep people from being malnourished or starved.

Political and civil rights have been united into an International Covenant on Civil and Political Rights (ICCPR). This treaty commits ratifying nations to protecting people from government infringement on their rights as well as rights violations by organizations and other people. This class of rights includes the right of human dignity, freedom of speech, the right to life, freedom of assembly, freedom of religion, rights to vote and have input into the community decision-making process, and the right to due process and a fair trial when accused of a crime. These kinds of rights protect people from torture and arbitrary detainment and promote gender equity and minority rights. The ICCPR is designed to protect people's right to participate in the civil and political actions of their communities and nations. Violations of the ICCPR may include capital punishment, the execution of children or mentally impaired people, and the failure to protect people from domestic violence.

Cultural rights protections include a wide variety of rights, such as the ability of people to profess and practice their own religion, to use their own language, to create both material and nonmaterial items, to have culturally relevant education and training, to share their culture with similar people and to participate in events that support that culture, to have materials available so that they can communicate with others in their own language, and to support their cultural identity and heritage. When cultural identity is not the norm of a society, those groups with fewer members may find themselves in a subordinate position and find that access to their own cultural background is not made possible. Violations can include discriminating against people on the basis of attributes that may include their race, religion, or cultural group, limiting the observance of religious practices, limiting or prohibiting languages and thereby inhibiting access to information and shared perspectives, limiting opportunities for cultural practice, restricting the preparation and serving of food, imposing restrictions on what people wear or how they style their hair, and making education in their own language unavailable to people.

Constitutional rights are those set forth in a nation's charter, such as in the Declaration of Independence and the Bill of Rights in the United States. A country's initial constitutional rights may be changed through amendments. Constitutional rights influence legal decisions, which can vary from time to time and place to place. For instance, drinking alcohol is legal in some nations but not in others. In the United States, alcohol use was legal, then made illegal, and then made legal again. Legal and constitutional rights are products of social construction and are more subjective than a natural law approach to rights.

All human rights, no matter what type they are (civil, political, etc.), are interlinked. For example, poverty makes it very challenging for an individual to reach their highest potential. If people cannot read or write, they will have a hard time finding a job or securing life necessities. When people are not well educated, sick, hungry, malnourished, homeless, and struggling to get by, it is less likely that they will be able to participate meaningfully in their communities and have input to advocate for themselves or for social change.

Three Generations of Rights Frameworks

What is considered a human right has evolved over time. Scholars sometimes group human rights movements into generations. The first generation, during the seventeenth and eighteenth centuries, focused on the concept of Liberty, pertaining to civil and political rights. The second generation of rights emerged in the nineteenth century during the Industrial Revolution, when there were significant technological changes and a demand for more workers. Many workers found themselves overworked, underpaid, and employed in dangerous occupations, working with machinery that could harm them. The second generation of rights, therefore, focused on equality and concerned economic, social, and cultural rights. The third generation of rights are referred to as solidarity or fraternity rights. These rights came to the forefront in a more contemporary timespan and address the rights of people of different genders, races, ethnicities, and abilities. These rights are part of a growing sense of an increasingly diverse and globally interconnected world and the inequalities that persist or arise in that world. Third-generation rights also focus on the collective needs of everyone to live in a safe, healthy, and sustainable environment.

These generations of rights may not be linear in nature or have followed the same path globally. Western and developed nations have sometimes responded differently to various rights movements than have developing countries. Civil and political rights have generally been higher order in Western nations than developing nations, whereas recognition of second- and third-generation rights has been slower. The cultural background and economic framework of a society influences its approach to human rights protections. However, especially in this time of massive social and technological change, distinguishing between types of rights may be becoming less relevant as awareness increases that human rights are interdependent and indivisible. This realization may create a new sense of obligation for states to respect, protect, promote, and fulfill their commitment to human rights (Viljoen n.d.).

Historical Contributions

Ancient World

Babylonia

One of the earliest references to human rights came from King Hammurabi of Babylon. The code of Hammurabi (1780 BCE) refers to the need to protect human dignity and freedom. Hammurabi's Code of 282 rules was carved onto a massive, finger-shaped black stone stele or pillar. It established standards for commercial interactions and set fines and punishments that were deemed appropriate. The code indicated that some laws are so fundamental to society that they apply to everyone, including the king. Hammurabi welcomed those who were oppressed to seek justice, particularly with respect to freedom of speech and protections for slaves, women, and those who were weak.

Cyrus II of Persia (c. 600–530 BCE) was a military strategist who expanded the Achaemenid Empire from the Aegean Sea to the Indus River. He became known as Cyrus the Great because he respected the cultures, religions, and customs of the people in the lands he acquired into his empire. He demanded no forced assimilation, did not denounce the local religions, and was regarded as a benevolent leader who championed religious minorities in conquered regions. When Cyrus arrived in Babylon to conquer it, he announced that he was chosen by the city's god, Marduk. The Babylonian king Nabonidus was unpopular, and both the common and elite members of the city viewed Cyrus as a more positive leader. The story of Cyrus's conquest of Babylon is written in cuneiform script on a clay cylinder and suggests that Cyrus was responsible for establishing a new social order that freed slaves, ended the Babylonian exile and allowed deported peoples to return to their homes, and restored shrines. Cyrus is credited for allowing Jews to return to Jerusalem, where they built the Second Temple. The Cyrus Cylinder, housed now at the British Museum, is acknowledged as the first document to formalize basic freedoms and has been described as the first "Charter of Human Rights" because the word "rights" appears on it.

Greece and Rome

The origins of human rights are also often traced back to the Greek philosophers Socrates, Plato, and Aristotle, who put forward ideas of natural rights, justice, and equality. Many thinkers in ancient Greece argued that human conduct should be judged according to the law of nature, and Aristotle (384-322 BCE) determined that there was a difference between natural and legal justice. He declared that natural law holds that the same rights apply to everyone everywhere, and that those rights are not dependent upon whether there are laws or public acceptance of them. Sophocles (c. 497-c. 406 BCE), in one of his classic plays, *Antigone*, writes about the death of Oedipus, the King of Thebes. The title character (Antigone) challenges state law and relies upon the law of nature to have higher authority. Romans developed the body of law Jus Civile for Roman citizens and Jus Gentium for people coming to Rome from elsewhere. Jus Gentium in Roman Law was virtually synonymous with natural law, which later became what we know today as human rights.

Ancient Greece and Rome included recognition of some rights for children. Greek philosopher Plato (c. 428-348 BCE), in *The Republic*, advocated for all children to receive an education and believed that children were born with an intuitive understanding of the world and what was right. Roman emperor Quintilian (35–95 CE) advocated that education should be through positive imitation, not intimidation. However, Roman law and Greek philosophy failed to recognize the rights of children in other ways. For instance, the Roman notion of *patria potestas* gave fathers absolute power over children, who were seen as parental property to do with as they wanted, which could include abuse or abandonment. Plato advocated infanticide as a form of eugenics. Adult Greek athletes commonly took male as well as female children to be sexual partners. Although early Greek and Roman influences helped build our understanding of human rights, these ancient societies did not necessarily embrace all rights for all people.

Ashoka the Great of India

Ashoka the Great (304-232 BCE) was a ruler in India who conquered the state of Klinga but became so troubled over how many people were killed or injured that he converted to Buddhism. He promised to never wage another war. He had his edicts inscribed upon pillars and walls so that they would be visible to the public and seen as the law of the Mauryan empire, which consisted of Afghanistan, Indiana, Bangladesh, Pakistan, and Nepal. He is important in the history of human rights because he advocated for peace rather than violence when engaging in the conquest of new societies.

Africa

Ancient Africa also produced a foundation for human rights concepts. Some indigenous African systems embraced a framework that celebrated people as social beings and the bearers of rights and duties. Within communities, people learned that human dignity was the basis and goal of this framework, and individualism was curbed with a balance between one's rights and one's duties to care for others. Public and personal wellness were integrated; wellness at one level was naturally reflected in the other. The African notion of justice is rooted not in individual claims against the state, but in the physical and psychic security of group membership, and this view supports the notion that community and personal rights are linked. Human rights were central in pre-colonial Africa even though they were not written down.

Aztec and Inca

The value of human rights was a lesson hard learned by early South American civilizations. The Aztec in Mexico (1325-1521 CE) and the Inca in Peru (1438-1532 CE) built mighty kingdoms that were technologically sophisticated and wealthy. Both societies are said to have built their wealth on the laborers they exploited and the people they taxed and stole valuables from. But their power ended with the arrival of Spanish conquistadors in the sixteenth century. These outsiders brought with them diseases like smallpox and influenza, which killed countless innocent people. The conquistadors wanted gold and other forms of wealth they saw in these civilizations, and they were ruthless in their attempt to gain power. The destruction of the town of Tenochtitlan marked the end of the Aztec civilization. The Spanish used their superior weapons and strategies to steamroll over the remaining fragile indigenous resistance, and the Inca empire fell when its emperor, Atahualpa, was executed (Smit 2019; Tolentino 2024).

Tales of both the Aztec and Inca civilizations demonstrate how their leaders exploited people to gain wealth, power, and privilege. The magnificent cultures they created were destroyed by the Spanish conquistadors, who also longed for wealth, power, and control, and who would do anything to get it. These experiences laid a foundation for the average person to long for their basic rights to be protected—for example, to not be killed, to not have their culture destroyed, to not work long hours only to have those in power take most of what they earned, and to have a say about the governance of their communities.

Europe

The Magna Carta

The Magna Carta, or Great Charter, is regarded as fundamental to the evolution of human rights. In 1215 in England, King John was imposing heavy taxes on barons to fund wars and crusades. The barons and other nobility bonded together and created a treaty that demanded peace without revenge and to create a balance of power between the king and the barons. They threatened revolt, and the king was forced to sign the document. The Magna Carta is seen as a statement asserting the dignity of a person against the abuses of those in political authority and a symbol of the need for human constitutions that address the needs of all people, not just the rich and powerful.

Hugo Grotius, the Father of International Law

Hugo Grotius (1583-1645) was a Dutch juror, poet, and student of Greek and Roman philosophy, which he integrated into his book, *On the Laws of War and Peace* (1625). In it he attempted to reconcile natural law with the laws of nations and concluded that there are certain human rights that are fundamental to human beings and vital to understanding human nature. His work became a model for modern international human rights law in that while he promoted non-intervention policies, he agreed that one country could step in against another if citizens were injured as a result of tyrannical rulers focusing on their own personal gain.

The Petition of Rights 1628

In England, Sir Edward Coke (1552-1634), a former judge and politician, filed a petition with Parliament because knights refused to pay imposed taxes unless the taxes were approved not just by King Charies I but also by those in Parliament. This case became fundamental in the argument of "taxation without representation."

English Bill of Rights

Tensions within the English government had been brewing and led to a revolution from 1688-9. King James abdicated the throne by leaving the country, and his daughter Mary and her husband, William of Orange, took charge. To do so, they had to agree that they were not absolute monarchs and that there would be an elected set of members to Parliament to advise the monarchs. This bill of rights was a form of checks and balances in the government and ensured some level of political representation.

Declaration of the Rights of Man and of the Citizen

In France, a revolution occurred in which the feudal system was attacked by peasants who no longer wanted to work without representation and fair treatment. The writings of philosopher Jean-Jacques Rousseau (1712-78), which promoted the concepts of "liberty, equality, and fraternity," influenced the French National Assembly, which declared that "all men are born free and equal in rights" and that it is the duty of the government to preserve and protect the natural rights of men, including the rights of liberty, property, security, and resistance to oppression. The 1789 Declaration of the Rights of Man and of the Citizen elevated the status of natural rights to legal rights. These views were common in the Age of Enlightenment, which emphasized the value of individual liberty and religious tolerance.

United States

The Virginia Declaration

Colonists from England settled in what was to become the United States. In 1776 the Virginia Constitutional Convention was adopted. It contained sixteen sections that listed rights that could not legitimately be taken away by government authorities. These included freedom of religion, separation of powers, and free elections. The declaration set the stage for the creation of the US Constitution.

Declaration of Independence

The Declaration of Independence of the United States announced the secession of the thirteen American colonies from Great Britain. Its construction embedded parts of the English Bill of Rights and the French Declaration of the Rights of Man and of the Citizen. Marquis de Lafayette, a French nobleman and military officer who joined the Continental Army under George Washington, and clergyman Emmanuel-Joseph Sieyes helped construct the declaration, which listed abuses under the sovereignty of King George III and declared that the colonies regarded themselves as independent states that were no longer subject to British rule. Thomas Jefferson, at the time a member of the Continental Congress, used philosopher John Locke's conception of natural rights in writing the Declaration of Independence, which was adopted by the fifty-six congressional delegates in Philadelphia, Pennsylvania, on July 4, 1776. Articles of Confederation were created in 1777 to define state representation in congress, presidential powers, and the slave trade.

Constitution and Bill of Rights

The 1777 Articles of Confederation and the 1789 Constitution that replaced them focused primarily on rights of the government but did not truly address the rights of the people. By 1791 the states that had declared their independence from Great Britain wanted greater constitutional protection for their civil liberties, so Representative James Madison drafted a Bill of Rights that contained ten amendments to the Constitution. The Bill of Rights (see document in Chapter 5) focuses on the right to due process, freedom of speech, freedom of religion, freedom to keep and bear arms, freedom of assembly, and freedom to petition, as well as the prohibition of cruel and unusual punishment, unreasonable search and seizure, and self-incrimination.

Civil War and the Emancipation Proclamation

Slavery was a regular part of early American society, and many of the founding fathers of the new nation, who professed the importance of freedom, owned slaves. Economic and political concerns, including whether to end the institution of slavery, differed between northern and southern states and created increasing conflict within the country. Eventually, the South decided to secede from the United States, which resulted in a bloody civil war. At the end of the war, President Abraham Lincoln proclaimed in 1863 that slaves were emancipated, or free. This advancement in human rights was significant not just for enslaved people and African Americans, but for all people.

Suffragette Movement and Equal Rights Amendment

The Constitution's statement that "all men are created equal" did not include women. Women were not allowed to vote and suffered discrimination in virtually every aspect of their lives. The fight for women's voting rights, known as the suffragette movement, had been active since before the Civil War. It took over 100 years for activists to see the 19th Amendment to the Constitution, stating that the right to vote could not be denied based on sex, ratified in 1920. This amendment finally acknowledged that American women deserved all the rights and responsibilities of citizenship as men. However, a proposed Equal Rights Amendment, which would prohibit discrimination based on sex, has not yet succeeded in obtaining ratification by the required three-quarters of states.

Civil Rights Movement

There have been many civil rights movements around the world. The civil rights movement in the United States gained much international publicity and influenced the struggles of other nations, as it fought for abolishing legal racial segregation but also addressed discrimination in many of its forms, including the disenfranchisement of women and other Americans. The civil rights movement employed actions such as protests, sit-ins, marches, and freedom riders, but it is noteworthy that many of these peaceful actions were met with violence from those in authority. In 1957 President Dwight Eisenhower signed a Civil Rights Act through which people who prevented others from voting could be prosecuted. President Lyndon Johnson signed the Civil Rights Act of 1964, a Voting Rights Act in 1965, and a Fair Housing Act in 1968. But the threat of violence against those who were fighting for human rights was real, as exemplified by the killing of protestors by police during the Bloody Sunday march in Birmingham, Alabama and the assassinations of President John F. Kennedy, Senator Robert Kennedy, and civil rights leaders Malcolm X and Martin Luther King.

International War

While national efforts were underway to establish human rights laws in particular countries, there was also a growing realization that there needed to be an overarching set of human rights standards that pertained to everyone, everywhere. Human rights concerns are global, even if different places tend to focus on different issues at different times. Some of the first international organizations designed to work together focused on specific concerns common to the nations involved. To address communication issues across borders, the International Telegraph Union was formed in 1865 and the Universal Postal Union in 1874. The Hague Conference was called together in 1898 by Russian Czar Nicholas II to create a permanent court of arbitration to settle international disputes and to address how wars should be fought and prisoners treated. A second Hague convention in 1907 expanded upon the contents of the 1898 accord with increased attention to naval warfare.

Discontent continued to exist, however, as did attempts to forcibly take territory or impose rule upon others. International conflicts in the late nineteenth and early twentieth century included the Boxer Rebellion in China (1899-1900), which involved a violent effort to drive foreigners out of the country and a multinational response to defeat the campaign. Other regional conflicts included the Italo-Turkish war (1911-12) and the Balkan wars in Europe, Turkey, and Libya (1912-13). The Irish war of independence (1919-21) and Irish civil war (1922-3) involved international disputes that continued through most of the century. The Spanish Civil War garnered much international attention, as have ongoing conflicts in the Middle East in Palestine and Israel.

While human rights involve a wide array of rights, wars and conflicts have focused attention on the numerous harms they cause to people and the importance of peace efforts in preventing those harms. War results in death, disability, and emotional trauma, destruction of businesses, homes, and infrastructure, separation of families, and catastrophic environmental impacts, to name just a few negative consequences. These problems motivate people to consider a better way, a way that will protect human rights. The following sections highlight two of the largest international conflicts of the twentieth century—called "world wars" for a reason—as well as some of the efforts to improve human rights that resulted from them.

World War I and the Paris Peace Conference

Relatively small conflicts have the potential to mushroom into widescale war, such as was the case with World War I. The "war to end all wars," as it was optimistically called, came about partly because of a power imbalance in Europe and increased economic competition among nations. The assassination of Austrian Archduke Franz Ferdinand exacerbated ongoing international tensions and resulted in a global conflict between many countries, including Germany, Italy, Bulgaria, France, the United Kingdom, Greece, Romania, the United States, and areas in the Middle East, Africa, Asia, and Asia-Pacific regions. The deadliest war in history at the time, 9 million military personnel and 8 million civilians died, and 23 million people were wounded. Heavy use of chemical warfare on both sides and regional genocide played a part in the large number of fatalities. The devastation of the war resulted in personal, economic, and military exhaustion. Russia signed an armistice, as did Bulgaria, the Ottoman Empire, and Austria-Hungary, and the war finally ended in 1918. This new form of war and its catastrophic impacts made it clear that preventing war in the future was a global imperative.

In 1919 a peace conference was held in in Paris at the Palace of Versailles. In the resulting treaty, Germany was disarmed, lost some of its territories, and was required to pay war reparations. The idea was to punish Germany for its involvement in instigating World War I and to curtail the country's ability to start another war. The Paris Peace Conference also included the Covenant of the League of Nations as part of its terms.

The Covenant of the League of Nations outlined a structure and function of the first worldwide intergovernmental organization with a mission to maintain world peace. Established in 1920, the League of Nations sought to bring about global security through international cooperation, by mutual disarmament, settling international disputes through negotiation and arbitration, and seeking conflict resolution via global governance. It created a platform for diplomacy to avoid war.

US President Woodrow Wilson championed the League of Nations. He created an ideological framework called Fourteen Points to move forward this vision of a new era of international relations and negotiations. However, the United States refused to become a member of the League of Nations because some members of Congress were afraid it would commit the country to military involvement in other countries without congressional approval, which would contravene its Constitution's provisions on war powers. The debate laid the foundation for further global conversations about human rights.

In 1924, the League of Nations adopted the Declaration of the Rights of the Child, drafted by British social reformer Eglantyne Jebb (1876-1928). The declaration states that children must be provided what they need for normal development, including food, healthcare, education, housing, and assistance when they are in distress. Children must also be protected from all forms of exploitation.

Another organization that emerged from the 1919 Paris Peace Conference was the International Labor Organization. After World War I, safeguards for social and economic rights became a heightened concern, adding to nineteenth- and early twentieth-century social and labor movements related to industrialization. Setting international standards for workers and providing the working class a fair standard of living became a priority. The International Labor Organization was helpful during post-war rebuilding and, in 1946, became a United Nations agency. It is still in operation today.

World War II and the United Nations

While World War I was touted as the war to end all wars, the seeds of discontent that led to that war had not disappeared. Between 1939 and 1945, almost the entire planet was engulfed in a second world war. Why did this war occur, despite efforts to prevent it? The rise of fascism in Europe led to conditions allowing Adolf Hitler (1889–1945) to gain power through the Nazi Party, with the ultimate goal of purifying the German race and conquering the world. The Spanish Civil War and Soviet-Japanese border conflicts were contributing factors in worsening the global conflict, as was war between China and Japan. Many nations were experiencing economic problems.

More than 85 million people died in World War II—a third of the world's population—many due to genocide, massacres, starvation, and disease. Millions more suffered disabilities due to the direct and indirect consequences of the war. Techniques of war had changed; weapons were more lethal and sophisticated. Bombing became more strategic, and population centers were targeted, which increased casualties. The United States dropped two nuclear bombs on Japan, ending the war. Children were orphaned, homes and communities were destroyed, and the social fabric of communities was ripped apart. After the war ended in Europe and then Asia, new national boundaries were drawn and new political alignments and socio-cultural structures were created that continue to endure. These events set the stage for future international conflicts, including the ongoing Israel-Palestine and Ukraine-Russia conflicts.

After World War II, there was a consolidated effort to prosecute perpetrators of war crimes. Two military tribunals were created to put alleged war criminals on trial: the Nuremberg trials in Nuremberg, Germany, and the Tokyo tribunals in Tokyo, Japan. Punishment for war crimes was sought in the interest of serving the human right to justice.

The United Nations (UN) was founded in 1945 with the goal of accomplishing what the League of Nations had not—to bring about world peace and justice for all. US President Franklin D. Roosevelt had proposed that the major international power-states of the United States, Soviet Union, United Kingdom, and China would resolve all major world problems at a Security Council. This format did not occur, largely because of the Cold War that had begun between the Soviet Union and European nations. Instead, fifty-one countries signed the UN Charter.

The UN, regarded as the world's largest international organization, is the premiere humanitarian organization advocating for justice for all. The organization has realized that peace is not possible when people are hungry, sick, and poorly educated, so it has expanded its human rights emphasis to include healthcare, education, safety, food and nutrition, water, housing, and civic engagement. Its diplomatic functions help to create peace and security, develop friendly relations among nations, achieve international cooperation, and serve as a center for harmonizing the actions of nations. In 2017, the UN adopted the Treaty on the Prohibition of Nuclear Weapons, acknowledging that weapons of mass destruction are considered a violation of human rights.

Wars, and the Quest for Peace, Continue

The quest for human rights is universally endorsed, and yet nations have been unable to live harmoniously together on this planet. Countless conflicts have occurred all over the world since World War II, and they continue to occur, creating havoc for human rights. However, wars can be seen as a motivator for further development of human rights protections. The physical, emotional, social, and financial costs of war are so extensive that it is common for people to say "no more." They then become more open to the benefits that human rights protections can offer. Wars are symbolic of both national and international tensions. These tensions include conflicts over sex, gender, race, ethnicity, immigration, political representation, economic equity, criminal justice, and essentials such as access to clean water and air, food, housing, and safety from violence. Discrimination and injustice set the stage for bigger and more lethal problems to arise. International human rights treaties have attempted to create a blueprint that governments and individuals can use to build a world respectful of human rights so that the horrors of war do not attend. The next section looks at some of these major human rights treaties.

Development of International Treaties

Efforts to create a human rights framework have resulted in part from global conflicts and injustices. Treaties are a relatively recent attempt to enable human rights realization at the personal, national, and international levels. Although there have certainly been efforts to further human rights at the individual and national levels, the United Nations has become the main bulwark against war and the primary advocate for the creation of individual and social wellbeing and the promotion of peace and justice for all.

After the UN Charter was adopted in 1945, a series of treaties were subsequently adopted by some of the member nations. The UN Economic and Social Council set up the Commission on Human Rights, which consisted of fifty-four elected governmental representatives. The Commission helped establish the Universal Declaration of Human Rights (UDHR) in 1948. As good as the UDHR is, it does not necessarily address all the human rights needs and violations that member countries encounter. This resulted in the creation of more conventions, charters, and treaties. Some of these treaties focused on a specific group of people (like children or immigrants) or experiences (like civil rights, torture, or economic wellbeing). Over time, different countries and geographic regions developed treaties that were more specifically aligned with their needs, and even sub-regional treaties have emerged. Some of the major treaties are described in the following sections to show the evolution of human rights development (Viljoen n.d.).

Human rights declarations and treaties are of little value if they are not implemented/enforced, however. This has been a concern because individual states make their own decisions about whether to sign and ratify the treaties. If they do, they are obligated to implement them. Many do, but some do not. Monitoring countries' practices and documenting their violations is difficult. How to hold a nation, or individual, accountable for rights violations is also challenging. In addition, new human rights issues emerge for which there are not necessarily treaties available. Examples include LGBTQ+ and gender rights, rights of people who retire, or rights around the use of social media or artificial intelligence.

UN Charter

The UN Charter, adopted in 1945, is considered the foundational document, or treaty, that lays forth the overall structure and function of the United Nations, how it is organized, ways it will govern members, and member requirements. It includes the roles of the Secretariat, General Assembly, Security Council Court of Justice, and Economic and Social Council. When a nation joins, the rules and obligations are binding for it. These include nondiscrimination, justice, and the pursuit of peace.

Universal Declaration of Human Rights

In 1948, the monumental UDHR was passed by the UN. It serves as a model for domestic constitutions, policies, laws, regulations, and practices. It was drafted by representatives from countries with different legal and cultural backgrounds. Eleanor Roosevelt is often credited for it, but it was a document that took years to construct, with input from people from all regions of the world. This Declaration was proclaimed by the United Nations General Assembly in Paris on December 10, 1948, as General Assembly resolution 217A. While it is not a legal document per se, it is customarily considered to be international law. It is a blueprint for how societies can live in a civil and respectful world and how governments should treat all people no matter who they are or where they live. The UDHR codified for the first time a common set of standards that announced that all people were entitled to fundamental rights that were to be universally protected. The UDHR is so important that it has been translated into over 500 languages so that all people everywhere can understand what their rights are. The UDHR has created a base of essential human rights that has allowed other rights to be clarified as new topic-specific treaties have emerged. There are now over seventy other human rights treaties that have grown from the UDHR foundation. However, not all member countries have ratified every treaty.

International Humanitarian Law and the Geneva Conventions of 1949

The International Humanitarian Law was signed in 1949 after World War II in hopes of preventing more war. It became part of what is referred to as the Geneva Convention, which had several parts. The first is designed to protect the rights of soldiers who are sick and wounded, while the second Geneva Convention expands rights to naval combatants and ship-bound non-combatants. The third identifies standards that are necessary for the treatment of prisoners of war. The fourth Geneva Convention expands civilian rights in occupied land or conflict areas.

The Refugee Convention

In 1951, this convention supplemented Article 14 of the UDHR with reference to people's right to asylum. It went into effect in 1954 and was amended in 1967. This document defines a refugee as someone who fears persecution because of their race, religion, sex, political opinion, or membership in a group that makes it unsafe or them to return to their country of origin as they seek refugee in a new country. It is designed to provide a safety net to guarantee their rights, freedom, and human dignity.

International Convention on the Elimination of All Forms of Racial Discrimination

The International Convention on the Elimination of All Forms of Racial Discrimination (ICERD) commits its members to the elimination of racial discrimination, the criminalization of hate speech, and the promotion of understanding among all races in 1965. While the UN Charter and the UDHR enshrined the principle of nondiscrimination, the UN recognized that as African states became independent and emerged from colonial rule, it was important to create a prominent legal instrument that promoted nations' obligations of nondiscrimination.

International Covenant on Economic, Social, and Cultural Rights

The International Covenant on Economic, Social, and Cultural Rights was adopted by the UN General Assembly in 1966. It was developed alongside the ICCPR. It commits parties to grant economic, social, and cultural rights that include the right to health, labor rights, the right to education, and the right to an adequate standard of living.

Convention on the Elimination of All Forms of Discrimination Against Women

The Convention on the Elimination of All Forms of Discrimination Against Women (CEDAW) is an international bill of rights for women, adopted by the UN General Assembly in 1979. It built upon the fundamental principles in ICERD, banning racial discrimination and applying the same principles to the protection of women everywhere.

Convention on the Rights of the Child

Just as ICERD recognized racial discrimination and CEDAW identified the need for women to be protected, in 1989 the UN passed the Convention on the Rights of the Child (CRC). This was a monumental decision because it declared that children were not property of parents but human beings who were entitled to their own identity and rights. The CRC articles focus on protecting the best interests of the child, particularly around issues of provision, protection, and participation. (The text of this document is presented in Chapter 5.)

Convention against Torture and Other Cruel, Inhuman or Degrading Treatment or Punishment

The Convention against Torture and Other Cruel, Inhuman or Degrading Treatment or Punishment is often referred to as the UN Convention against Torture. Around the world, people in power have treated others in cruel, inhuman, and degrading ways. Torture has been used as a form of punishment and to gain compliance, and individuals have been transported from nations in which torture was illegal to other countries, where it was not. This 1984 treaty forbids such actions.

International Convention on the Protection of the Rights of All Migrant Workers and Members of Their Families

The International Convention on the Protection of the Rights of All Migrant Workers and Members of Their Families was signed by the UN in 1990 and entered into force in 2003. It is a comprehensive international treaty that came about because of the increased economic exploitation of migrant workers around the world. Millions of people from many countries move to build better lives and to find work, so this was a concern not clearly delineated in the UDHR. It emphasizes the fact that migrant workers are entitled to human rights and worker protections, no matter where they come from or what country they move to.

Convention on the Rights of Persons with Disabilities

The Convention on the Rights of Persons with Disabilities was drafted in 2006. People with disabilities are a major minority group around the world who have been systematically ignored and ill-treated. This treaty is designed to promote, protect, and ensure the human rights of people with ability challenges and to have those rights legally protected.

International Convention for the Protection of All Persons from Enforced Disappearance

The International Convention for the Protection of All Persons From Enforced Disappearance (ICPPED) was drafted in 2006 as an acknowledgment of the forced disappearance of individuals. First recognized as a human rights issue in the 1970s due to military dictatorships in Latin America, victims all around the world are abducted, illegally detained, and tortured. They may be killed and their bodies hidden to reduce evidence of their death. These are crimes against humanity that are addressed in the ICPPED.

Modern Threats to Human Rights

Certain trends in politics and society continue to threaten human rights around the world. Among these are an increasing prevalence of authoritarianism and disinformation, continued discrimination against certain groups, and health crises related to climate change, environmental degradation, and war.

Authoritarianism

Authoritarian governments and far-right extremists have emerged around the world. They are attempting to mobilize factions and embolden their financial power. Terrorists and hate groups have increased in number and strength. Once seen as splinter groups of foreign agents, terrorists today are more likely to be domestic and home-grown (Morgan 2021). In a US congressional testimony highlighted in Chapter 5, Venezuelan human rights activist Leopoldo Lopez provides an analysis of conditions that are contributing to the rise of both national and global authoritarianism. Warnings have existed for years that the rise of external sources of authoritarianism will trigger internal governments to move in that direction. This trend is preventable, but it will require mobilization of the majority of people across the world who want to live in nations focused on human rights and not countries led by authoritarianism regimes (Adler et al. 2022; Lopez 2023; Svolik 2012).

Oligarchies are government forms that are run by a small number of people, and these people may not represent the majority of the citizens under their control. Wealthy individuals may yield disproportionate influence in this type of government, and corporations may take a major role in constructing social policies and laws. When rich individuals and businesses control government, the decisions, policies, and practices they create may be designed to bolster their own best interests—not the interests of the general population. Corporate and political corruption has been on the rise. Multinational corporations yield revenues that far exceed the gross national product of many nations. Globalization has led to porous boundaries, allowing the wealthy to slip between the laws of different countries to promote the growth of their power, privilege, and pockets. Their ability to hire attorneys makes it difficult to challenge their actions and self-serving positions, further creating inequity at all levels. Autocratic and oligarchic societies are especially susceptible to abuses related to human rights.

Disinformation

Anti-democratic regimes and ideologies may be flourishing in part due to an increase in disinformation, presented as legitimate but having malicious intent. Social media is responsible for much of this increase, as bad actors can reach countless people all over the global, attempting to sway the public or cause confusion or terror by spreading untruths (Livingston and Miller 2024). Misuse of Big Tech business models such as X (Twitter), TikTok, Facebook, and other social media platforms has been shown to promote dangerous and false information, information that has been found to increase mental distress and ferment hatred and polarization between groups. The impact of disinformation on the human rights of marginalized communities is, therefore, particularly concerning. Related technologies, such as artificial intelligence, global spyware, and methods of electronic surveillance are pervasive and have not been controlled by an oversight organization like the UN to make sure that they meet human rights standards.

Discrimination

There are certain human rights trends that seem to be pervasive across the globe. Racial and ethnic discrimination stimulate the rise of global tensions and conflicts. This is visible in the conflict between Israel and the Occupied Palestinian Territories (Gaza), which has resulted in countless deaths, hostage-taking, destruction of infrastructure, and a humanitarian disaster that has left people homeless and starving. Discrimination can also be found at the root of the conflicts in Myanmar, the Sudan, Ethiopia, in China with the Uyghurs, and between Russia and Ukraine.

Polarization and nationalism foster discrimination. Seeing groups of people as "the other" is a way to dehumanize them and nurture beliefs that see them as deserving of ill-treatment. Resentment over migrants or refugees arriving from another nation to seek a better life can lead to a push for them to go back to where they came from—or anywhere else. The systematic oppression of women around the world is the result of gender discrimination. Women's reproductive rights, including their right to use contraception, is frequently challenged, leaving women in a position where they are not necessarily in control of their own bodies. Homophobia and the oppression of LGBTQIA+ people are rooted in discrimination based on sexual orientation and gender identity. Gender violence, domestic violence, and social marginalization are occurring worldwide. Economic disparity divides people into the haves and the have-nots. Economic devastation promotes not just poverty, but poor physical and mental health, a rise of crime and substance use, and a distrust of those in authority.

Disparity and discrimination of all kinds set the stage for violence and the adulteration of law. Rights protections provided by law are not static; they can be changed as societal ideas and political administrations change. Disinformation, as discussed in the previous section, can lead to the promotion of discriminatory ideas, regimes, and laws that fail to protect human rights, encouraging the use of violence to control groups of people who are perceived as a threat.

Health Crises

Healthcare availability and affordability is a significant global concern, exacerbated by climate change, economic inequality, globalization, and conflicts. No place on earth is immune from the adverse effects of climate change and environmental exploitation. Events such as fires, floods, air pollution, hurricanes, tornadoes, earthquakes, droughts, and toxic dumping impact the health and safety of everyone but are disproportionately affecting marginalized communities. Globalization has also made worldwide pandemics, like the one caused by COVID-19, more of a threat. Positions and policies that would help protect human rights are often ignored as governments and corporations continue to support their own short-term interests at the expense of global health concerns. Environmental justice includes providing protection and assistance for those most impacted and least able to address these catastrophes and their resulting health effects.

The UN Security Council has largely been ineffective in its attempts to address human rights health issues related to global conflict. For example, the UN Working Group on Children and Armed Conflict has not been able to achieve consensus on grave violations against children in Afghanistan, Myanmar, Somalia, and Syria after years of negotiations. Getting humanitarian aid to people in Gaza has been extraordinarily challenging for a variety of reasons.

Snapshot of Human Rights around the World

Human rights protections and violations vary depending upon where one lives geographically. Some regions of the world, and some countries within a given region, are more respectful of these rights than others. Reports from several organizations, including Amnesty International, Human Rights Watch, the Human Rights Measurement Initiative (HRMI), and the University of Washington, help to paint a general picture. This section provides a general overview of the human rights issues faced in different parts of the world. The further reading section at the end of the chapter includes additional resources for readers to learn more about specific rights in specific areas.

Africa

Africa is a huge continent consisting of fifty-four nations confronting different challenges and attempting different solutions to the human rights issues they face. In Burkina Faso, Cameroon, the Central African Republic, the Democratic Republic of the Congo, Mali, Nigeria, Somalia, and Sudan, ongoing violence and armed conflict has included attacks and sexual violence on civilians, while leaders have shown little regard for international humanitarian laws. Protesting and criticizing government actions and corrupt leaders has resulted in brutal crackdowns in many African nations, effectively muzzling large numbers of people who fear for their lives if they complain. Life for the average person is challenging due to high food prices, food insecurity, climate change problems, corruption, armed conflict, and targeted violence against girls, women, and those who are LGBTQIA+. Poverty, extreme weather conditions, and armed conflicts have forced millions of people to migrate, become refugees, and to seek asylum or homes in other areas. When people have dared to protest in Angola, Ethiopia, Kenya, Mali, Mozambique, Senegal, and Somalia, police have arrested or killed protestors who seek to repress all forms of dissention and peaceful assembly, and courts have ordered long imprisonments to those who thought they had the right to peacefully protest or freely associate with different groups and individuals. Arbitrary arrests and detention remain widespread, especially in Ethiopia, Botswana, Burundi, Niger, Zimbabwe, the Democratic Republic of the Congo, Equatorial Guinea, and Mali. Torture is common for those imprisoned. People have been executed or simply "disappeared" if the government has seen them as troublesome. Amnesty International and Human Rights Watch reports highlight the high rate of hunger, evictions, and lack of healthcare, as well as how children's right to education was denied or impeded in many countries. Human rights defenders have found it difficult to obtain truthful information, justice, and reparations. They implore governments across Africa to do a better job implementing and protecting human rights for all people. In short, while there are areas where rights are being defended, securing high level human rights in Africa has been challenging (Chiwanza 2022).

North America

North America is typically said to include twenty-three countries, although the seven countries that connect Mexico to Columbia in South America are sometimes referred to as Central America. The United States, Canada, and

Mexico are by far the largest and most powerful of the countries in North America. Many of the smaller countries, including some island nations of the Caribbean, and have been at risk from external pressures that have watered down human rights protections.

Findings from both Amnesty International and Human Rights Watch conclude that in most North American countries, civic space has shrunk, and democracy is threatened. Human rights defenders in Canada, Cuba, Ecuador, El Salvador, Guatemala, Haiti, Honduras, Mexico, and Nicaragua have become targets of violence because a robust human rights system does not exist there. Journalists especially have been targets of harassment, violence, and criminalization. Honduras has the highest number of human rights defenders killed per capita in the world. Peaceful protestors have been met by violence, even from police. Excessive and unnecessary use of force, including lethal force, by police was found to occur particularly in Canada, Cuba, the Dominican Republic, Honduras, Mexico, Puerto Rico, and the United States. Turks and Caicos Islands recorded the highest murder rate in Latin America, followed by Jamaica and St. Lucia. Laws diluting legal obligations on the use of force were passed in several countries, and sixteen US states introduced bills restricting the right to protest.

People's rights to life, liberty, and fair trials have been violated in many countries. For instance, in El Salvador there were over 73,000 arbitrary detentions recorded in a two-year period, with most detainees accused of illegal associations. Detainees are often tortured, ill-treated, or forcibly disappeared. Gender-based violence has increased for both women and LGBTQ+ individuals. Abortion rights have been set back, even in countries like the United States, where abortions had been legal. Indigenous people continue to be oppressed, and their rights have been adversely affected. About a third of the population of Latin America live in poverty conditions.

Throughout the Americas, there have been humanitarian, economic, and political crises. These have resulted in a dramatic increase in people leaving their homes to find a better life, but migrants, refugees, and asylum seekers have not always been welcomed and assisted, and in some places they are met with extreme violence or death. Migrants from the Central American "triangle" of Honduras, Guatemala, and El Salvador have learned, as they have made the dangerous journey to the border of the United States, that successfully finding a safe and supportive new home elsewhere is fraught with challenges.

Canada and the United States have been major contributors to global greenhouse gas emissions. Demand for oil has increased, and most North

American nations, including most notably Canada, Ecuador, Mexico, and the United States, have failed to take sufficient and effective measures to mitigate the effects of the climate crisis and ensure people's right to a healthy environment. Indigenous peoples have been most extremely impacted by environmental health issues.

In the United States, after the COVID-19 tax relief packages ended, economic inequality rose dramatically, as did the incarceration rate, which has been one of the highest rates in the world, especially for Black people. The poorest 50 percent of the US population owns just 1.5 percent of the nation's wealth. Youth justice remains low throughout the North America; children may be tried as adults or given sentences of life without parole in some countries, despite international standards forbidding these practices. The United States is the only country in the world where children sentenced for a crime may spend their lives and die in prison. Child labor has increased as well. Child labor protections have been rolled back, allowing young children to work for low pay and long hours in often harmful situations where they are exposed to chemicals and dangerous machinery. Drug use remains high, and countries rely more on criminalization than prevention or health strategies that are more effective and humane. Hunger and homelessness have increased as wages cannot keep up with rising costs. Rights for people who are older, younger, disabled, female, LGBTQ+, or BIPOC (Black, Indigenous, and people of color) are particularly compromised. Educational systems at every age are under-funded, and disinformation through social media is prevalent.

In the 2024 presidential election, Donald Trump was victorious for a second term. He and his administration have been accused of not being supportive of human rights for all and instead of favoring policies that benefit corporations and wealthy individuals (Columbia University 2024; Human Rights Watch 2024e). In his past administration, he pulled the nation out of human rights and other international treaties, and he has been accused of being an autocrat and turning the US government into an oligarchy as he has vowed for social change. What that change will look like, pending future political and legal actions, and how it will affect human rights protections in the United States and other countries has yet to unfold (Schmidt 2019).

South America

South America comprises twelve countries and includes the Amazon rainforest, which covers 30 percent of South America's total geographic area. Poverty, drug gangs, oppression of women and minorities, and insurgence of multinational corporations exploiting the environment for riches at the expense of indigenous peoples are all concerning human rights violations. According to Amnesty International's report, over 201 million people (32 percent) live in poverty in Latin America. Brazil is a major contributor to greenhouse gas emissions and experienced the second highest number of COVID-19 fatalities, after the United States.

Political instability in governments is not uncommon. Human Rights Watch reports that South America has an alarming rate of human rights challenges and reversals of basic freedoms. Human rights activists have been targets for harassment and prosecution in Brazil, Chile, Columbia, Ecuador, Peru, and Venezuela. In Brazil, an average of three human rights activists have been murdered every month over the past four years. Excessive force by police was found to occur particularly in Argentina, Brazil, and Peru. Venezuela has one of the highest murder rates in Latin America. Many people have attempted to flee some regions because of the economic situation and safety fears, but travel is dangerous and expensive, and they need somewhere to go where they will be accepted.

Asia

Asia is the most populated continent, consisting of fifty countries and 60 percent of the world's population. Its countries are widely dispersed geographically—so much so they are often subdivided into regions for the purposes of discussion: the Middle East, South Asia, Russia, etc. The grouping of countries is not always consistent, however, in reports by organizations concerned with human rights. Discussion of the Middle East, for instance, often includes countries in North Africa as well as Afghanistan, which is sometimes considered part of South Asia. To complicate things further, country boundaries do not always coincide with cultural boundaries. For the purposes of this very general overview, a precise division of countries into regions is unnecessary. Given the vast number of human rights concerns associated with China and Russia, those two nations are discussed in the Chapter 2, allowing for more attention to other Asian nations here.

In the area generally referred to as the Middle East, human rights violations are common. Women are often required to dress a certain way, are not allowed to travel without a man to oversee their actions, and have limited freedom for education, employment, and social opportunities. Regionally, members of racial, ethnic, national, and religious communities experience discrimination in both law and practice that impacts their rights to worship, enjoy equal access to employment and healthcare, and live free of persecution, among other serious human rights abuses. Attacks on the rights of LGBTIQ+ people have intensified. There are concerns about how refugees and asylum seekers are treated. Economic inequality exists, and there are political tensions with neighboring countries.

South Asia, when defined to include Afghanistan, Bangladesh, Bhutan, India, the Maldives, Nepal, Pakistan, and Sri Lanka, is about 90 percent Hindu, 96 percent Sikh, and 31 percent Muslim, with smaller numbers of Christians and Buddhists. Tension between religious groups has led to conflicts. Historically, much of South Asia was controlled by colonial interests, particularly Britain. In the 1940s British rule was effectively challenged by Mahatma Gandhi (1869–1948), with the result of India gaining its independence. Geographic lines designating country boundaries have resulted in conflict in the region over the years. Primary conflicts have occurred between India and Pakistan, with disputes over Kashmir and the creation of the independent nation of Bangladesh. Nearby countries of China and Russia have influenced the area as the former colonies have sought to establish their own nations and identities.

India has the largest population in the world and is becoming a technology powerhouse. In 2021, Prime Minister Narendra Modi's government in India was downgraded from a free democracy to a "partially free democracy" by global rights organizations and is regarded as a country of concern for its use of systematic, ongoing, and egregious freedom violations. Attacks on human rights defenders, journals, and activists have increased, and there are concerns that calls for genocide against Muslims and Christians have risen. Pakistan has continued to have problems with its economy, which has contributed to the rise of terrorism and military-political instability. Bangladesh is growing fast economically and becoming more powerful within the region. But enforced disappearances, abductions, torture and extrajudicial killings by its security forces occur with impunity. Human rights defenders, including opposition leaders, activists, journalists, business people, and critics have systematically disappeared, or have been targeted with surveillance, politically motivated charges and arbitrary detention. Afghanistan has had a history of political instability and discrimination against minorities and females. The Taliban rule has had a devastating impact on the lives of Afghan women, girls, journalists, and human rights defenders as it continues to oppress them and use intimidation to control them. Throughout South Asia there is a concern about the oppression of religious minorities, increased use of police and military control, and risks for human rights defenders and the freedom of information and autonomy.

Throughout Asia, censorship and surveillance technologies are used to find out what people are doing and to suppress dissent. Social media companies may require users to disclose their identity and other private information about themselves. For instance, countries like Vietnam and Thailand use Predator or Pegasus spyware to violate human rights standards, especially the rights of human rights defenders and civil society activists. Asian nations, including Laos, the Philippines, Pakistan, China, Vietnam, and Hong Kong, exhibit a pattern of intimidation, arbitrary detention, enforced disappearances, and murder to silence critics. Free speech and freedom of expression and association are not possible without concerns of retaliation. In Malaysia and Mongolia, authorities used repressive laws to stop people's right to peaceful protest.

There are voting and election concerns in most nations, actions that prevent trade unions from supporting workers, and problems with access to due process and fair trials. Economic problems are plentiful, as skyrocketing inflation has occurred in most countries. Poverty results in lack of access to food, healthcare, and daily essentials. Corporate accountability in many of Asian businesses is elusive. Throughout Asia, environmental challenges—floods, hot temperatures, typhoons, and cyclones—may be worsening because of climate change. These events can result in loss of housing, businesses, schools, electricity, safe water, access to the internet, and passable roads.

Attacks by armed groups are common. Attacks and discrimination against minority groups and forced dislocations have occurred. For example, the Uyghurs in China have had their homes razed and been put into resettlement locations, otherwise known as concentration camps. The rights of women and girls are systematically violated from a human rights perspective, as are rights of LGBTQ+ individuals. Trafficking and sexual exploitation are common. Treatment of migrants is often harmful, torturous, or even deadly. Children's rights in general are not protected in Asian nations, as their governments fail to provide for them, protect them, or allow them to participate meaningfully in matters that impact their lives. Freedom of religion and beliefs have been, and remain, under threat.

Australia and Oceania

The south Pacific region consists of fourteen countries, Australia being the largest, and many territories. Human Rights Watch noted that Australia has been a vibrant democracy that has tended to protect the civil and political rights of its citizens. But Australia has been criticized for cruel treatment of refugees and asylum seekers, as well as systemic discrimination against First Nations peoples, who are over-represented in its prisons. The country has had a turn-back policy of sending seekers who arrive by boat back to their countries of departure. Detention of refugees is also a concern.

Australia is the only Western country without a national human rights act or constitutional charter. A 2023 Royal Commission on Violence, Abuse, Neglect, and Exploitation of People with a Disability found that people with disabilities are over-represented in child protection allegations and that Indigenous people are 28 percent less likely to receive care than others. The country has mixed reviews on youth justice and youth rights. The Commission recommended that social media be controlled through government measures to demand transparency from companies or face fines. Australia is a top twenty global greenhouse emitter, the world's largest coking coal exporter, and a leading exporter of natural gas.

The Oceania Human Rights Commission has sought to build human rights protections through ratification of the UN CRC. Along with other countries and territories in Oceania, Samoa is facing significant challenges due to climate change as rising seas impact many of their economic, health, social, and cultural rights. Human rights education is a priority in Samoa, where it must be provided from kindergarten through university levels.

Europe

Europe is composed of fifty-one countries and is the most developed continent. Europe has demonstrated a higher commitment than other regions described in this book to ratify human rights treaties and implement them. The Council of Europe is Europe's oldest intergovernmental organization, dedicated to defending human rights, rule of law, and advancing democracy in the region. All Council of Europe member countries have committed to the European Convention on Human Rights, a regional human rights treaty implemented by the member states and overseen by the European Court of Human Rights. People who believe their rights have been violated can contact ombudspeople and courts for help and to seek legal remedies. This regional commitment to promote and protect human rights has resulted in higher levels of health, life satisfaction, and wellbeing.

The European Union (EU) is the biggest economic and political union in the world. It has adopted a Charter of Fundamental Rights and has embedded human rights education into schools so that people will know what their rights are and how to use them. The Charter is an important document that includes the EU's range of rights and principles, including civil and political rights, social and economic rights, rights to life, liberty, dignity, nondiscrimination, and freedom of expression, and rights regarding issues such as data protection, ethics, and organizational transparency. To assist EU institutions and member states to promote and protect human rights across the EU, the EU Agency for Fundamental Rights collects data and publishes reports on various human rights issues, giving expert advice to policy and decision makers. The EU has also developed National Human Rights Institutions to promote human rights. The European Network of National Human Rights Institutions connects, strengthens, and supports forty of these institutions across Europe. The European Network of Equality Bodies (Equinet) facilitates cooperation among and supports and promotes the work of institutions that promote equality and fight discrimination at the national level. The EU has also developed systems that protect human rights defenders at the local and regional levels. In response to the threats climate change poses to human rights issues, the Paris Climate Accord and other EU endeavors have sought to limit pollution, greenhouse gas emissions, and other environmental problems.

However, that is not to say that there are no human rights violations in Europe. There are. Some nations have more challenges than others. Chapter 2 includes discussion of human rights violations in the conflict between Ukraine and Russia. Ireland suffered from problems before and after civil war tore the country apart. Scotland is contemplating leaving the United Kingdom. Belarus shut down its main human rights group, Viasna, and other civil society organizations. Increased migration has created resource, economic, and political dilemmas as refugees and asylum seekers from the Middle East, Africa, and other areas have made dangerous travels north to Europe to build new lives. There is a need to work toward greater inclusivity throughout Europe, given the wide variety of nations, cultures, and languages in the region. Racism and intolerance must be confronted. Hatred and disinformation, exacerbated by social media, occurs in Europe as it does elsewhere. How to contain or mitigate it is now an important strategy for reducing intolerance and terrorism.

Further Reading

Adler, P. S., Adly, A., Armanios, D., et al. (2022). Authoritarianism, populism, and the global retreat of democracy. *Journal of Management Inquiry*, 32 (1): 3–20. https://doi.org/10.1177/10564926221119395.

Amnesty International. (2023a). Africa. https://www.amnesty.org/en/location/africa/report-africa (accessed March 31, 2025).

Amnesty International. (2023b). South America. https://www.amnesty.org/en/location/americas/south-america (accessed March 31, 2025).

Amnesty International. (2024b). Asia. https://www.amnesty.org/en/location/asia-and-the-pacific/report-asia-and-the-pacific (accessed March 31, 2025).

Amnesty International. (2024c). North America. https://www.amnesty.org/en/location/americas/north-america/united-states-of-america/report-united-states-of-america (accessed March 31, 2025).

Amnesty International. (2024d). The state of the world's human rights 2024. https://www.amnesty.org/en/documents/pol10/7200/2024/en (accessed March 31, 2025).

Chakrabarti, Shami. (2024). *Human Rights: The Case for the Defence*. Allen Lane.

Chiwanza, Tadukzwa Hillary. (2022). A brief history of human rights in Africa. *Africa Rebirth*. https://www.africarebirth.com/the-brief-history-of-human-rights-in-africa (accessed March 31, 2025).

Columbia University. (2024). Trump administration human rights tracker. https://trumphumanrightstracker.law.columbia.edu (accessed March 31, 2025).

Dworkin, Ronald. (2011). *Justice for Hedgehogs*. Harvard University Press.

EU Agency for Fundamental Rights. (2024). Fundamental rights report 2024. https://fra.europa.eu/sites/default/files/fra_uploads/fra-2024-fundamental-rights-report-2024_en.pdf (accessed March 31, 2025).

Gensler, H. (2013). *Ethics and the Golden Rule*. Routledge.

Hoffman, V. (2019). *Making the New Middle East: Politics, Culture, and Human Rights*. Syracuse University Press.

Human Rights Measurement Initiative. (2024). The state of human rights (by country or region). https://humanrightsmeasurement.org/the-state-of-human-rights-in-south-asia (accessed March 31, 2025).

Human Rights Watch. (2024a). Egypt. https://www.hrw.org/world-report/2024/country-chapters/egypt (accessed March 31, 2025).

Human Rights Watch. (2024b). Iran. https://www.hrw.org/world-report/2024/country-chapters/iran (accessed March 31, 2025).

Human Rights Watch. (2024c). Iraq. https://www.hrw.org/world-report/2024/country-chapters/iraq (accessed March 31, 2025).

Human Rights Watch. (2024d). Latin America. https://www.hrw.org/news/2022/01/13/latin-america-alarming-reversal-basic-freedoms (accessed March 31, 2025).

Human Rights Watch. (2024e). Second Trump term is a threat to the US, world. https://www.hrw.org/news/2024/11/06/us-second-trump-term-threat-rights-us-world (accessed March 31, 2025).

Human Rights Watch. (2024f). United States. https://www.hrw.org/world-report/2024/country-chapters/united-states (accessed March 31, 2025).

Kundal, Navjeet Sidhu. (2023). The evolution and impact of human rights. *International Journal of Science and Research*, 12: 11. https://www.ijsr.net/archive/v12i11/SR231118171059.pdf (accessed March 31, 2025).

Livingston, S., and Miller, M. (2024). *Connective Action and the Rise of the Far-Right: Platforms, Politics, and the Crisis of Democracy*. Oxford University Press.

Lopez, Leopoldo. (2023). Testimony of Leopoldo Lopez to US Senate Foreign Relations Committee. March 28, 2023. https://www.foreign.senate.gov/imo/media/doc/45179b35-ff38-bb09-829a-641cb1d81a84/032823_Lopez_Testimony2.pdf (accessed March 31, 2025).

Morgan, M. (2021). Understanding the rise of global authoritarianism. Stanford University News. https://fsi.stanford.edu/news/understanding-global-rise-authoritarianism (accessed March 31, 2025).

Schmidt, A. (2019). Trump's alarming human rights agenda. American Progress. https://www.americanprogress.org/wp-content/uploads/sites/2/2019/12/Human-Rights3.pdf (accessed April 18, 2025).

Smit, Jana Louise. (2019). Ancient civilizations timeline: The complete list from Aboriginals to Incans. *History Cooperative*, December 15, 2019. https://historycooperative.org/ancient-civilizations (accessed March 31, 2025).

Svolik, Milan. (2012). *The Politics of Authoritarian Rule*. Cambridge University Press.

Tolentino, Cierra. (2024). The evolution, growth, and history of human rights. History Cooperative. https://historycooperative.org/history-of-human-rights (accessed March 31, 2025).

UN Commission on Human Rights. (2024). What are human rights? https://www.ohchr.org/en/what-are-human-rights (accessed March 31, 2025).

University of Washington. (2015). Human rights in the Middle East. https://digital.lib.washington.edu/server/api/core/bitstreams/a4be94e5-9d8f-4f56-a065-d6623abbd305/content (accessed April 18, 2025).

Viljoen, Fraz. n.d. International human rights law: A short history. United Nations. https://www.un.org/en/chronicle/article/international-human-rights-law-short-history (accessed March 31, 2025).

RTA

2

Problems, Controversies, and Solutions

Human rights are universal, inalienable, and indivisible. Human rights treaties have been designed to help us to avoid problems and to live more harmoniously with each other. If we all agreed on how to solve a social problem, we would work together so there would be no problem. Although people may agree that rights are important, they may disagree about whose rights are more important when there are competing rights. When a human rights violation occurs, people may debate about why it exists, who it affects, and what to do about it.

People of every gender, race, nationality, ethnicity, age, religion, and other category have worked in defense of human rights. Some have put their own lives on the line to protect the rights of others. However, if human rights were respected by everyone everywhere, the world would look different than it does today. This chapter explores some of the major types of human rights violations that exist around the world.

There are, of course, many different types of human rights that merit analysis. This chapter explores a set of human rights that are in concert with those identified by major international human rights data collection organizations. The Geneva Academy of International Humanitarian Law and Human Rights (Zipoli 2024) reports that during the last decade the human rights landscape has undergone a significant transformation and that our understanding of it has improved thanks to the use of digital human rights tracking tools and databases. The information gathered has helped us to better understand what is going on across the world and has improved how human rights are implemented,

---

Afghani girls attend a ceremony commemorating the opening of a new girls' high school building in Kabul in 2011. Since the Taliban returned to power in 2021, it has banned education for girls beyond the 6th grade. Over 130 million girls are denied access to education worldwide. (ResoluteSupportMedia via Flickr, Creative Commons license CC-BY-2.0)

reported, and monitored. Better data has assisted our understanding of how well the world is complying with the UN's 2030 Sustainable Development Goals (SDGs), which are designed to promote a more humane, healthy, sustainable, and just world. Collecting systematic data on human rights through metrics, such as those from digital human rights tracking tools and databases and the HRMI, helps societies to obtain a comprehensive, cross-national assessment of human rights practices. These evaluations include objective, consistent measures of what types of efforts people feel are desirable, important, and useful. This information can help guide policy priorities, inform strategies, budgeting, accountability, and assessment of human rights impact and be used by policy makers, government leaders, practitioners, and everyday people alike (Brook, Clay and Randolph 2020; Zipoli 2024).

The HMRI identifies three broad types of human rights—Quality of Life, Safety from the State, and Empowerment—with sub-groups in each. Quality of Life rights include the right to education, right to housing, right to health, and the right to work. Safety from the State rights include freedom from arbitrary arrest, freedom from enforced disappearance, freedom from the death penalty, freedom from torture and ill-treatment, and capital/corporal punishment. Empowerment rights include the right to assembly and association, right to opinion and expression, right to participate in government, and freedom of religion and belief.

This chapter includes a few human rights indicators for analysis in addition to those listed by the HRMI. These include, under the Safety from the State heading, war, terrorism, autocracy, and mass shootings. Under Empowerment rights, additional topics include diversity, equity, and inclusion (DEI), the rise of disinformation, narratives that endorse hatred and discrimination (with emphasis on gender, sex, race, religion, and migrants), as well as climate and demographic changes.

Quality of Life Rights Issues

HRMI (2025a) general quality of life data for eighty-seven countries found that the nations with the highest quality of life rating were Germany, Belgium, Estonia, Chile, and Poland. The countries with the lowest quality of life rating were Niger, Sudan, Tanzania, Madagascar and Ethiopia. The following sections take a closer look at specific factors that influence quality of life around the world.

Education

All human rights treaties acknowledge that people—especially children—have a right to education. This includes math, social studies, humanities, history, language, physical fitness, music, and art, as well as human rights education. The UDHR states that education is fundamental for both individuals and societies because a community cannot grow to be productive and kind unless people are provided the skills to help them to be well-rounded human beings. Primary education is to be free, compulsory, and universal for all children. A movement exists toward making secondary education free, compulsory, and universal as well. In a few communities, higher education or vocational training is free, although this varies significantly around the world (UNESCO 2020).

Implementation of education is required in nations that have ratified the UN CRC. This international human rights treaty has been ratified by all of the UN member countries except for one—the United States. Nations that have ratified and implemented the CRC report higher educational scores, student satisfaction, teacher satisfaction, less crime, and greater wellbeing (Lundy et al. 2022). Human rights education content can be scaffolded from preschool through higher education and professional training programs and has been found to be very effective in creating rights-respectful individuals, schools, and societies (Vissing 2023).

Not all countries have made education available to all students. UNESCO (2023) reports that about 258 million children are not in school. Around 155 countries legally guarantee nine years or more of compulsory education, but only ninety-nine guarantee twelve years of free education. Over 102 million children lack basic literacy skills, and only six in ten youth will finish secondary school in 2030. Over half, 3.7 million of the world's 7.1 million refugee children, do not attend school. Worldwide, girls are provided with less access to education than are boys, creating gender disparity that will impact the totality of female's lives. Over 130 million girls around the globe are denied the access to education (United Nations 2023d). In countries that require that all children receive primary education, girls' education may end at that level, as secondary schooling is not allowed or possible for females.

The quality of education may vary significantly depending upon where someone lives. Educational quality is related to the amount of financial investment a community or nation is willing to provide for education. HMRI (2025b) data found that 153 countries vary widely in how well they achieved income-adjusted benchmarks for educating students. The five nations achieving the highest benchmarks were Burundi, Singapore, Vietnam, Japan, and Poland, while the countries that ranked lowest in achieving income-adjusted educational benchmarks were Niger, Mali, Mauritania, Pakistan, and Ghana.

Qualifications and training of teachers vary dramatically around the world as well. In some places, teachers are required to have a college education and professional license, while in other places teachers may have no formal training at all. This is especially the case in early childhood education. While the early years of a child's life are fundamental in brain, cognitive, social, and physical development, many children are taught by people who have not been trained on how to help children to achieve their highest potential. Investing in education and healthcare are proven factors that can significantly improve the lives of individuals and societies (Alexander 2023; Harvard Center for the Developing Child 2023).

Human Rights Watch (2023a, 2023b) identifies that a variety of actions that can be considered "attacks on education" are increasing throughout the world. These attacks include bombings, school shootings, attacks on teachers and students, occupation by police or the military, recruitment of students into gangs or soldiering, or destruction of buildings, books, or educational resources. Conceptually, curricula are under attack, as information on sex, race, history, or anything deemed controversial may be banned. Books and educational materials may be removed from libraries or even burned (Vissing and Juchniewicz 2022). The CRC articles support children's access to educational materials so that they can be empowered to make their own decisions; refusing to let children have equal access to education may have negative social repercussions as communities and educational systems evolve.

Public education is based on a democratic principle of equality. If all children in a community are taught at the same school by the same teacher using the same books and tested in the same way, then all children have equal access to learn the same material and succeed. This should enable them to get the same quality of jobs no matter who they are or what they look like. However, public education in many areas has come under attack. Schools may not be available, their curriculum are not comprehensive, and public schools are being replaced with for-profit schools, charter schools, private schools, and edubusinesses whose main goal is business profit, not necessarily high-quality student education (Nadworny 2023; Schrecker 2010).

Food

One of the most fundamental human rights is having enough to eat. Food also needs to be nutritious in order for the human body to operate properly and remain healthy. Access to sufficient quantity and quality of food varies enormously both across the globe and within a given country, with some categories of people going hungry at much higher rates than others. Over 828 million people in seventy-two countries are experiencing a hunger crisis, and the numbers are steadily increasing worldwide. In 2021, 2.3 billion people, or 29.3 percent of the world's population, were moderately to severely food insecure after the rise of COVID-19. About 924 million people, or almost 12 percent of the world's population, became severely food insecure—an increase of 207 million—in a span of only two years. Of the people who do have food, over three billion cannot access or afford to eat a healthy diet. Non-nutritious food generally costs less than nutritious food and is more widely available. At the time of this writing, famine is a particular problem in Gaza, South Sudan, and Mali (World Food Programme 2024; World Health Organization 2022a). HRMI (2025b) measured how well a country is using its resources to ensure people's right to food is fulfilled. Of 136 nations, those that use their resources most effectively include Tuvalu, Tonga, Taiwan, South Korea, and Latvia, while those nations that are least successful in doing so are Papua New Guinea, Guatemala, Timor-Leste, Libya, and Angola. Hunger is predicted to continue unless global action is taken.

Why is hunger occurring? The World Health Organization (2022b) and the World Food Programme (2024) point out that hunger is a human made problem as well as one related to environmental issues and climate change. War and conflict are responsible for over 70 percent of the hungry people in the world. As observed in conflict areas such as Ukraine, Palestine, and parts of Africa, war dislocates people from their homes where they could store food and cook, obliterates access to food in stores, and results in people losing their jobs and incomes so they cannot pay for whatever meager foods might be available. Food production can also be curtailed in conflict areas. Bringing food in from outside sources may be almost impossible.

Climate change is destroying the typical cycle for food production. Droughts, floods, high temperatures, hurricanes, tornadoes, tsunamis, earthquakes, and fires are increasing in intensity and frequency around the world. These climate shocks destroy crops and the ability of people to grow enough to feed themselves. Crops once sold for money may be devastated by the weather so that farmers cannot support themselves or provide others with food. Fertilizer prices have increased dramatically, as have gas prices, which has impacted imports and exports and reduced food supplies. Agribusinesses make it harder for farmers to obtain seeds and grow crops in ways that helped to sustain them in the past.

Hunger is related to poverty, which is related to the economic condition of the state or community. Poverty is highest worldwide for women and children. The World Health Organization (2022c) reports that 45 million children under age five suffer from wasting, a form of malnutrition that increases a child's risk of death by twelve times, and that 249 million children have stunted growth and development due to poor nutrition. Two out of three children are not fed diet that is minimally nutritious, required for their to grow and develop properly.

Health

Access to good health is a fundamental human right present in human rights treaties. This includes both physical and mental health. However, gross disparities exist globally and within nations in people's living conditions, which can affect their health. Access to healthcare providers and people's ability to afford healthcare also vary greatly. Where we live impacts our health, but so does who we are, from a demographic perspective. People of different genders, races, ethnicities, abilities, and ages may not have access to good health conditions where they live, and they may not be able to obtain good quality care when they need it. In this section some of the main health disparities are examined from a human rights issues perspective. These include hunger and nutrition, housing and homelessness, access to physical healthcare services, reproductive healthcare, access to mental healthcare, and access to vaccines and the prevention of epidemics such as COVID-19 (DeLaet and DeLaet 2015). HMRI (2025a) measured whether a country is using its resources to ensure people's right to health is fulfilled. Of 141 countries, those countries most successful in doing so include Finland, France, Nicaragua, and Germany while the least successful are Nigeria, Equatorial Guinea, Somalia, and Chad.

Physical Health

Healthcare providers are keenly aware that poverty and inequality impact how healthy someone will be, how long they will live, and what the quality of their life will be like. While nutritious food and safe housing are foundational to good health and the prevention of health problems, access to physical healthcare services is also a mainstay human right. Tackling health inequities and identifying how climate change exacerbates negative health conditions are among the high priority issues for the human rights community.

Epidemiologists indicate that noncommunicable diseases constitute seven of the top ten causes of death. These include heart disease, cancer, diabetes, and other disorders. Cardiovascular diseases, including stroke, high blood pressure, and ischemic heart disease are the leading causes of death globally, accounting for 28 percent of total deaths in 2021. Dementia is increasing worldwide, which is posing unique new challenges for healthcare providers and families who care for their loved ones. Respiratory infections, especially respiratory syncytial virus and influenza, are on the rise. The public health community is also concerned about the impact of "long-COVID," the long-term health effects that some people have experienced after battling the COVID-19 virus. Access to and the cost of pharmaceuticals, including life-saving drugs like insulin, as well as drug resistance, are global concerns (World Health Organization 2022c; 2024c).

People with disabilities suffer many more healthcare challenges than people who do not have ability challenges. Access to healthcare providers is more limited in lower income communities, where the quality of care is technologically and pragmatically considerably lower. Climate change and violence impose burdens on people in lower and middle-income countries, where their life expectancy is thirty-four years lower, infant mortality 100 times higher, and suicide and interpersonal violence thirty times higher than for people in higher income communities.

Common measures of health include morbidity (or presence of illness) and mortality (or death). Child mortality is an indicator of the effectiveness of a nation's healthcare system. Children are at the mercy of parents and adults to ensure that their lifestyles are safe and healthy. Historically, one in two babies died before age fifteen, but today that number is only 4 percent, thanks to better preventive care. Yet child mortality continues to be a huge global problem, with 6 million children under age fifteen dying each year—1,600 per day, or a child death every eleven minutes (Dattani et al. 2023). The greatest number of infant deaths are occurring in African nations (World Population Review 2024b). Worldwide, the main causes of child mortality include malnutrition, infectious diseases (e.g., pneumonia, malaria, HIV/AIDS), accidents, and child abuse. In the United States, main causes of child death include firearms, drug overdoses, and car accidents (USA Facts 2023).

Comparative data shows that while the United States spends much more for healthcare than other countries, most developed nations have population health outcomes that are much healthier. Some reports show that out of thirty-five developed nations, the United States comes in last on most health indicators, and this has been the trend since 2004. Scandinavian countries tend to fare well on health and happiness measures. From a human rights perspective, access and affordability are key factors in healthcare disparity. For instance, when comparing lower income people in the United States and the UK, costs prevented half of those in the United States from getting care but only 12 percent of those in the UK. About a quarter of higher-income people in the United States found that money was a barrier to getting care but only 7 percent in the UK. Among the developed nations surveyed, the United States is the only one without universal health insurance coverage (Commonwealth Fund 2021; Howard 2023).

Reproductive Health

Sexual and reproductive healthcare is a human right, one that is critically important to women worldwide (United Nations Population Fund 2024). Globally there are 257 million women who want to avoid pregnancy but have few options for doing so. They may have been raped or unable to prevent intercourse or have no access to methods of safe contraception, as well as a host of other reasons. They may be prevented from terminating an unwanted pregnancy as well. The UN Population Fund found that 60 percent of unintended pregnancies end in an abortion, many of which are illegal and half are unsafe, causing death to the woman.

Rape is a common war tactic that increases the incidence of unintended pregnancies. Dr. Natalia Kanem of the UN reported that the staggering number of unintended pregnancies worldwide represents a global failure to uphold women and girls' basic human rights. "For the women affected, the most life-altering reproductive choice—whether or not to become pregnant—is no choice at all. By putting the power to make this most fundamental decision squarely in the hands of women and girls, societies can ensure that motherhood is an aspiration and not an inevitability" (World Health Organization 2024b).

Viewing reproductive healthcare as a human right is nothing new. Thirty years ago, the International Conference on Population and Development in Cairo, Egypt, identified that all people had sexual and reproductive health and human rights, and in 2004, 191 member states of the World Health Organization created resolutions that were based on gender equality and the importance of sexual health. Their global strategy focused on family planning resources, physical and sexual healthcare, eliminating unsafe abortions, and preventing sexually transmitted infections. Their actions have reduced HIV infection by 38 percent since 2010, made human papillomavirus vaccine available in 60 percent of member states with the aim of eliminating cervical cancer as a public health problem, and increased access to contraception and family planning from 467 million women in 1990 to 874 million in 2022. Over sixty countries have liberalized abortion laws in the past thirty years to safeguard the health of women and adolescent girls. The World Health Organization position is that sexual and reproductive health should never be relegated to the margins of healthcare but recognized as critical for the overall wellbeing of individuals and communities (World Health Organization 2024b; United Nations Population Fund 2024). However, recent years have seen a rollback of some reproductive rights, including in the United States, where some states have enacted more restrictive legislation on abortion since the Supreme Court overturned the *Roe v. Wade* decision that had previous ensured a right to abortion at the federal level.

Mental Health

A cause-and-effect relationship exists between physical health and mental health. One can directly and indirectly influence the other, and both are influenced by one's socioeconomic status and where one lives. Increased attention by medical and social scientists has led to a greater understanding of mental illness and its relationship to physical and social factors, resulting in a greater general awareness of the importance of mental health. But increased awareness does not mean that there are sufficient services available to address mental health concerns. Even in developed nations, where there are mental health services available than in poorer countries, there are not enough.

Over one billion people reportedly have mental illnesses, although the actual number of people is likely much higher. The website Our World in Data (2024) provides a map showing the prevalence of mental illness worldwide, although it relies on reported data, limited by the fact that some countries do not have accurate reporting systems. That said, the countries with the highest reported mental illness include the United States, Australia, Greenland, Brazil, Iran, and Spain. The United Nations World Health Organization found that 70 percent of people with psychotic disorders do not get the help they need, and the gap is greatest for people in less developed nations. Seven in ten people receive psychosis related treatment in high-income countries but only 12 percent in low-income countries. For people suffering from depression, only 20–30 percent of people in high-income countries receive care, only 3 percent do in lower income countries (United Nations 2022c; World Health Organization 2022b).

Mental disorders are a leading cause of disability worldwide, with no evidence of a decrease ahead. The impact of the COVID-19 pandemic, war, and violence on mental health is regarded as a human rights priority. With supports and treatment, people with mental illness can do very well and live happy, productive, successful lives. Without treatment, people are on their own and may experience not only degradation of physical health but also discrimination. Stigmatization by people who do not understand mental illness makes it less likely that people will seek treatment. Investment in social services and mental health and recovery organizations is recommended in human rights treaties. Having greater public awareness about mental illness, its causes, its effects, and the positive outcomes from care could have positive global benefits for individuals and societies alike.

Access to Vaccines

The COVID-19 pandemic brought vaccines to the forefront as an international human rights issue in two ways. One pertained to access—who got the vaccines and who did not. The other revolved around whether mandating vaccines was a human rights protection or a violation of human rights.

Historically, many diseases have existed that have killed millions of people. In 1796 a vaccine was created to protect people from the deadly disease of smallpox. This was followed by rabies vaccine in 1885, whooping cough vaccine in 1914, flu vaccine in 1945, and polio vaccine in 1955. Measles, mumps, and rubella vaccines were developed in the 1960s. In the 2000s vaccines for Zika, MERS, SARS, and COVID-19 were created (Mayo Clinic 2024). There are now over twenty deadly diseases preventable by vaccines. These vaccines have saved millions of lives around the world, preventing an estimated 5 million deaths per year.

Vaccines have been so effective in controlling disease outbreaks that healthcare leaders at the World Health Assembly created a global vision strategy called the Immunization Agenda 2030 (IA2030) that they believe could save over 50 million lives in the next decade (World Health Organization 2024c). UNICEF (2024b) supports the IA2030 because closing the immunization gap and ensuring that all people are protected against communicable diseases could save millions of lives. The plan requires a global partnership in which healthcare providers, governments, and local leaders invest in primary healthcare. During the COVID-19 pandemic, there emerged a global disinformation campaign about the efficacy of vaccines. In some countries, like the United States, vaccines became a political issue, and some parents refused to let their children (and themselves) be vaccinated because they thought the vaccines would make them sick, even though data consistently proves that the vaccines save lives (Wilkenfeld and Johnson 2022).

Some countries and people have difficulty obtaining vaccines, partly because new vaccines are often initially in short demand. Over 2.7 million children were not adequately vaccinated in 2023. Over half of unvaccinated children live in thirty-one countries, most of which have conflict or fragile economies. They are at high risk for the next pandemic, which Harvard University's School of Public Health (2024) describes as a matter of "not if, but when." The United Nations and World Health Organization are doing their part to prepare (United Nations 2023e). Vaccine development and accessibility will continue to be pressing human rights health issues in the future.

Housing

Housing is another fundamental human right that directly and indirectly impacts one's health and wellbeing. Having a home allows people to keep and prepare food to eat; it provides places for people to toilet, bathe, and wash. Homes give us places to rest and sleep, places where we can be safe from outside dangers. Homes also provide us with support from family and neighbors.

As the population has grown, housing has become both more expensive and harder to access around the globe. The HRMI (2025a) measured the degree to which a nation defended its population's right to housing. Cyprus, Hungry, Ireland, Finland, Albania were strong defenders of this right. Countries such as Niger, Ethiopia, Chad, the Congo, and the Central African Republic were reported to have the greatest struggles ensuring housing. It is challenging to secure accurate numbers of how many people are homeless worldwide because many countries do not have data gathering systems to count them, while some countries wish to downplay the actual number of homeless people because it might tatter their reputation.

Often homeless people prefer to be invisible out of fear that there could be social penalties applied to them if authorities find that they are homeless.

Homelessness, or rough sleeping, had been on the rise before the COVID-19 pandemic and has increased significantly since that time. The World Economic Forum (Henry 2021) reported that over 150 million homeless people, or 2 percent of the world's population, are homeless. The World Population Review (2024d) created a map that shows how much homelessness exists in each country. It shows that the countries with the largest homeless populations are in Asia and Africa. China and India have big homeless populations, but the birth rate in India is higher than China's, which makes their housing problem significant for the future. Nigeria has over 4.5 million homeless people, partially due to economic disparity and partly because of high immigration rates with people needing housing who do not have adequate financial resources. The United States has one of the biggest problems with homelessness when compared with impoverished countries, with a half-million people with nowhere to sleep each night and a housing policy that tends to criminalize them because they are homeless.

In a Kaiser Family Foundation study (Hamel et al. 2024), homelessness was found to increase socioeconomic, physical, and mental health challenges. People without housing are less likely to get the care they need. Healthcare providers seldom ask people about their work, housing, childcare, access to food or transportation, or social support resources, even though these factors can significantly impact their wellbeing. The Kaiser study recommends that healthcare providers ask questions about such resources and link individuals to needed services as part of their healthcare visits.

Homelessness occurs largely because of a lack of available, accessible, affordable housing. The problem of a housing shortage has been predicted for decades, with warnings that communities needed to prepare for an increase in the world's population. Opportunities to provide affordable housing exist but require changing the predominant existing paradigms used to address housing shortages. Communities that have embraced innovative approaches have found that homeless people can live stably in their own homes and make positive contributions to their family and communities (Henry 2021; Vissing, Hudson, and Nilan 2020).

Work

The right to earn a decent living is universal in human rights treaties. Work is also a way for people to use their skills and talents for personal and social fulfillment. But having access to work, and being paid a fair wage, is not universal. Economic inequality is one of the biggest drivers of human rights violations. All types of human rights—economic, civil, social, political, and cultural—are interdependent. Two agreements, the ICCPR and the International Covenant on Economic, Social, and Cultural Rights were both passed in 1966. The UN's 2030 Agenda for Sustainable Development was been built upon the importance of economic equality, as it is directly related to conflicts, environmental crises, and the spread of disease globally.

The HMRI (2025b) asked people if they had access to good jobs and whether they earned (or were provided from another source) a decent living in 152 countries. They found that people in the United Arab Emirates, Iceland, Slovenia, Switzerland, Maldives, Finland, and Luxembourg were responded most favorably, while people in Madagascar, Burundi, Congo, Malawi, and Mozambique responded least favorably. The gap between the "haves" and the "have nots" has grown significantly larger as a social problem in recent years, but as Hassell et al. (2023) observe from intensely analyzing global economic data, although inequality in many countries is high and rising, it is not rising everywhere. In some countries, economic inequality has remained stable or even fallen. For instance, economic inequality has risen in recent years, resulting in a U-shaped curve over time in the United States, Canada, the United Kingdom, and Italy in recent years. Countries that experienced declines in economic inequality in the twentieth century and maintained stable levels of inequality, resulting in an L-shaped curve, are Japan, Sweden, France, Spain, and the Netherlands. Inequality is the result of social decisions, policies, laws, and investments. This means that economic equity could also be achieved if government and business leaders had the will to do so.

The World Bank (2023) has found that addressing economic inequality is challenging because of its intersecting environmental, political, and social factors. The world's poorest nations have the greatest challenges. These include bouncing back from the COVID-19 pandemic, climate change, war and conflict, food insecurity, rising refugee numbers, and employment challenges. A report from the World Economic Forum (Myer 2021) finds that globally, on average, a person's income is estimated to be around US$23,380, but someone from the top 10 percent will earn $122,100 while someone from the bottom 50 percent will earn only $3,920. The richest 10 percent of the global population has cornered 52 percent of the world's income while the poorest half receives only 8 percent.

When one considers wealth, which is not just income but also includes property, stocks, jewelry, art, and other assets of value, the richest 10 percent owns 76 percent of all wealth, while the poorest 50 percent of the world owns only 2 percent of global wealth. There are over 2,769 billionaires in the world who have increased their incomes enormously in the last few years, while over 3.4 billion people live in poverty, or on less than $5.50 per day (Oxfam 2025).

The United Nations (2020) Department of Economic and Social Affairs reports that income inequality has increased in most developed countries and some middle-income countries. It found that the richest 1 percent of the population have gained substantial economic benefits since 1990, while the majority of people across the world have struggled to maintain the same standard of living or found that they had lost ground. Income disparities create stress, frustration, physical and mental health problems, job insecurity, protests, conflicts, immigration, and discontent that trickles down into new generations.

But it does not have to be that way. The United Nations (2021) notes that states or nations have an obligation to respect, protect, and fulfill economic, social, and cultural rights for their citizens. This means that they are required to create long-term plans for economic sustainability and take immediate action to help balance income equality. People who are suffering the most require intervention for their survival. Efficient and effective distribution of resources is one of the duties of all governments. Applying a human rights approach to address economic inequality can reduce poverty and lead to greater social justice in nations around the world (Lienbenberg and Slade 2023).

There are many alternatives for creating economic justice and improving the lives of everyone everywhere. What may work in one location may not in another, so research to identify best practices is necessary. Some solutions may include ensuring a universal income, changing tax laws so that corporations and rich individuals pay more, giving the poor and lower classes tax credits, increasing benefits such as social security, healthcare, education, childcare, housing, food, transportation, retirement and pensions, and access to the internet. Increasing the minimum wage, having a cap on how much people can earn, sharing stock options with workers, and creating more education and job opportunities for traditionally marginalized groups could help reduce gender, race, and ability economic and social disparity. Workers also need labor protections to keep them from working in harmful conditions and for minimal pay. Labor unions are under attack or forbidden in some areas, which puts workers at risk for exploitation.

Safety from the State Rights Issues

This section addresses safety measures that are associated with human rights of individuals and groups in relation to states. Rights protections put in place by national laws and international treaties may involve policies or obligations concerning arrests, detainments, capital and corporal punishment, terrorism, gun control, terrorism, and war.

Arbitrary Arrest

Arbitrary arrests are a violation of human rights. During this type of arrest, people are typically given no rational explanation for why they are being arrested and shown no arrest warrants. They may be denied access to communication or their location may be concealed. According to Article 9 of the UDHR, no one shall be denied their liberty and subjected to arbitrary arrest, detention, or exile regardless of circumstances. The ICCPR specifies the protection of individuals from arbitrary arrest and detention.

Alleged violations that lead to arbitrary arrest are just that—arbitrary. Arbitrariness, according to resolution 1997/50 of the UN Commission on Human Rights (2024a), is interpreted broadly to include elements of inappropriateness, injustice, lack of predictability, and due process of law. Common examples include arresting asylum seekers, immigrants, or refugees and arresting someone for alleged drug or substance abuse violations, alleged threats against the government, or engaging in protests, particularly when they concern political or rights issues (Amnesty International 2019). In 2021, over 35,000 people were arbitrarily detained in Belarus alone for alleged violations against the government (UN Commission on Human Rights 2021). HRMI (2025a) data finds that countries such as New Zealand, Australia, South Korea, and Taiwan protect people from arbitrary arrests, which are more likely to occur in China, India, the Democratic Republic of the Congo, or Bangladesh.

Arrests and criminal prosecution of women and girls who have defied Islamic dress code laws have increased in Iran. This is an example of arbitrariness violating human rights. Iran began ramping up the enforcement of mandatory hijab wearing after Mahsa Amini, a young woman who was detained for allegedly improper hijab wearing, died while in police custody. "Morality police" arrested over 500 females for noncompliance of hijab wearing on one day alone, and the arrests have continued under what is called the Noor plan. Women arrested are often also the targets of physical violence (U.S. Institute for Peace 2024). The Syrian Network for Human Rights provided the UN with documentation of over 226 cases of arbitrary arrests in Syria in May 2023 alone, including women and children. They reported that every detainee is tortured from the first moment of their arrest and that many never see their families again and are later categorized as forcibly disappeared (Relief Web 2023).

Forced Disappearance

Forced or enforced disappearance of individuals is characterized by the United Nations (2024a) as arrest, detention, abduction, or depriving someone of their liberty at the hands of people authorized by the state to conceal their fate or whereabouts. Forced disappearance practices conflict with mandates from the Declaration on the Protection of All Persons from Enforced Disappearance. HRMI (2025a) data reports the people living in New Zealand, Australia, Nepal, South Korea, and Singapore are least likely to worry about forced disappearance, but those in the Democratic Republic of the Congo, China, Mexico, Saudi Arabia, and Venezuela have fewer protections. Sri Lanka has one of the highest global rates of disappearance, with over 100,000 people missing since 1980 (Amnesty International 2024).

Forced disappearance, as well as subjecting individuals to torture, is used as a strategy to seed terror within societies and exert control over a population. Families are often ignorant of what happened to their disappeared loved ones and suffer emotional distress ranging from despair, uncertainty, hope, fear, and loss. Human rights defenders, journalists, key witnesses, relatives of these people, and lawyers seem to be particularly targeted. An estimated 1,000 people are disappeared each day around the world (United Nations 2024a).

In recent years, greater awareness of the disappearance of "invisible" people—people of low status—has led to increased attention to the problem. Examples include Indigenous women and girls and children in residential schools (Morris 2023). African girls have been kidnapped and disappeared from the schools they were placed in for education and protection (Busari 2024). Disappearance of women and girls is a global concern, one that has often been ignored because of the lower status of these victims (Kapur and Alshaibi 2023).

Capital Punishment

Capital punishment is typically referred to as the death penalty. It is an authorized killing of a person by the state as punishment for a crime that they are thought to have committed. Types of capital punishment have included shooting, beheading, electrocution, clubbing, hanging, drowning, and lethal injection. Capital punishment has been used throughout history and around the world, but in the last century its use has been abolished in many countries as inhumane. The death penalty is not in use in 112 countries. It is still on the books in fifty-five countries, but it is sparingly used. Countries that continue to execute people include China, Iran, Saudi Arabia, Egypt, Vietnam, Yemen, Iraq, and the United States. Although meant, at least in part, to serve as a deterrent to others, the death penalty has not been proven to eradicate the types of crimes to which it is applied. Even so, the number of executions has risen globally in recent years with over 2,016 deaths in 2022 in fifty-two countries. Amnesty International projects that over 28,282 people were under death sentences in 2022 globally. China executes the most people (883 recorded in 2022), but those numbers are likely underestimates since China does not release records about the use of its death penalty. Amnesty International also suspects that North Korea uses the death penalty but cannot confirm that (BBC 2024).

There is a fine line between officially sanctioned executions and those that are conducted unofficially. Some executions may be performed without judicial authorization. Use of torture and aggression that leads to mortality may be used by members of the military or police or by vigilantes (Adachi 2017; Project on Government Oversight 2024).

Corporal Punishment

Corporal punishment is any punishment in which physical force is used and intended to cause some degree of pain or discomfort. The term is usually used in reference to the treatment of children. Corporal punishment can include hitting, smacking, slapping, spanking, kicking, shaking, throwing, scratching, pinching, biting, burning, scalding, pulling hair, boxing ears, attacking children with a hand or implement, forcing children to stay in uncomfortable positions, or the forced ingestion of dangerous substances. Non-physical corporal punishment are actions designed to be cruel and degrading that belittle, humiliate, denigrate, scapegoat, threaten, scare, or ridicule a child (World Health Organization 2024a).

Corporal punishment is found around the world, in homes, schools, and organizations who are supposed to provide oversight to children's wellbeing. The WHO reports that at least 60 percent of children age two to fourteen regularly suffer physical punishments by adults, and in some areas it can be as high as 100 percent, with boys, girls, rich, and poor students all subject to this form of treatment. Prevalence remains high despite research that documents that corporal punishment provides no positive outcomes and, in fact, increases children's emotional, physical, cognitive, social, criminal, educational, and behavioral problems. A 2030 Agenda for Sustainable Development goal, Target 16.2, seeks to "end abuse, exploitation, trafficking and all forms of violence against and torture of children." Corporal punishment and its associated harms are preventable.

Life in Prison Without Parole

Some people are kept on death row or are imprisoned for the rest of their life, many without the chance for parole. Life imprisonment has become a global human rights concern (Reade 2018). The UN Standard Minimum Rules for the Treatment of Prisoners is known as the Nelson Mandela Rule, which advocates that imprisonment be the vehicle for rehabilitation and reducing recidivism. Life in prison without parole (LPWP) is contradictory to that goal. It removes the opportunity for rehabilitation. It is also a dehumanizing lifestyle that undermines dignity and the possibility of making contributions to society. Globally, around 5,000 criminal offenses are associated with life sentences, but some crimes are nonviolent (applying to 24 percent of those sentenced to LPWP in the United States), which brings into question the appropriateness of the sentence for certain crimes. The only nation that has laws affirming that children can be put into jail for life sentences without the chances of parole is the United States. This is a violation of children's rights standards as set in the CRC. There is variation concerning how long children may be put into jail in other countries (Child Rights International Network 2015).

Terrorism

Intolerance breeds violence that can be used to invoke terror on others. Terrorist activity and the increased visibility of hate groups is a globally pervasive human rights problem. Terrorism consists of violence that uses fear, or terrorizes people, to further some aim. It can be difficult to define if it does not have a clear political goal or organized group behind it. Terrorism is an ancient concept but is sometimes associated with the French Revolution's Reign of Terror. The concept of terrorism has gained worldwide attention since the 1970s, with well publicized events such as airplane hijackings and violence associated with nationalist movements in Ireland.

Far-right extremism is regarded by foreign policy experts as a global problem. The Center for Strategic and International Studies (2024) produced a global terrorism risk assessment for 2024 surveying terror as an international threat. Violent far-right and far-left extremist ideologies have become more prominent around the world, especially in groups like Hamas and Hezbollah. Analysis by Statista (2024b) identifies that trends in the Middle East and Northern Africa by radical Islamists have shaped increased international terrorism, while there has been a decrease of terrorist attacks in Europe and Asia since 2017. Terrorism is also common in Central and South America as well as throughout Africa.

The US Government Accountability Office (2023) finds that an increase in domestic terrorism is more of a terrorist threat than international terrorism. Far-right movements spread ideas of white supremacy and pursue discriminatory policies that restrict basic human rights and dignity and interfere with promoting human rights issues. Domestic hate groups are directly associated with violent hate-motivated incidents, violent crimes, and mass terror attacks occurring across multiple countries.

International terrorism is also on the rise. The CIA reports that there are more than sixty-five terrorist groups designated by the US State Department as Foreign Terrorist Organizations. Some of the most well-known international terrorist leaders have included Hassan Nasrallah, Secretary-General of Hezbollah; Hossein Salami, Commander-in-Chief of Iranian terrorist organization IRGC-Quds Force; Ismail Haniyeh, Hamas political chief; Robert Rundo, Serbia's co-founder of Rise Above Movement; Haibatullah Akhundzada, Emir of the Taliban; Sirajuddin Haqqani, Commander of the Haqqani network and Interior Minister of the Taliban; Abdul-Malik al-Houthi, Yemen's leader of the Houthis; Ayman al-Zawahiri, Afghanistan's head of al-Qaeda; Shahab al-Muhajir, an ISIS-K leader; and Ahmad al-Hamidawi, the Secretary-general of Iraq's Kata'ib Hezbollah.

The desire to terrorize others may have specific purposes, such as taking over their land, their government, or brutalizing others just because they are hated.

Intolerance breeds hate and create stereotypes that are used to dehumanize others. Therefore, addressing intolerance is central to decreasing terror. Data on an accurate amount of the global prevalence of intolerance is challenging to obtain, but estimates are that there are thousands of hate and terror groups around the world. The Southern Poverty Law Center (SPLC) in the United States has collected data on hate groups that give a barometer about what may be happening else. It documented 1,430 hate and anti-government extremist groups in 2023 that are hate groups run by white supremacists (2023, 2024). These groups have both online and physical organizational infrastructures that have been shown to oppose inclusive democracy, attempt to legitimize insurrections, promote hate as virtuous, and promote disinformation and false conspiracy theories that justify the oppression of others. Hate groups exist from coast to coast, but some geographic and cultural centers seem to ferment support for ideological hate groups. SPLC reports (2019, 2023, 2024) indicate that hate is transmitted to others through social media and that hate rhetoric in one region may promote it in others. For instance, anti-immigrant and anti-LGBTQ+ hate are common in the United States but are also rising in many other parts of the world.

Guns and Mass Shootings

Intolerance and hate can quickly escalate into violence, especially when guns and other weapons are available. Guns are identified as a public health problem because gun violence is common and can impact both physical and emotional health. However, experts acknowledge that a health-focused approach to the problem is insufficient by itself because gun violence is also a criminal justice problem associated with inequalities, education, trust in institutions, peer pressure, toxic masculinity and power, and commercial interests, and pressure to change laws (Lancet 2023). Using a human rights perspective approach to prevent gun violence could cut across these institutional divides.

From a human rights perspective, it is useful to understand the origin of gun proliferation. The United States has less than 5 percent of the world's population but over 46 percent of its civilian-owned guns. It is the only nation in the world where civilian-owned guns outnumber people, with 120 guns for every 100 Americans, according to the Switzerland-based Small Arms Survey. For comparison, in the Falkland Islands there are sixty-two guns per 100 people, a gun ownership rate is almost half that of the United States. Yemen has the third-highest gun ownership rate at fifty-three guns per 100 people. The United States also has the highest rate of homicide by guns of any nation. In 2019, the number of US deaths from guns was four per 100,000 people, which is eighteen times the average rate in other developed countries. Since the COVID-19 pandemic, gun manufacturing and ownership has increased substantially, as have gun-related deaths of all types (Fox 2024; Masters 2022).

Mass shootings have had variable responses worldwide. In some countries, like Australia, Canada, Germany, South Africa, and the United Kingdom, shootings have prompted governments to tighten gun laws, but in the United States and other nations, there has either been no curtailment of gun control legislation or lukewarm attempts that have little impact. In Mexico, there is reportedly only one gun store in the country, and it is controlled by the military. Australia found that after banning assault-style weapons and tightening licensing rules, gun deaths dropped by 51 percent, while after the UK Parliament tightened gun laws and banned private ownership, gun-related deaths fell by 25 percent (Fox 2024; Masters 2022).

After a US assault weapons ban ended in 2004, and with gun manufacturers winning authorization to streamline export approvals in 2020, over 3.7 million semiautomatic American-made guns have been pouring into countries around the world in the past few years. While the majority of assault weapons are sold within the United States, the export of such weapons has an enormous impact on other nations and the safety of their citizens. In some countries, such as Canada, there are strict regulations of such weapons, but in others, such as Guatemala, there are few regulations at all. According to Tom Malinowski, US Assistant Secretary of State for Democracy, Human Rights and Labor from 2014 to 2017, "if you look at how civilians die in armed conflicts around the world, it's hard not to conclude that the true weapons of mass destruction are these small arms that are subject to the fewest controls" (Riley 2023). The company that sells the most weapons and makes the most money from gun sales, is Sig Sauer Inc., a company that has enormous influence on politicians and gun legislation in the United States. The firearm industry has weakened gun-control laws not just in the United States but in other countries around the world, particularly in Latin America.

The Biden administration issued an order that would prioritize human rights as a factor in weapons sales, but it is very difficult to enforce this order or track where guns sold end up and how they are used, as oversight changes for gun manufactures reduced Congress's ability to monitor gunmakers' sales abroad

(Riley 2023). Because there is little monitoring of gun sales or their use, current trends would predict the rise of guns of all types being used in non-military assaults, in which innocent people are victims. Many of these gun assaults are strategically designed to evoke terror.

War

Wars and violent conflicts have occurred throughout human history. Ongoing conflicts in 2024 include those in Ukraine, Gaza, Sudan, Myanmar, Ethiopia, Haiti, the Sahel region of Africa, and Armenia and Azerbaijan. The Council on Foreign Relations (2024; Koup 2021) maintains a global conflict tracker that shows the countries in which wars and violent conflicts are occurring, and it makes clear that there are few places in the world that escape human rights violations resulting from conflict.

The definition of what constitutes a war can be confusing. Not every armed conflict is considered as a war, and not all wars are officially declared to be one. In general, war is defined as a state-based conflict in which at least 1,000 battle-related deaths occur within a year (Uppsala Conflict Data Program 2024). The main reasons for war include economic gain, territorial gain, religion, nationalism, revenge, civil war, revolutionary war, and defensive war (Goodman 2024).

The number of people directly killed in wars throughout history is approximated at 1 billion, but this does not count the vast number of people who were collateral damage and died later from injury, exposure to toxins, starvation, or torture. In addition to death and disability, victims of war suffer from the loss of family, friends, home, and community. There may be no safe place to go, as even schools and hospitals may become military targets. Food may be difficult to find, available water may be polluted, and transportation systems can be overwhelmed or broken. Normal structures and infrastructures may be compromised or destroyed. Humane, civil behavior may be replaced with aggression and self-defense. Shadow crime systems may emerge that exploit innocent victims. Increased use of drugs, violence, psychological warfare, and rape as war tactics are common, which result in traumas that can be pervasive for the rest of one's life and cut lives short (Center for Strategic and International Studies 2024).

The UDHR was designed after World War II to prevent more wars from occurring. The United Nations is the world's peacekeeper and has tried to work with global leaders and nations to create conditions that will support the development and sustainability of peace and justice. The UN Security Council has primary authorization to promote peace and security around the world. The various human rights treaties described in Chapter 1 of this book were designed to directly and indirectly promote peace through the actions that individuals and nations take. Peacekeeping actions, like diplomacy and economic incentives, have been challenged as conflicts around the world become more intertwined, with economic, multinational, and geopolitical alignments shifting the global landscape.

War is big business. The military–industrial complex benefits through the development, sale, and distribution of weapons and reaps huge financial benefit through maintaining global violence. Lobbyists pressure governments to finance military endeavors. The US Pentagon has a budget that is larger than the GDP of all but seventeen countries in the world (Semler 2022). China has the largest military, followed by the United States, India, North Korea, and Russia. Fourteen of the world's twenty largest militaries are in developed nations (Hedges 2003). The types and numbers of people who make money directly and indirectly from war are enormous, so the financial incentives of keeping perpetual war going are huge (Bloomfield 2021).

There are always at least two sides to any story, and in war, conflicting stories and interests complicate a human rights resolution. The following sections explore two examples of contemporary wars, showing how disputes about rights issues tend to keep war going. No matter what the conflict, high emotional and financial stakes are on the line.

Ukraine and Russia

The history and current conflict between these two nations goes back hundreds of years. Briefly, the Russian Empire was controlled by czars, who were overthrown in a 1917 Russian Revolution. As a result of the revolution, the land was divided into a set of socialist republics, one of which was Ukraine. These republics became known collectively as the Union of Soviet Socialist Republics (USSR). In 1918 Ukraine declared independence from Russia, as did other nations. But three years later, the new independent Ukrainian Soviet Socialist Republic government was overthrown by Soviet troops and taken back by the USSR. Joseph Stalin was a Soviet ruler whose policies killed millions of people, primarily starving ethnic Ukrainians. During World War II, Nazi troops invaded and occupied Ukraine and caused enormously devasting conditions for the people.

After the war, Nikita Khrushchev became president of the USSR. An ethnic Russian and former head of the Communist Party of Ukraine, Khrushchev gave Ukraine more political and cultural freedoms and transferred Crimea away from Russia. The USSR was experiencing economic stagnation and political strife in trying to control the different ethnicities across its regions, and in 1991 many of the USSR countries declared their independence. Other nations, including Ukraine, followed.

Ukrainian citizens overthrew President Viktor Yanukovych because he was too friendly to Russia. A popular pro-democracy opposition leader, Viktor Yushchenko, who later became president, unexpectedly fell ill, and doctors confirmed that he had been poisoned. The tension between Russia and Ukraine continued, with Russia attempting to take over areas that were Ukraine's, and festering resentments between groups of citizens. In 2019, Volodymyr Zelensky was elected by a large majority as president of Ukraine on a promise to make peace with Russia and restore the Donbas region back to Ukraine. Russian president Vladimir Putin, who is reportedly the richest man in the world, waged a brutal set of attacks to take over land. He has removed Ukrainian children and transported them against their will to Russia, where they are undergoing "resocialization" to become aligned with Russia.

Russia and Ukraine were once the same nation. Russia feels it has a right to take the land back, while Ukraine has been trying for 100 years to be an independent country. Russia has regularly prevented that from occurring in a peaceful way. Russia is the most sanctioned country in the world for human rights violations. While Ukraine too is engaging in warfare, Russia has international condemnation for its aggression and extensive crimes against humanity (Davis 2024; Groch 2023; Sullivan 2022).

Israel and Palestine

This region of the world has experienced violence and human rights violations since World War II. The current humanitarian and human rights crisis in Gaza and Israel appears to have no plausible resolution at this time. Both sides feel they are right in their positions. Essentially, the main Israeli and Palestinian issues revolve around who the land belongs to, whether there should be a two-state solution, the presence of Israeli settlements, refugee treatment, and the "ownership" of Jerusalem.

A 2023 attack by Hamas, the Palestinian political and military authority in Gaza, at an Israel concert resulted in murders and hostage taking that led to Israel's decision to bomb and control the Gaza region. The Hamas attack resulted in 1,200 Israeli deaths and 253 hostages, after which Israel responded with a military campaign in which over 33,000 Palestinians have been killed. Houses, schools, businesses, hospitals, and communities have been destroyed, refugees forced to move multiple times with little access to food, water, electricity, or safety. The result has been the slow death of innocent people, particularly children. The Gaza-Israel conflict is regarded as a major humanitarian crisis by all human rights organizations.

To understand today's conflict, one must go back in time. The Ottoman Empire ruled the region for 400 years, during which it was inhabited largely by Arab Muslims. Jewish people lived elsewhere, largely in east-central Europe. Due to persecution and the rise of antisemitism, the creation of a homeland for Jews and immigration to "the land of Israel" became a Zionist political movement in 1897. Post-World War I political alignments resulted in the Ottoman Turks being defeated by Britain, which then occupied Palestine. The Balfour Declaration created a Jewish homeland on both sides of the Jordan River with the condition that Palestine be an area of Arab independence. Tensions resulted in the Peel Commission of 1937, which proposed a two-state solution in which Palestine would be divided into two states, one Arab and one Jewish.

The rise of Fascism and Nazism and World War II drew Palestine into the conflict. Without going into detail about this complicated and conflictual time, the post-war result was the United Nations giving 55 percent of the land for a Jewish state and 45 percent for the state of Palestine. But Israel came to control three-quarters of Palestine, and Palestinians were expelled from the new Israel state into the areas of Gaza and the West Bank. Egypt controlled Gaza for twenty years until the 1967 Six-Day War, after which Israel controlled Gaza and began building settlements there. In 2005 under international pressure, Israel left the area to be governed by the Palestinian Authority.

This resulted with many Palestinians moving to an ever-smaller piece of land. Gaza became one of the most densely populated areas of the world, with half of its population being under nineteen years of age. A political group called Hamas took control of Gaza in 2006. In 2007 Israel created a blockade on Gaza to protect its border from Hamas. But the UN, the International Committee of the Red Cross, and organizations like Human Rights Watch found the blockade illegal and in violation of the Geneva Convention. The blockade prevents both people and goods from entering or leaving Gaza, creating an unemployment rate of 70 percent for young people who have limited opportunities for socioeconomic growth and access to the outside world. Human Rights Watch and other human rights organization reported that Israel's occupation of Palestine and Gaza committed multiple violations of international human rights law, including unlawful killings, forced displacement and segregation of Palestinians, restrictions of their movement, creation of new settlements, and policies that disadvantage Palestinians. By occupying Palestine by force, Israel incurs international responsibilities and remains accountable for violations of the rights of the Palestinians individually and as a people.

The Israelis feel they are right to protect their people from attack and to protect land that they feel is rightfully theirs. The Palestine people feel that it is their land, that they have a right to their own independent state, and that their treatment by Israel is oppressive and violates human rights. There are major political, economic, religious, and historic issues and international alignments that complicate the question about whose rights are more right in the current crisis between these peoples, but most human rights organizations report that Israel's treatment of innocent citizens in Gaza is unacceptable by human rights standards (Amnesty International 2023; Human Rights Watch 2017; Mayroz 2024; Reuters 2024; Salam 2023; United Nations 2022a).

Empowerment Rights Issues

Empowerment rights are central to people's ability to claim and defend their human rights. This category of rights includes people's rights to gather, associate, and express themselves freely, to practice their chosen religion without persecution, and to have a say in their government and the policies and decisions that affect their daily lives. Empowerment rights involve freedom from discrimination based on characteristics such as age, race, gender, and ability. Population growth and globalization, including migration, have created conditions that threaten human rights, as have climate change, authoritarian systems, and disinformation.

Assembly and Association

The UN Commission on Human Rights (2024c) reports that everyone has the right to freedom of peaceful assembly and association and that these are essential components of democracy. The right of peaceful assembly includes the right to hold meetings, sit-ins, strikes, rallies, events, or protests, both offline and online. The right to freedom of association involves the right of individuals to communicate and organize themselves to express, promote, pursue, and defend their common interests. Freedom of peaceful assembly and of association serve as a vehicle for the exercise of many other rights guaranteed under international law, including the rights to freedom of expression, right to form unions, and the right to conduct public affairs. The right to freedom of peaceful assembly and association is protected by article 20 of the UDHR. The UN provides a tool-kit that police and officials may use to ensure that people's right to assemble and voice their opinions are protected during public protests.

HRMI (2025a) surveys asked if people were able to express themselves freely and fully participate in public life. They found that the countries in which people were most likely to do so included New Zealand, Taiwan, Brazil, Liberia, and Australia while people in the following countries were least likely to be able to do so: Saudi Arabia, China, Hong Kong, Vietnam, and Venezuela.

Opinion and Expression

To be able to have an opinion and voice it is fundamental to human rights, as are journalistic freedoms. HRMI (2025a) surveys asked if people were allowed to hold opinions and express themselves freely. They found that in twenty-eight countries surveyed, people in Taiwan, New Zealand, Papua New Guinea, Brazil, and Australia were most likely to do so, while people in Saudi Arabia, China, Vietnam, Venezuela, and Hong Kong were least likely to be able to express their opinions. The Facts Institute (Caitriona 2024) examined freedom of the press by 180 countries according to Reporters Without Borders. It found that the countries most like to provide journalists freedom are Norway, Denmark, Sweden, Netherlands, Finland, Estonia, Portugal, Ireland, Switzerland, and Germany. Countries where freedom of the press is most curtailed are Eritrea, Syria, Afghanistan, North Korea, Iran, Vietnam, and China. The United States was ranked 55—after Ghana, Chile, and the Ivory Coast and just ahead of Gabon. Of the 180 countries, only 8 (or 4 percent) can boast a favorable climate for journalistic freedom. The data shows that the Middle East and North Africa are the most dangerous places for journalists. In these places, as well as in Asia, there is pressure to avoid writing about sensitive topics.

Religious Freedom

Government actions and religious freedom are directly related. The consolidation of power in autocratic and fundamentalist governments has led to increased violation of religious freedoms as well as human rights in general. Some examples include terrorist attacks and destruction of religious heritage and symbols in Turkey and Syria and proliferation of anti-conversion laws and financial restrictions related to religion in Southeast Asia and the Middle East. The international community and religious leaders have increasingly ignored atrocities committed by autocratic regimes that are strategically valuable to them politically. Violence against people who are of the "wrong" religion has become normalized in many areas of the world. One example is the brutal persecution of the Uyghurs in China. Within religions, divergent trends can lead to persecution of one group by another. For example, Shi'a Muslims have often faced genocide where the Sunni Muslim sect has held power as the majority. Individuals in the West who have adopted more progressive beliefs have increasingly been harassed by religious traditionalists.

According to Catholic Aid organization Aid to the Church in Need (2023), more than 4.9 billion people live in countries where religious freedom was violated, and citizens in sixty-one countries faced severe violations of their religious freedoms. Of the twenty-eight countries with the highest religious persecution (where 4 billion people live, constituting over 51 percent of the world's population), almost half (thirteen) are in Africa. The HRMI (2025a) asked people if they were able to practice, express, or change their religion and beliefs freely. Data from twenty-nine nations reflected that people living in Mexico, Papua New Guinea, Tonga, Brazil, and Taiwan were most able to do so, while people in Maldives, Vietnam, Saudi Arabia, China, and India were least likely. The International Institute for Religious Freedom has created a freedom data spectrum that identifies religious freedom in countries across the world. Pew Research (2024) found that government restrictions and social hostilities tend to go hand in hand. Countries experiencing religion-related wars, militant activity, or ongoing sectarian violence include Afghanistan, Bangladesh, Egypt, India, Iraq, Israel, Nigeria, Pakistan, Sri Lanka, Syria, Thailand, and Yemen.

Participation in Government

Human rights treaties hold that everyone should have equal input into decisions that impact their lives, and that governments need to be receptive to addressing the needs of all citizens. Historically, however, this has not always been the case. Sociologist C. Wright Mills (1956) points out that governments are often led by elite people who have more power than others and who construct laws and social orders that will benefit themselves more than others. Improved participation in government is a goal of human rights advocates, and scholars debate how better participation might be most effectively achieved (Durkee 2022). Civic education can encourage individual participation in governance, so more active incorporation of this type of education could yield results (Chanda 2024). Increasing digital participation may help by involving individuals at grassroots levels, mobilizing groups of like-minded people for social action, problem solving, and political participation that may otherwise not be possible (Mao et al. 2024). Voting is just one part of the right to participation.

There is wide variability internationally in being able to participate in government. The HRMI (2025a) asked people if they were able to vote and participate in public life. In the twenty-eight countries surveyed, people in New Zealand, Liberia, South Korea, Nepal, and Australia were most likely to do so, while people in Saudi Arabia, Hong Kong, Vietnam, Venezuela, and China were least likely to be able to vote and participate in public life. Global Citizen data (Liao 2020) reports that over 2 billion voters in fifty countries have been able to vote to elect their leaders and express their desire for leaders to be held accountable for taking certain actions. In 2015, Saudi women were granted the right to vote and run for office. In Brazil and Nicaragua, people can vote at age sixteen. Austria became the first European Union country to adopt this voting age, increasing Austria's voter base by 200,000. Bolivia has a compulsory voting policies that requires all citizens to cast a ballot. Not doing so can result in fines or being denied their salary.

India has the world's largest vote within its massive population, but not everyone is allowed to vote. A 2019 Citizenship Amendment Bill prohibits migrants without documentation from becoming Indian citizens and denies them the right to vote. The bill allows people from Afghanistan, Pakistan, and Bangladesh the right to apply for Indian citizenship but only if they are Hindu, Christian, Sikh, Jian, Parsi, or Buddhist, thereby prohibiting Muslims from voting, especially those fleeing Myanmar, where Rohingya Muslims have been persecuted.

Diversity, Equity, and Inclusion

The concept of DEI refers to a set of values associated with human rights that address how people should be treated (Arsel, Crockett, and Scott

2021). The idea of DEI has become polarizing in contemporary society, with some groups supporting its integration into policies while others oppose it. Operationally, DEI is controversial because it can refer to differing definitions, measurements, and applications (Esparza et al. 2022). The term diversity generally refers the range of people that make up a group, including characteristics related to identity (such as gender, race, age, ethnicity, sexual orientation, and ability), as well as their life experiences, perspectives, and beliefs. The E in DEI sometimes stands for equality and sometimes for equity in different usages, but these terms are not equivalents. Equality refers to the equal distribution of goods, services, resources, and treatment, while equity focuses on equal access and removal of barriers for historically disadvantaged groups. Inclusion refers to practices, policies, and processes that shape how organizations operate, aiming to create environments where all people are valued and respected and people feel free to share their opinions and be themselves (Beavers 2018).

DEI as a concept emerged during the 1960s civil rights movement and gained popularity in recent years because of discrimination in schools and workplaces that led to the threat of lawsuits due to rights violations. DEI programs are designed to promote tolerance and respect for differences, so that all people have access to the same opportunities. Issues of diversity, equity, and inclusion are embedded into human rights treaties. Human rights education in schools could potentially provide future workers with the skills to be rights-respectful toward others. Critics allege that DEI policies do not work, are insincere or surface-level only, prioritize diversity initiatives over merit-based rewards, involve reverse discrimination, or are poorly implemented. Although human rights advocates see DEI programs as analogous to human rights treaty protections, the DEI approach has become politicized as dangerous and is being rejected by many schools and businesses (Arsel, Crockett, and Scott 2021; Beavers 2018; Esparza et al. 2022; Gomstyn 2023; Vissing 2023; Zheng 2022).

Gender and Sexual Orientation

According to the United Nations (2022b), gender equity is at the heart of human rights, and discrimination based on gender is prohibited in every human rights treaty. Even so, globally, millions of girls and women face discrimination every day, a situation largely attributable to a narrative of female inferiority that is systematically embedded into cultural norms and institutional practices. People who do not conform to typical gender and sexual orientation roles are also subject to discrimination.

Gender is often used as a justification for controlling people's bodies, identities, and lives. Forms of gender discrimination include restrictions on reproductive rights, inequalities in pay and access to employment, limits on social participation and political representation, discriminatory marriage laws, and differential treatment based on stereotypes or assumptions about a person's ability or character based on their gender. Gender discrimination is seen at the macro, meso, and micro levels of society. Macro forms of discrimination are those that are institutionally and often legally based, such as females not being allowed to go to school or drive cars, only being authorized to work in certain types of occupations, and not having choices regarding marital partners or reproduction. Micro discrimination occurs at interpersonal levels and may include women not being able to go out alone or without male supervision and other interactions that deny them of their dignity, equality, and autonomy. Gender-based violence is common, both in the home and within communities, and is sometimes sanctioned by authorities despite international standards protesting such actions.

The UN's Gender Social Norms study, looking at seventy-five countries, found that none had achieved gender equality. About 50 percent of men said they had more right to a job than women, and a third of respondents thought it was acceptable for men to hit their partners. Zimbabwe had the highest amount of bias against women, while Andorra reported the least bias. In Zimbabwe and the Philippines, over 90 percent of people reported that they thought the use of physical violence against women was acceptable and opposed women having control over their own reproductive rights. The study also found a decrease of women in major governmental leadership positions (BBC 2020).

Data gathered by the organization UN Women (2022, 2023a, 2023b) found that the world is failing women and girls, despite international awareness of the importance of curbing discrimination against them. The organization's study on how well the UN's SDGs for 2030 are being achieved found that

> if current trends continue, more than 340 million women and girls—an estimated 8 per cent of the world's female population—will live in extreme poverty by 2030, and close to one in four will experience moderate or severe food insecurity. The gender gap in power and leadership positions remains entrenched, and, at the current rate of progress, the next generation of women

will still spend on average 2.3 more hours per day on unpaid care and domestic work than men. (UN Women 2023b)

The World Economic Forum (2023a) analyzed global gender trends and identified long-standing gender discrimination patterns that continue to exist. It found that the participation of women in the economic sector of the world has diminished in recent years, with the greatest disparities between men and women occurring in the Middle East, North Africa, and Southern Asia. These are the regions where women face the lowest pay as well as substandard working conditions. The regions with the greatest involvement of women in the workforce are North America and Europe. Women are most likely to obtain jobs the informal sector, part of the economy that is often not taxed or monitored by governments. They are also likely to work in healthcare, social services, education, and consumer services. A lack of good available childcare is a global problem for women of all educational levels who attempt to seek employment. Men continue to make more money than women and to secure the majority of leadership positions in most fields around the world. Even among college-educated women, the disparity is great, with women earning 71 cents for every dollar of a similarly qualified man (Savage 2024).

Domestic violence occurs throughout the world and includes assault, rape, verbal and emotional abuse, financial exploitation, social isolation, and a host of other demeaning, degrading, and devastating impacts on women's physical and emotional wellbeing. Rates of domestic violence against women increased during the COVID-19 pandemic (Kippert 2023). Protections for women's rights are particularly poor in the Middle East, parts of Asia, and Africa, where practices intended to exert control over women, including violence, are common. In some areas, women's clothing is regulated, their movements constrained to the home unless supervised by a male. They are not allowed to go to school or engage in paid work outside of the home. Women may be murdered if their partner disapproves of their actions, a practice known as femicide. Over 81,000 women were killed in 2021 (UN Women 2022). In a procedure known as female genital mutilation, over 230 million women have undergone nonconsensual procedures involving partial or total removal of the female external genitalia or other injury to the female genital organs for non-medical reasons (UNICEF 2024a). These procedures are most common in the Middle East, Africa, and Asia, and are often not performed in medical facilities.

Gender identity and sexual orientation are often targeted by the same discriminatory policies. Over sixty nations have created laws that criminalize private consensual sexual relationships and punish people for how they dress, for the groups to which they may wish to belong, for what bathrooms they wish to use, or even what pronouns they prefer. Homophobia, biphobia, transphobia, and discriminatory attitudes toward intersex people remain deeply embedded in many cultures around the world. LGBTQIA+ individuals risk being arrested, blackmailed, stigmatized, extorted, and—in at least six countries—executed. The United Nations (2023b, 2024b) has taken an active position to protect the rights of LGBTQIA+ individuals through their establishments of treaties, Special Rapporteurs, and other mechanisms.

Social movements have emerged around the world to demand rights protections for gender and sexual orientation. These include feminist movements, the #MeToo movement, and a variety of LGBTQIA+ movements. These movements attempt to bring the public's attention, as well as the attention of government officials, the need for greater rights protections.

Race

The World Justice Project (2023) analyzed data from around the world, concluding that racism is pervasive and that its prevalence has increased in three-fourths of the studied nations since 2015. Finland was found to have the least discrimination based on race, while Afghanistan was found to have the most discrimination, closely followed by Sudan and Nicaragua. Of high-income nations, the United States and Hungary were found to have the most discrimination; the United States ranked 103 of 140 countries studied, a drop of 13 percent since 2015.

Despite some international improvements resulting from human rights treaties such as the UDHR (1948) and the 1965 ICERD, racism, xenophobia, and related forms of intolerance and discrimination continue to exist (United Nations 2024g). In a Pew Research Center survey (Silver 2021) study of seventeen developed nations about people's attitudes toward racial and ethnic discrimination, respondents from fourteen countries indicated that discrimination was a problem. In only three of the surveyed countries—Japan, Singapore, and Taiwan—did people not see discrimination to be a serious issue. Countries including New Zealand, South Korea, Canada, Japan, the Netherlands, Spain, and Sweden believed that discrimination was more prevalent in the United States than in their own countries. Younger people, women, and people who were ideologically progressive saw discrimination as a greater problem than did men, older people, and those whose who were ideologically conservative.

The Convention on the Elimination of All Forms of Racial Discrimination employs the term racial discrimination to refer to "any distinction, exclusion, restriction or preference based on race, colour, descent, or national or ethnic origin which has the purpose or effect of nullifying or impairing the recognition, enjoyment or exercise, on an equal footing, of human rights and fundamental freedoms in the political, economic, social, cultural or any other field of public life." Scientists now agree that race is a socially constructed concept, not a biological one. They have found that genetic differences within a "race" may be greater than variation between perceived races. Globally there are many more people engaging in racial intermarriage than in the past. This trend is resulting in biracial children who form families with other biracial children, which results in a blending of identity that is not racially or ethnically bound (Telles, Esteve, and Castro 2023). The World Economic Forum (2023b) has identified that traditional definitions and measures of race and ethnicity may no longer work and that alternate measures of diversity and inclusion need to be developed.

Race and social class variables have often been confounded. Research indicates that social class influences lifestyle and opportunity; the lower one's socioeconomic status, the greater the chance for poverty and accompanying distress factors, such as poorer physical and mental health, increased incarceration, lower education, and less access to well-paying high-prestige jobs. Homelessness is associated with one's lack of income, and while homelessness is present in one in eight adults, the rates are one in five among Black and American Indian or Alaska Native adults (Hamel et al. 2024).

There are both direct and indirect forms of racism, types that may be overt or covert. Racism hurts individuals in a variety of ways, such as in health conditions that increase exposure to acute, communicable, and chronic diseases, stressors that harm mental health, with morbidity that results in earlier mortality or shorter lifespans. Racism and poverty are correlated, which puts individuals at risk of both macro and micro aggressions that limit their personal, social, and career opportunities, their wellbeing, social participation, where they live, and lifestyle (Abubakar et al. 2022; Lewsley and Slater 2023). Racism also hurts communities and society. Systematic or structural racism may not be as obvious, but it is insidious and results in segregation, political disempowerment, biased policing and sentencing (particularly of Black males), voter suppression, economic practices that discriminate, placement of roads, and residential areas that are adjacent to toxic environmental areas (Braveman et al. 2022).

Age

The United Nations (2024d) posits that age-based discrimination is intolerable from a human rights perspective and that countering ageism and eliminating discrimination based on age is a starting point for the full enjoyment of all people's human rights. Ageism can include people of all ages, and age discrimination can be found in both macro and micro elements of societies. As with gender, sexual orientation, and race, attitudes toward and treatment of individuals of certain age groups are socially constructed. No one age is better than another, but age may greatly influence a person's status and opportunities (Riley 1987).

The UN's CRC is the most ratified human rights treaty in the history of the world. This treaty is a blueprint for communities and leaders to follow in defending children (birth to age eighteen) as human rights holders. It has fifty articles that pertain to children's protections, provisions, and participations.

While the CRC addresses children's rights, an equivalent treaty to protect older persons does not exist, although there is some international movement in that direction. Protection against age discrimination for these people varies considerably around the world (Fritz 2024). For example, in some countries, like the United States, a person is no longer forced to retire in most occupations at age sixty-five, but in other countries like Iceland, there is a forced retirement age. Even if a person is qualified and interested in contributing to their profession and wants to work, they may not be allowed to do so. In the United States, age discrimination at work was addressed in the 1967 Age Discrimination and Employment Act.

Ability

A society that is respectful of human rights requires intentional social justice to include people with equity challenges (Jones 2022). The United Nations (2024e) identifies that over a billion people live with disabilities, and that number is increasing. Disabilities can include physical and mental health challenges, mobility and dexterity issues, processing and cognitive conditions, and emotional reactions, to name but a few. Ability challenges may impact a person's performance as well as their social treatment. Some disabilities are visible, such as losing a limb or eye, while others are invisible, such as mental health or cognitive challenges. Because many disabilities are invisible, the actual number is likely higher (Institute on Disability 2011). People with disabilities may also face stigma, which can contribute to people not wanting others to know about their challenges. Some may not receive treatment, which contributes to undercounting as well.

Part of the reason for the increase in people living with disabilities is that people are living longer, largely due to medical advances. The World Health Organization (United Nations 2023a) has found that 80 percent of people who have disabilities live in developing countries, and in countries where people live beyond age seventy, people spend about 12 percent of their life, or eight years, living with some sort of disability. Disabilities are more common in people who are impoverished and those who are poorly educated. Women and street youth experience more disabilities, which often contributes to their exclusion and marginalization in society. Studies from around the world consistently report that people who have disabilities are subject to more abuse of all types. This is true for people across the age spectrum, from the very young to the very old. Social maltreatments are common for people with disabilities even in schools, social services, and medical facilities. People living with a disability are less likely to be employed, and when they are, they may be paid lower wages and endure substandard working conditions. Despite disability legislation and awareness that discrimination of people with disabilities is a violation of their human rights, only forty-five countries have anti-discrimination laws that are disability specific (United Nations 2023a).

Population Growth and Migration

The world's population is growing, and with it grows the problem of protecting everyone's human rights. This challenge has long been predicted. Thomas Malthus in 1798 wrote an essay that predicted the natural human tendency to be sexually active would lead to population growth and that, sooner or later, the increased human need for food, water, and space would be greater than the environment could sustain. The result, he warned, would be poverty, misery, and famine for the bulk of the world (Malthus 1993). The same basic conclusion was reached in the 1972 "Limits to Growth" study (Meadows and Randers 2013), which analyzed a variety of demographic variables in multiple combinations to see how Malthus's catastrophe could be avoided. The authors of that study employed computer modeling to reach their results. This report was controversial. Some economists and scholars argued that the predicted resource collapse would not occur because people would marry later and have fewer children, choosing to offer a higher quality of life to their children by reducing family size. These theorists believed that these types of tempering factors could save the planet (Kahn 2022), but they also acknowledge that our choices today shape future conditions for life on Earth.

The ten countries with the largest populations, in decreasing order, are India, China, the United States, Indonesia, Pakistan, Nigeria, Brazil, Bangladesh, Russia, and Mexico. In addition to problems associated with population growth, the protection of human rights is experiencing challenges related to the migration of people around the planet. Movement from one area to another results in changes in population size as well as other demographic changes, creating challenges as nations attempt to accommodate newcomers. Pew Research found that the number of international migrants, people moving to places outside of their country of birth, grew to 281 million in 2020, or 3.6 percent of the world's population. This number increased by 128 million since 1990 and was over three times the estimated number in 1970. The United States has the most international migrants, followed by Germany then Saudi Arabia. About 86.7 million international migrants lived in Europe and 85.6 million in Asia. Latin America and the Caribbean have the fastest-growing migrant population (Natarajan, Moslimani, and Lopez 2022). Nations vary in their willingness to accept immigrants. Those regarded as most welcoming include Canada, New Zealand, Iceland, Australia, and Sierra Leone. Those most resistant to immigrants are Hungary, Serbia, Croatia, North Macedonia, and Bosnia (Statista 2024a).

Why do people migrate? The main reasons include searching for a better quality of life, seeking employment, seeking a good education, fleeing violence or poverty, and moving because of problems resulting from climate change. Migration can be thought of as an effort by people to improve access to their human rights (Edmond 2020). The Migration Data Portal (2023) reports that there were 27.1 million refugees and 4.6 million asylum seekers worldwide. About 38 million internal displacements occurred in 2021, with 23.7 million due to disasters and 14.4 million due to violence and conflict. Children under eighteen accounted for 13 percent of migrants and females 28 percent. Migrant workers numbered 169 million, 62 percent of the international migrant population. Their presence is critically important to the economic systems of nations.

Health and political conditions influence the rate of migration. A report for the International Organization for Migration (McAuliffe and Triandafyllidou 2022) found that COVID-19 caused major disruption in traditional migration patterns due to travel restrictions. Since those restrictions ended, migration has increased. Migration patterns will likely continue to shift due to changing social influences.

Traveling to new locations can be dangerous, but desperation leads many to make the attempt. There were over 52,100 migrant deaths and disappearances from 2014 to 2022. About 5,000 people died while migrating globally in 2022 (Migration Data Portal 2023). Although people immigrate with hope for a better life, they may find that they are not welcome when they arrive. This is particularly the case when cultures collide or when hosting countries bear economic burdens they are not prepared to carry. A global shift from national homogeneity to heterogeneity creates challenges as different cultures figure out how to live with each other. Power, ideology, familiarity, and other factors may impact whether migrants are seen as an asset and are welcomed or as invaders who are a burden, asking for much but offering little in return (DeLaet 2000; McMichael and Weber 2021).

The degree to which immigrants are accepted by societies is also influenced by whether their arrival is through legal channels or not. People may immigrate legally through a nation's formal immigration system. However, migrants often move abruptly, sometimes under desperate circumstances, and do not have the time or ability to work through formal immigration systems. Illegal immigrants are sometimes referred to as aliens, indicating a certain level of resistance to their arrival. Others are regarded as refugees or asylum seekers. Resentment toward these groups may grow, especially when large numbers of illegal immigrants require services from their new communities, including education in different languages, housing, food, healthcare, documentation, social services, and legal assistance. Anti-immigrant sentiment can result, with people taking a "not in my backyard" attitude or a "go back where you came from" stance. Young immigrants are particularly vulnerable if their new communities cannot or will not provide support for them (Leitao and Vissing 2023).

Climate Change and the Environment

No matter who we are or where we live, we are one under the sun. What happens in one part of the planet impacts everyone and everywhere else, either directly or indirectly. We are at the mercy of our environment, with devastation from wildfires, floods, droughts, earthquakes, tornadoes, tsunamis, and extreme temperatures creating problems for human rights. Our rights to life, safety, health, food, water, air, transportation, and sanitation are affected by environmental threats. The ability of people to survive and thrive is directly associated with what is going on in their environment.

Climate change has occurred more rapidly than many experts predicted or hoped. Scientists have found that climate change is occurring ten to 100 times faster than in the past (Mulkern 2013). As a result, ecosystems are finding it difficult to adjust. Climate scientists have documented in detail how global warming is impacting the planet and why it is essential to curb it immediately (Hansen et al. 2023). Over a dozen scientists from around the world have studied data from polar ice cores, tree rings, climate models, and observational data and conclude that the earth is in a climate emergency that must be addressed for the future of the planet and all living species on it.

The Bulletin of Atomic Scientists in 1947 created a Doomsday Clock to warn humanity about risks related to technologies we have created and to encourage the avoidance of global catastrophe. The clock striking midnight represents doomsday, a point of no return for human life on the planet. In January 2024, the clock was set at 90 seconds to midnight, in part due to threats posed by climate change and extreme weather. Although the clock is merely a symbol meant to inspire social change, it indicates that citizens of the planet have little time to waste in avoiding global catastrophe through scientific developments, international cooperation, and changes in lifestyle (Mecklin 2024).

For centuries, the environment was taken for granted as people assumed it would always be able to sustain them. But there has become a greater recognition that the environment and all the creatures that live on the planet who depend upon it needed protection. The United Nations and world community created a mandate concerning human rights and the environment in March 2012, the UN Special Rapporteur on Human Rights and the Environment. This mandate intended to protect the land, water, air, climate, and all living beings. It created a framework that applies human rights to an environmental context. The 16-point framework is recommended as a way for all 193 member nations to work together in partnership to fend off global environmental catastrophe, because what happens in one part of the world naturally impacts other areas. Nature does not abide by geographic or national boundaries. The mandate recommends a set of concrete actions and indicates that the framework provides "an unassailable moral and legal justification for immediate and urgent action to protect the environment for the benefit of all persons." Environmental sustainability and the promotion, protection, and fulfillment of human rights are central to global sustainable development goals. The mandate underscores that businesses have an obligation to operate in ways that do no harm and respect human rights and the rights of the planet. If violations occur, businesses and governments have a responsibility to create effective remedies (United Nations Environment Program 2018).

In 2022 the UN General Assembly declared that everyone on the planet has a right to a healthy environment. The resolution identified climate change and environmental degradation as a major threat to humanity's future and the future of the planet. It called upon nations to create legislative, legal, commercial, and practical efforts to curb climate destruction to preserve our human right to a clean, healthy, and sustainable environment.

Autocracy and Authoritarianism

Autocracy is on the rise globally (Koenigsbauer 2022). The world is seeing a shift in governmental rule away from democracy and toward more authoritarian and autocratic forms of government. Although authoritarian and autocratic regimes may have similarities and the terms are sometimes used interchangeably, they can have different dimensions.

Authoritarian governments reject political differences and employ centralized power systems to control people. There are different types of authoritarian governments, including monarchies, military regimes, and those that are ideologically based. What they have in common is centralized power, limited political pluralism, restricted civil liberties, lack of accountability, censorship, propaganda, suppression of opposition, economic control, and a limited rule of law. Examples of authoritarian leaders/countries are Viktor Orban and his Fidesz party in Hungary, Alexander Lukashenko of Belarus, Recep Tayyip Erdoğan of Turkey, Bashar al-Assad of Syria, as well as Saudi Arabia, China, and other countries (Jacobson 2020).

An autocracy is a governmental system in which a single leader or small group has absolute power over individuals and how the government operates. Therefore, an autocratic government is generally more oppressive and controlling than other authoritarian forms of government. Dictatorships are forms of autocracy. Totalitarianism is also a form of autocracy. Monarchies may be as well.

Autocracies tend to place the needs of groups who support the autocratic leader over the needs of the general population. This means suppressing opposition and controlling the opportunities of people who may wish to challenge their leadership. Totalitarian governments include Italy under Benito Mussolini, the Soviet Union under Joseph Stalin and Russia today under Valdimir Putin, Germany under Adolf Hitler, Japan under Hirohito, China under Mao Zedong, Cuba under Fidel Castro, France under Napoleon Bonaparte, North Korea under the Kim dynasty, and Venezuela under Nicolas Maduro. Autocracies are often divided into two forms, elected or closed. In an elected form, public elections supposedly give citizens a chance to choose a leader, but these elections are often fixed and lack safeguards that would allow them to be free and fair. In closed forms, autocratic leaders are not chosen; they simply assume power.

Autocracies are related to oligarchies. An oligarchy consists of rule by a small group of individuals, typified by wealth that leads them to wield significant power and control over aspects of government and social life. Oligarchies differ from autocracies in that a few individuals or a dominant class influence governance, whereas in an autocracy the rule is dominated by a single person or small group. In both cases, people in high positions may make decisions with little or no input from others. They control nearly every aspect of their respective nations, including organizations, the media, financial distribution, and how a country's major businesses and industries are run.

Autocracies may find defending human rights interferes with their goals, and human rights violations are rarely punished in autocracies. Those who speak out against human rights violations may be targeted for retaliation and punishment. Human rights defenders, therefore, are at risk under autocratic governments. Countries that are regarded as autocracies by the World Population Review (2024a) include Afghanistan, Bahrain, Burkina Faso, Chad, China, Cuba, Eritrea, Eswatini, Guinea, Haiti, Hong Kong, Iran, Jordan, Kuwait, Laos, Libya, Mali, Morocco, Myanmar, North Korea, Oman, Qatar, Saudi Arabia, Somalia, South Sudan, Sudan, Syria, Turkmenistan, United Arab Emirates, Uzbekistan, Vietnam, and Yemen.

Pulitzer Prize-winning historian Anne Applebaum (2024) alleges that autocracy in the twenty-first century is markedly different from previous autocratic regimes. She finds that autocrats today are united only by a "ruthless, single-minded determination to preserve their personal wealth and power," and no longer on a shared ideology. They are self-serving in every sense of the word. While they may have no common ideological foundation, the new autocrats employ similar strategies. These include dissemination of propaganda, control of the media, trading in weapons and technology, and laundering money so that their corruption is not so apparent. Money laundering is commonly achieved through real estate, businesses, and shell companies as well as sending money to other countries for safeguarding. Use of fake news, false narratives, and other forms of disinformation are universal strategies. Stoking fear about groups or individuals autocrats perceive as threats to their interests is common. They promote themselves as defenders and protectors for individuals and the heart of the nation, employing lawyers who can counter any arguments that opponents may wage against them. Applebaum stresses that democratic societies need each other now more than ever, as "their democracy are not safe—nobody's democracy is safe."

Disinformation

Disinformation is regarded as a major challenge in the twenty-first century. As pointed out in the previous section, autocrats rely upon the use of disinformation to manipulate the public and to preserve their positions of authority and privilege. Misinformation is defined as the inadvertent transmission of untrue information without intent to harm, while disinformation is regarded as false information that is designed to intentionally mislead others. Disinformation is spread deliberately, and its impact is calculated to cause confusion and make people believe that fiction is truth.

The strategic use of spreading false information to influence public opinion is nothing new, but due to the availability and spread of social media globally, its use has increased in both amount and the degree to which it results in dangerous consequences (Broda and Strömbäck 2024). Scholars have attempted to dissect the threat level to social harm caused by disinformation and identified how social platforms (particularly Twitter or X) actively spread it (Suarez-Lledo and Alvarez-Galvez 2021). One analysis (Muhammed and Mathew 2022) of disinformation on politics, health, and disasters found that strategic misrepresentation of facts to sway readers to certain untrue positions or beliefs was common. Another study (Adams et al. 2023) concluded that the rise of computer technology and social media is spreading false information narratives around the world. A third (Ecker et al. 2022) identified that psychologically, the spread of disinformation has long-term consequences, even when people know that the information is not true. A residue of belief in false information persists and affects opinions on related topics, long past the time the disinformation is debunked. Disinformation is not just a problem in one nation or in relation to one aspect of society. It is pervasive and highly dangerous in respect to the harm that it can cause from a human rights view. Chapter 3's perspective essay by Dr. Steven Livingston explores disinformation further.

Conclusion

A common thread unites the issues outlined in this chapter. This is the use of power and control to shape social narratives and the reactions that stem from them. This strategy is most impactful when set by the policies and practices of government leaders. It is reflective of how reality is socially constructed. Human rights have often relied upon diplomatic action and intervention, but these strategies have waned in their effectiveness (Ero and Atwood 2024). As sociologist Howard Becker (1967) reminds us, what we see and what we believe is often dependent upon "whose side we are on."

War, terrorism, discrimination, racism, sexism, and other forms of hatred and intolerance are interlinked human rights issues. These factors are also related to living on a sustainable planet that can continue to nurture us. From a prevention of violence perspective, promoting greater tolerance for one another's differences is a good starting point. Tolerance and respect can be obtained through inclusion and diversity opportunities that help people to find commonalities between and among groups. Social media's perpetuation of disinformation is a contributing factor to the attack on human rights, but media could also be a means to defend them, by changing social narratives.

People want to be physically and emotionally healthy and happy, have good jobs, receive quality education, to be respected and treated with dignity no matter who they are, and to have input into how their governments operate. They want to be able to own their beliefs, religions, and lifestyle. A lack of equity between people of different groups and from those who hold power hinders access to these rights. The trend for leaders and nations to absorb as much power, money, and privilege as they can is increasingly moving human society away from a reality of equality and justice for all. Governments that are democracies tend to be more supportive of human rights than governments that are not. The 2024 Democracy Index identified twenty-four countries of the world as full democracies, fifty as flawed democracies, thirty-four as hybrid regimes, and fifty-nine as authoritarian regimes (World Population Review 2024a). This data confirms other findings that authoritarian governments and autocracies are ruling most citizens across the world. It also supports information provided throughout this chapter about where human rights are most protected and where they are most violated.

As multinational corporations have grown and governments have bowed to prioritize business interests over those of the general population, the result has been social, environmental, and cultural conditions that have led to increased inequality. The gap between the rich and poor nations, as well as the rich and poor individuals who live within those nations, has been increasing. As the United Nations and other major international economic organizations have pointed out, economic disparity is not in the best interest of the planet. It is an obstacle to achieving sustainable health, peace, and justice for all. Individuals, organizations, businesses, and governments all have a role to play in defending human rights.

Further Reading

Abubakar, I., Gram, L., Lasoye, S., Achiume, T., et al. (2022). Confronting the consequences of racism, xenophobia, and discrimination. *Lancet*, 400 (10368): 2137–46. https://www.thelancet.com/journals/lancet/article/PIIS0140-6736(22)01989-4/fulltext (accessed March 31, 2025).

Adachi, J. (2017). Police militarization. American Bar Association. https://www.americanbar.org/groups/crsj/publications/human_rights_magazine_home/2016-17-vol-42/vol-42-no-1/police-militarization-and-the-war-on-citizens (accessed March 31, 2025).

Adams, Z., Osman, M., Bechlivanidis, C., and Meder, B. (2023). (Why) Is misinformation a problem? *Perspectives on Psychological Science*, 18 (6): 1436–63. doi: doi:10.1177/17456916221141344.

Aid to the Church in Need. (2023). Global report. https://acninternational.org/religiousfreedomreport/reports/global/2023 (accessed March 31, 2025).

Alexander, D. (2023). Investing in children. Presentation at Children's Human Rights Conference. April 10. Salem State University, Salem, Massachusetts.

Amnesty International. (2019). Arbitrary arrests. https://www.amnesty.org/en/latest/press-release/2019/09/hong-kong-arbitrary-arrests-brutal-beatings-and-torture-in-police-detention-revealed (accessed March 31, 2025).

Amnesty International. (2023). Israel and Palestine. https://www.amnesty.org/en/location/middle-east-and-north-africa/middle-east/israel-and-occupied-palestinian-territories/report-israel-and-occupied-palestinian-territories (accessed March 31, 2025)./

Amnesty International. (2024). Enforced disappearance. https://www.amnesty.org/en/what-we-do/enforced-disappearances (accessed March 31, 2025).

Applebaum, A. (2024). *Autocracy, Inc.: The dictators who want to run the world.* Doubleday.

Arsel, Z., Crockett, D., and Scott, M. (2021). Diversity, equity, and inclusion (DEI). *Journal of Consumer Research*, 48 (5): 920–933. https://doi.org/10.1093/jcr/ucab057.

Ashby, H. 2021. Far right extremism is a global problem. *Foreign Policy*. https://foreignpolicy.com/2021/01/15/far-right-extremism-global-problem-worldwide-solutions (accessed March 31, 2025).

BBC. (2020). Gender study finds 90% of people are biased against women. https://www.bbc.com/news/world-51751915 (accessed March 31, 2025).

BBC. (2024). How many countries have the death penalty? https://www.bbc.com/news/world-45835584 (accessed March 31, 2025).

Beavers, D. (2018). Diversity, equity, and inclusion framework. Greenlining. http://greenlining.org/wp-content/uploads/2018/05/Racial-Equity-Framework.pdf (accessed March 31, 2025).

Becker, H. (1967). Whose side are we on? *Social Problems*, 14 (3): 239–47. doi: 10.2307/799147.

Bhattacharya, A. (2024). Political campaigns embrace AI to reach voters across language barriers. MSN. https://www.msn.com/en-us/money/other/political-campaigns-embrace-ai-to-reach-voters-across-language-barriers/ar-AA1qPJAX (accessed March 31, 2025).

Bloomfield, D. (2021). Ike was right. War is good for business—too good. *Jerusalem Post*. https://www.jpost.com/opinion/ike-was-right-war-is-good-for-business-too-good-681213 (accessed March 31, 2025).

Bomboy, S. (2024). A national TikTok ban and the first amendment. Constitution Center. https://constitutioncenter.org/blog/a-national-tiktok-ban-and-the-first-amendment (accessed March 31, 2025).

Braveman, P. (2021). Systemic and structural racism. *Health Affairs*, 41 (2). https://www.healthaffairs.org/doi/10.1377/hlthaff.2021.01394 (accessed March 31, 2025).

Braveman, P. A., Arkin, E., Proctor, D., Kauh, T., and Holm, N. (2022). Systemic and structural racism: Definitions, examples, health damages, and approaches to dismantling. *Health Affairs*, 41 (2): 171–8. doi: 10.1377/hlthaff.2021.01394.

Broda, E., and Strömbäck, J. (2024). Misinformation, disinformation, and fake news: Lessons from an interdisciplinary, systematic literature review. *Annals of the International Communication Association*, 48 (2): 139–66. doi: doi: 10.1080/23808985.2024.2323736.

Brook, A., Clay, C., and Randolph, S. (2020). Human Rights Data for Everyone: Introducing the Human Rights Measurement Initiative (HRMI). *Journal of Human Rights*, 19 (1): 67–82.

Busari, S. (2024). Chibok boarding school kidnapping. CNN. https://www.cnn.com/2024/04/14/africa/chibok-girls-ten-years-as-equals-intl-cmd/index.html (accessed March 31, 2025).

Caitriona, M. (2024). Countries ranked by freedom of the press. Facts Institute. https://factsinstitute.com/ranking/countries-ranked-by-freedom-of-press (accessed March 31, 2025).

Caruso, C. (2022). COVID-19 lesson for future pandemics. Harvard University. https://hms.harvard.edu/news/covid-19s-lessons-future-pandemics (accessed March 31, 2025).

Center for Strategic and International Studies. (2024). Global terrorism threat assessment 2024. https://www.csis.org/analysis/global-terrorism-threat-assessment-2024 (accessed March 31, 2025).

Chan, A. (2022). 11 global health issues to watch in 2023. Health Data. https://www.healthdata.org/news-events/insights-blog/acting-data/11-global-health-issues-watch-2023-according-ihme-experts (accessed March 31, 2025).

Chanda, T. (2024). Civic education and citizen participation in local governance. *International Journal of Research Publication and Reviews*, 5, 4628–37.

Chatterjee, M. (2024). What AI is doing to campaigns. *Politico*. https://www.politico.com/news/2024/08/15/what-ai-is-doing-to-campaigns-00174285 (accessed March 31, 2025).

Child Rights International Network. (2015). Inhumane sentencing: Life imprisonment of children. https://archive.crin.org/sites/default/files/life_imprisonment_children_global_0.pdf (accessed March 31, 2025).

Commonwealth Fund. (2021). US health system ranks behind 11 countries. https://www.commonwealthfund.org/press-release/2021/new-international-study-us-health-system-ranks-last-among-11-countries-many (accessed March 31, 2025).

Council on Foreign Relations. (2024). Global conflict tracker. https://www.cfr.org/global-conflict-tracker (accessed March 31, 2025).

Counter Extremism. (2024). Top 20 most dangerous extremists in the world. https://www.counterextremism.com/content/top-20-extremists (accessed March 31, 2025).

Creary, S. (2024). Is DEI going away? Wharton the University of Pennsylvania. https://knowledge.wharton.upenn.edu/article/is-dei-going-away-heres-what-experts-say (accessed March 31, 2025).

Dattani, S, Spooner, F., Ritchie, H, and Roser, M. (2023). Child mortality. Our World in Data. https://ourworldindata.org/child-mortality (accessed March 31, 2025).

Davis, D. (2024). Why did Russia invade Ukraine? U.S. News. https://www.usnews.com/news/best-countries/articles/explainer-why-did-russia-invade-ukraine (accessed March 31, 2025).

DeLaet, D. (2000). *US immigration policy in the age of rights.* Praeger.

DeLaet, D., and DeLaet, D. (2015). Global health in the 21st century: The globalization of disease and wellness. Routledge.

Durkee, M. J. (2022). Rethinking participation in global governance. *American Journal of International Law*, 118 (1): 219–24. doi:10.1017/ajil.2023.60.

Ecker, U. K. H., Lewandowsky, S., Cook, J. et al. (2022). The psychological drivers of misinformation belief. *Nat Rev Psychol*, 1:, 13–29. doi: 10.1038/s44159-021-00006-y.

Edmond, C. (2020). Global migration. World Economic Forum. https://www.weforum.org/agenda/2020/01/iom-global-migration-report-international-migrants-2020 (accessed March 31, 2025).

Ero, C., and Atwood, R. (2024). 10 conflicts to watch in 2024. Foreign Policy. https://foreignpolicy.com/2024/01/01/conflicts-2024-gaza-sudan-china-iran-myanmar-ukraine-ethiopia-sahel-haiti-armenia-azerbaijan-iran-hezbollah (accessed March 31, 2025).

Esparza, C., Simon, M., Bath, E., and Ko, M. (2022). Doing the work—or not. Public Health, *22*(10). doi: 10.3389/fpubh.2022.900283.

Fox, K. (2024). How US gun culture stacks up with the world. CNN. https://www.cnn.com/2021/11/26/world/us-gun-culture-world-comparison-intl-cmd/index.html (accessed March 31, 2025).

Fredman, S., and Goldblatt, B. (2015). Gender equality and human rights. UN Women. https://www.unwomen.org/sites/default/files/Headquarters/Attachments/Sections/Library/Publications/2015/Goldblatt-Fin.pdf (accessed March 31, 2025).

Fritz, J. M. (2024). Retirement around the world. In J. Zajda and Y. Vissing (Eds.), *Globalisation and Human Rights* (pp. 28–41). Springer.

Global Project Against Hate and Extremism. (2024). Country reports. https://globalextremism.org/country-reports (accessed March 31, 2025).

Gomstyn, A. (2023). DEI is a multi-billion dollar industry that doesn't work. Chief. https://chief.com/articles/dei-multi-billion-dollar-industry-that-doesnt-work-how-to-change-it (accessed March 31, 2025).

Goodman, P. (2024). Main reasons for war. https://owlcation.com/social-sciences/The-Main-Reasons-For-War (accessed March 31, 2025).

Groch. S. (2023). Putin is one of the world's richest men, but the money isn't in his name. Sydney Morning Herald. https://www.smh.com.au/world/europe/putin-is-one-of-the-world-s-richest-men-but-the-money-isn-t-in-his-name-20230308-p5cqbl.html (accessed March 31, 2025).

Hamel, L., Pillai, A., Artiga, S., and Rudowitz, R. (2024). Racial equity and health policy. Kaiser Family Foundation. https://www.kff.org/racial-equity-and-health-policy/poll-finding/health-and-health-care-among-adults-with-previous-experiences-of-homelessness (accessed March 31, 2025).

Hansen, J, Sato, M., Simons, L., et al. (2023). Global warming in the pipeline. *Oxford Open Climate Change*, 3 (1). doi: 10.1093/oxfclm/kgad008.

Harvard Center for the Developing Child. (2023). Place matters: What surrounds us shapes us. https://developingchild.harvard.edu/resources/infographics/place-matters-what-surrounds-us-shapes-us (accessed March 31, 2025).

Harvard University. (2024). The next pandemic—not if but when. https://hsph.harvard.edu/news/next-pandemic-not-if-but-when (accessed March 31, 2025)./

Hassell, J., Rohenkohl, B., Arriagada, P., Ortiz-Ospina, E., and Roser, M. (2023). Economic inequality. OurWorldinData.org. https://ourworldindata.org/economic-inequality (accessed March 31, 2025).

Hedges, C. (2003). What every person should know about war. *New York Times*. https://www.nytimes.com/2003/07/06/books/chapters/what-every-person-should-know-about-war.html (accessed March 31, 2025).

Henry, P. (2021). Innovative projects tackling homelessness around the world. World Economic Forum. https://www.weforum.org/agenda/2021/10/innovative-projects-tackling-homelessness-around-the-world (accessed March 31, 2025).

Howard, J. (2023). US spends most for healthcare but has the worst outcomes. CNN. https://www.cnn.com/2023/01/31/health/us-health-care-spending-global-perspective/index.html (accessed March 31, 2025).

HRMI Rights Tracker. (2025a). Health measures. https://rightstracker.org/metric/health (accessed March 31, 2025).

HMRI Rights Tracker. (2025b). Indicators. https://rightstracker.org (accessed April 18, 2025).

Hulett, J. (2011). *Age discrimination: An epidemic in America affecting people of all ages*. AuthorHouse.

Human Rights Watch. (2017). Israel. https://www.hrw.org/news/2017/06/04/israel-50-years-occupation-abuses (accessed March 31, 2025).

Human Rights Watch. (2023a). Alarming increase of attacks on education worldwide. https://www.hrw.org/news/2023/09/07/alarming-increase-attacks-education-worldwide (accessed March 31, 2025).

Human Rights Watch. (2023b). Attacks on education. https://www.hrw.org/topic/childrens-rights/attacks-education (accessed March 31, 2025).

Institute on Disability. (2011). Report finds significant health disparities for people with disabilities. University of New Hampshire. https://www.unh.edu/unhtoday/news/release/2011/08/25/report-finds-significant-health-disparities-people-disabilities (accessed March 31, 2025).

Jacobson, V. (2020). Hungary's road to authoritarianism. University of Denver School of Law. https://djilp.org/hungarys-road-to-authoritarianism-through-the-demise-of-a-liberal-democracy-and-free-judiciary (accessed March 31, 2025).

Jones, K. (2022). Confronting ableism on the way to justice. Learning for Justice. https://www.learningforjustice.org/magazine/fall-2022/confronting-ableism-on-the-way-to-justice (accessed March 31, 2025).

Juma, C. (2016). Why do people resist new technologies? World Economic Forum. https://www.weforum.org/agenda/2016/07/why-do-people-resist-new-technologies-history-has-answer (accessed March 31, 2025).

Kahn, M. (2022). What the controversial "Limits to Growth" report got right. The Conversation. https://theconversation.com/what-the-controversial-1972-limits-to-growth-report-got-right-our-choices-today-shape-future-conditions-for-life-on-earth-184920 (accessed March 31, 2025).

Kapur, A., and Alshaibi, S. (2023). The impact of enforced disappearances on women. In J. Heath and A. Zahedi (Eds.), *Book of the Disappeared: The quest for transnational justice* (pp. 62–90). University of Michigan Press. http://www.jstor.org/stable/10.3998/mpub.11953892.7 (accessed March 31, 2025).

Kinsey, A. C., Pomeroy, W. B., and Martin, C. E. (1948). *Sexual Behavior in the Human Male.* Saunders.

Kippert, A. (2023). Why domestic violence is a public health crisis. https://www.domesticshelters.org/articles/ending-domestic-violence/why-domestic-violence-is-a-public-health-crisis (accessed March 31, 2025).

Koenigsbauer, T. (2022). Global rise of autocratic regimes. Organization for World Peace. https://theowp.org/reports/the-global-rise-of-autocratic-regimes (accessed March 31, 2025).

Koup, A. (2021). Where are the world's conflict today? Visual Capitalist. https://www.visualcapitalist.com/mapped-where-are-the-worlds-ongoing-conflicts-today (accessed March 31, 2025).

Lancet. (2023, October 21). Understanding global gun violence, and how to control it. *Lancet*, 402 (10411). doi: 10.1016/S0140-6736(23)02347-4.

Leitao, S., and Vissing, Y. (2023). *Child and Youth Refugee Resettlement and Community Formation Issues.* Vernon Press.

Lewsley, J. and Slater, R. (2023). Effects of racism on health and mental health. Medical News Today. https://www.medicalnewstoday.com/articles/effects-of-racism (accessed March 31, 2025).

Liao, K. (2020). Voting rights around the world. Global Citizen. https://www.globalcitizen.org/en/content/voting-rights-around-the-world (accessed March 31, 2025).

Liebenberg, Uni S., and Slade, B. (2023). Applying a human rights lens to poverty and economic inequality. *Federal Law Review*, 51 (3): 296–314. doi: 10.1177/0067205X231188637

Lundy, L., MacNaughton, G., Frey, D., and Porter, C. (2022). *Human Rights and Economic Inequalities.* Cambridge Press.

Malthus, T. (1993). *An Essay on the Principle of Population.* Oxford University Press.

Mao, Z., Zhang, W., Zou, Q., and Deng, W. (2024). The effects of e-participation on voice and accountability. *Information Technology for Development*, 1–26. doi: 10.1080/02681102.2024.2373745.

Marchant, N. (2020). Extinction facts. World Economic Forum. https://www.weforum.org/agenda/2020/11/extinction-facts-wildlife-attenborough (accessed March 31, 2025).

Masters, J. (2022). US gun policy—global comparisons. Council on Foreign Relations. https://www.cfr.org/backgrounder/us-gun-policy-global-comparisons (accessed March 31, 2025).

Mayo Clinic. (2024). History of disease outbreaks and vaccine timeline. https://www.mayoclinic.org/diseases-conditions/history-disease-outbreaks-vaccine-timeline (accessed March 31, 2025).

Mayroz, E. (2024). Why do Israelis and the rest of the world view the Gaza conflict so differently? And can this disconnect be overcome? The Conversation. https://theconversation.com/why-do-israelis-and-the-rest-of-the-world-view-the-gaza-conflict-so-differently-and-can-this-disconnect-be-overcome-223188 (accessed March 31, 2025).

Mazure, C. (2021). What do we mean by sex and gender? Yale Medical News. https://medicine.yale.edu/news-article/what-do-we-mean-by-sex-and-gender (accessed March 31, 2025).

McAuliffe, M., and Triandafyllidou, A. (2022). World migration report 2022. International Organization for Migration (IOM), Geneva. https://worldmigrationreport.iom.int (accessed April 18, 2025)..

McMichael, P., and Weber, H. (2021). *Development and Social Change*. Sage.

Meadows, D. H., and Randers, J. (2013). *Limits to Growth*. Chelsea Green Publishing.

Mecklin, J. (2024). The doomsday clock. https://thebulletin.org/doomsday-clock/current-time (accessed March 31, 2025).

Migration Data Portal. (2023). Final report summary. https://www.migrationdataportal.org/sites/g/files/tmzbdl251/files/2023-03/One-pager-2023-EN-Final.pdf (accessed March 31, 2025).

Mills, C. W. (1956). *The Power Elite*. Oxford University Press.

Mino, L. (2020). The dark side of homeschooling. Harvard Gazette. https://news.harvard.edu/gazette/story/2020/05/law-school-professor-says-there-may-be-a-dark-side-of-homeschooling (accessed March 31, 2025).

Morris, C. (2023). Disappearance of Indigenous peoples. *Law and Technology Resources for Legal Professionals*. https://www.llrx.com/2023/03/the-disappeared-indigenous-peoples-and-the-international-crime-of-enforced-disappearance (accessed March 31, 2025).

Muhammed, T. S., and Mathew, S. K. (2022). The disaster of misinformation. *International Journal of Data Science and Analytics*, 13 (4): 271–85. doi: 10.1007/s41060-022-00311-6.

Mulkern, A. (2013). Today's climate change. *Scientific American*. https://www.scientificamerican.com/article/todays-climate-change-proves-much-faster-than-changes-in-past-65-million-years (accessed March 31, 2025).

Myers, J. (2021). Global income inequality. World Economic Forum. https://www.weforum.org/agenda/2021/12/global-income-inequality-gap-report-rich-poor (accessed March 31, 2025).

Nadworny, E. (2023). For-profit schools. https://www.kqed.org/news/11962723/feds-announce-new-protections-against-for-profit-schools-that-leave-students-with-a-worthless-degree (accessed March 31, 2025).

Nario-Redmond, M. R. (2024). Ableism: The many manifestations of disability prejudice. In G. Bennett, and E. Goodall (Eds.), *The Palgrave Encyclopedia of Disability*. Palgrave Macmillan. doi: 10.1007/978-3-031-40858-8_8-1.

Natarajan, A., Moslimani, M., and Lopez, M. H. (2022). Key facts in global migration. Pew Research. https://www.pewresearch.org/short-reads/2022/12/16/key-facts-about-recent-trends-in-global-migration (accessed March 31, 2025).

Our World in Data. (2024). Mental and substance disorders. https://ourworldindata.org/grapher/share-with-mental-and-substance-disorders (accessed March 31, 2025).

Oxfam. (2025). Billionaire wealth surges. United Nations. https://www.oxfam.org/en/press-releases/billionaire-wealth-surges-2-trillion-2024-three-times-faster-year-while-number (accessed March 31, 2025).

People Powered. (2024). Participation to solve social problems. https://www.peoplepowered.org/news-content/best-of-2024 (accessed March 31, 2025).

Peterson Institute for International Economics. (2024). How to fix economic inequality. https://www.piie.com/microsites/how-fix-economic-inequality (accessed March 31, 2025).

Pew Research Foundation. (2019). How people around the world view gender equality. https://www.pewresearch.org/global/2019/04/22/how-people-around-the-world-view-gender-equality-in-their-countries (accessed March 31, 2025).

Pew Research Foundation. (2024). Religious restrictions around the world. https://www.pewresearch.org/religion/feature/religious-restrictions-around-the-world (accessed March 31, 2025).

Powell, J. (2014). 6 policies to reduce economic inequality. https://belonging.berkeley.edu/six-policies-reduce-economic-inequality (accessed March 31, 2025).

Project on Government Oversight. (2024). Poisoning our police. https://www.pogo.org/analysis/poisoning-our-police-how-the-militarization-mindset-threatens-constitutional-rights-and-public-safety (accessed March 31, 2025).

Reade, K. (2018). Life imprisonment. Penal Reform. https://www.penalreform.org/blog/life-imprisonment-a-practice-in-desperate-need-of (accessed March 31, 2025).

Relief Web. (2023). Syrian arbitrary arrests. https://reliefweb.int/report/syrian-arab-republic/least-226-arbitrary-arrestsdetentions-documented-may-including-six-children-and-11-women (accessed March 31, 2025).

Reuters. (2023). What's the Israel-Palestine conflict about? https://www.reuters.com/world/middle-east/israel-palestinian-dispute-hinges-statehood-land-jerusalem-refugees-2023-10-10 (accessed March 31, 2025).

Reuters. (2024). What is the history of the Israel-Palestine conflict? US News. https://www.usnews.com/news/world/articles/2024-01-13/explainer-whats-the-israel-palestinian-conflict-about-and-how-did-it-start (accessed March 31, 2025).

Riley, M. W. (1987). On the significance of age in sociology. *American Sociological Review*, 52 (1): 1–14. doi: 10.2307/2095388.

Riley, M. (2023). How the US drives gun exports and fuels violence around the World. Bloomberg. https://www.bloomberg.com/graphics/2023-us-made-gun-exports-shootings-violence-sig-sauer (accessed March 31, 2025).

Salam, Y. (2023). Gaza strip explained. NBC. https://www.nbcnews.com/news/gaza-strip-controls-s-know-rcna119405 (accessed March 31, 2025).

Saloni D., Spooner, F., Ritchie, H., and Rosner, M.(2023). Child and infant mortality. OurWorldInData.org. https://ourworldindata.org/child-mortality (accessed March 31, 2025).

Savage, C. (2024). Why is there still a gender pay gap in 2024? Associated Press. https://apnews.com/article/equal-pay-day-gender-wage-gap-pay-gap-women-889af690259722284241539984855758 (accessed March 31, 2025).

Schrecker, E. (2010). *Corporatization and the Assault on Academic Freedom*. New Press.

Semler, S. (2022). How the military industrial complex gets its power. https://jacobin.com/2022/10/pentagon-budget-military-contractors-lobbyists-biden (accessed March 31, 2025).

Shivaram, D. (2021). Across federal workforce, people with disabilities see need for more representation. National Public Radio. https://www.npr.org/2021/07/31/1020746037/disability-access-representation-ada (accessed March 31, 2025).

Sifry, M. (2024). How AI is transforming the way political campaigns work. *The Nation*. https://www.thenation.com/article/politics/how-ai-is-transforming-the-way-political-campaigns-work (accessed March 31, 2025).

Silver, L. (2021). More people globally see racial and ethnic discrimination as a serious problem. Pew Research. https://www.pewresearch.org/short-reads/2021/11/02/more-people-globally-see-racial-ethnic-discrimination-as-a-serious-problem-in-the-u-s-than-in-their-own-society (accessed March 31, 2025).

Southern Poverty Law Centers. (2019). Global hate: Hate travels. https://www.splcenter.org/fighting-hate/intelligence-report/2019/global-hate-hate-travels (accessed March 31, 2025).

Southern Poverty Law Center. (2023). Countering hate and extremism through policy and data. https://www.splcenter.org/year-hate-extremism-2023/countering-hate-extremism-policy-data (accessed March 31, 2025).

Southern Poverty Law Center. (2024). The year in hate and extremism 2023. https://www.splcenter.org/resources/year-hate-extremism-2023 (accessed March 31, 2025).

Statista. (2024a). Countries most and least accepting of migrants. https://www.statista.com/chart/10804/the-countries-most-and-least-accepting-of-migrants (accessed March 31, 2025).

Statista. (2024b). Terrorism. https://www.statista.com/topics/2267/terrorism (accessed March 31, 2025).

Suarez-Lledo V., and Alvarez-Galvez, J. (2021). Prevalence of health misinformation on social media. *Journal of Medical Internet Research*, 23 (1): e17187. doi: 10.2196/17187.

Sullivan, B. (2022). Russia's war with Ukraine. NPR. https://www.npr.org/2022/02/12/1080205477/history-ukraine-russia (accessed March 31, 2025).

Telles, E., Esteve, A., and Castro, A. (2023.) Black-white intermarriage in global perspective. *Demographic Research*, 49 (28): 737–68.

Tetrault, J. E. C. (2021). What's hate got to do with it? *Current Sociology*, 69 (1): 3–23. doi: 10.1177/0011392119842257.

UN Commission on Human Rights. 2021. Arbitrary detention. https://www.ohchr.org/en/2021/07/over-past-year-more-35000-people-have-been-arbitrarily-detained-belarus-special-rapporteur (accessed March 31, 2025).

UN Commission on Human Rights. (2024a). About arbitrary detention. https://www.ohchr.org/en/about-arbitrary-detention (accessed March 31, 2025).

UN Commission on Human Rights. (2024b). Forced disappearance. https://www.ohchr.org/en/special-procedures/wg-disappearances/about-enforced-disappearance (accessed March 31, 2025).

UN Commission on Human Rights. (2024c). Freedom of assembly and association. https://www.ohchr.org/en/topic/freedom-assembly-and-association (accessed March 31, 2025).

UN Women. (2021). What does gender equality look like today? https://www.unwomen.org/en/news/stories/2021/10/feature-what-does-gender-equality-look-like-today (accessed March 31, 2025).

UN Women. (2022). Gender related killing of women. Femicide. https://www.unodc.org/documents/data-and-analysis/briefs/Femicide_brief-_Nov2022.pdf (accessed March 31, 2025).

UN Women. (2023a). 11 biggest hurdles for women's equality. https://www.unwomen.org/en/news-stories/feature-story/2023/09/the-11-biggest-hurdles-for-womens-equality-by-2030 (accessed March 31, 2025).

UN Women. (2023b). The world is failing girls and women. https://www.unwomen.org/en/news-stories/press-release/2023/09/press-release-the-world-is-failing-girls-and-women-according-to-new-un-report (accessed March 31, 2025).

UNESCO. (2020). What you need to know about your right to education. https://www.unesco.org/en/articles/what-you-need-know-about-right-education (accessed March 31, 2025).

UNESCO. (2023). New methodology shows 258 million children are not in school. https://uis.unesco.org/sites/default/files/documents/new-methodology-shows-258-

million-children-adolescents-and-youth-are-out-school.pdf (accessed March 31, 2025).

UNICEF. (2024a). Female genital mutilation. https://data.unicef.org/topic/child-protection/female-genital-mutilation (accessed March 31, 2025).

UNICEF. (2024b). Global childhood immunization levels stalled in 2023. https://www.unicef.org/press-releases/global-childhood-immunization-levels-stalled-2023-leaving-many-without-life-saving (accessed March 31, 2025).

United Nations. (2020). Sustainable Outlook 2020. Department of Economic and Social Affairs. https://www.un.org/development/desa/dpad/publication/sustainable-development-outlook-2020-achieving-sdgs-in-the-wake-of-covid-19-scenarios-for-policymakers (accessed April 18, 2025).

United Nations. (2021). Equality is the heart of human rights. https://www.ohchr.org/en/2022/01/equality-heart-human-rights (accessed March 31, 2025).

United Nations. (2022a). Commission inquiry finds Israeli occupation unlawful. https://www.ohchr.org/en/press-releases/2022/10/commission-inquiry-finds-israeli-occupation-unlawful-under-international-law (accessed March 31, 2025).

United Nations. (2022b). Gender equality and human rights. https://www.ohchr.org/en/topic/gender-equality-and-womens-rights (accessed March 31, 2025).

United Nations. (2022c). Mental health around the world. https://news.un.org/en/story/2022/06/1120682 (accessed March 31, 2025).

United Nations. (2023a). About the human rights of persons with disabilities. https://www.ohchr.org/en/disabilities/about-human-rights-persons-disabilities (accessed March 31, 2025).

United Nations. (2023b). Free and Equal campaign. https://www.ohchr.org/en/sexual-orientation-and-gender-identity/un-free-equal-global-campaign-promote-equal-rights-lgbti-people (accessed March 31, 2025).

United Nations. (2023c). Human rights based approaches to migration. https://www.ohchr.org/en/publications/training-and-education-publications/towards-human-rights-based-approach-migration (accessed March 31, 2025).

United Nations. (2023d). The world is failing 130 million girls denied education. https://www.ohchr.org/en/press-releases/2023/01/world-failing-130-million-girls-denied-education-un-experts (accessed March 31, 2025).

United Nations. (2023e). World must be ready to respond to the next pandemic. https://news.un.org/en/story/2023/05/1136912 (accessed March 31, 2025).

United Nations. (2024a). About enforced disappearance. https://www.ohchr.org/en/special-procedures/wg-disappearances/about-enforced-disappearance (accessed March 31, 2025).

United Nations. (2024b). About LGBTI people and human rights. https://www.ohchr.org/en/sexual-orientation-and-gender-identity/about-lgbti-people-and-human-rights (accessed March 31, 2025).

United Nations. (2024c). Economic, social and cultural rights. https://www.ohchr.org/en/human-rights/economic-social-cultural-rights (accessed March 31, 2025).

United Nations. (2024d). Eliminate ageism. https://www.ohchr.org/en/stories/2021/09/eliminate-ageism-and-age-discrimination-says-un-expert (accessed March 31, 2025).

United Nations. (2024e). Factsheet on persons with disabilities. https://www.un.org/development/desa/disabilities/resources/factsheet-on-persons-with-disabilities.html (accessed March 31, 2025).

United Nations. (2024f). Irrefutable need for global AI regulation. https://news.un.org/en/story/2024/09/1154541 (accessed March 31, 2025).

United Nations. (2024g). Racism, xenophobia and intolerance. https://www.ohchr.org/en/topic/racism-xenophobia-intolerance (accessed March 31, 2025).

United Nations Development Group. (2017). Human rights and the environment. https://unsdg.un.org/sites/default/files/2020-03/Human-Rights-and-the-Environment.pdf (accessed March 31, 2025).

United Nations Environment Program. (2018). Framework principles on human rights and the environment. https://www.unep.org/resources/policy-and-strategy/framework-principles-human-rights-and-environment (accessed March 31, 2025).

United Nations Environment Program. (2022). UN declares healthy environment as a human right. https://www.unep.org/news-and-stories/story/historic-move-un-declares-healthy-environment-human-right (accessed March 31, 2025).

United Nations Population Fund. (2024). Half of all pregnancies are unintended. https://www.unfpa.org/press/nearly-half-all-pregnancies-are-unintended-global-crisis-says-new-unfpa-report (accessed March 31, 2025).

Uppsala Conflict Data Program. (2024). Definition of war. https://ucdp.uu.se/encyclopedia (accessed March 31, 2025).

US Government Accountability Office. (2023). Domestic terrorism. https://www.gao.gov/blog/rising-threat-domestic-terrorism-u.s.-and-federal-efforts-combat-it (accessed March 31, 2025).

US Institute for Peace. (2024). Iran primer. https://iranprimer.usip.org/blog/2024/sep/16/un-report-oppression-women-iran (website now closed).

USA Facts. (2023). Child deaths. https://usafacts.org/data-projects/child-death (accessed March 31, 2025).

Vissing, Y. (2023). *Children's Human Rights in the USA: Challenges and Opportunities*. Springer.

Vissing, Y., and Juchniewicz, M. (2022). Children's book banning. In J. Zajda (Ed.) *Globalisation, Values Education and Teaching Democracy* . Springer Publishers.

Vissing, Y., and Leitao, S. (2021). *The Rights of Unaccompanied Minors*. Springer.

Vissing, Y., Hudson, C., and Nilan, D. (2020). *Changing the Paradigm of Homelessness*. Routledge.

Wilkenfeld, D. A., and Johnson, C. M. (2022). In defense of vaccine mandates. *Public Health Ethics*, 15 (1): 27–40. doi: 10.1093/phe/phac005.

World Bank. (2023). Growing inequality. https://www.worldbank.org/en/news/feature/2023/12/18/2023-in-nine-charts-a-growing-inequality (accessed March 31, 2025).

World Economic Forum. (2023a). Gender gap in the workforce. https://www.weforum.org/publications/global-gender-gap-report-2023/in-full/gender-gaps-in-the-workforce (accessed March 31, 2025).

World Economic Forum. (2023b). Racial and ethnic diversity. https://www.weforum.org/agenda/2023/01/davos23-reporting-racial-ethnic-equity-improve-diversity (accessed March 31, 2025).

World Food Programme. (2024). Global hunger crisis. https://www.wfp.org/global-hunger-crisis (accessed March 31, 2025).

World Health Organization. (2022a). Global hunger. https://www.who.int/news/item/06-07-2022-un-report--global-hunger-numbers-rose-to-as-many-as-828-million-in-2021 (accessed April 18, 2025).

World Health Organization. (2022b). Mental health. https://iris.who.int/bitstream/handle/10665/356119/9789240049338-eng.pdf?sequence=1 (accessed March 31, 2025).

World Health Organization. (2022c). 10 global health issues. https://www.who.int/news-room/spotlight/10-global-health-issues-to-track-in-2021 (accessed March 31, 2025).

World Health Organization. (2024a). Corporal punishment and health. https://www.who.int/news-room/fact-sheets/detail/corporal-punishment-and-health (accessed March 31, 2025).

World Health Organization. (2024b). Sexual and reproductive health. https://www.who.int/news/item/16-05-2024-sexual-and-reproductive-health-for-all-20-years-of-the-global-strategy (accessed March 31, 2025).

World Health Organization. (2024c). Vaccines. https://www.who.int/health-topics/vaccines-and-immunization#tab=tab_1 (accessed March 31, 2025).

World Justice Project. (2023). Discrimination is getting worse globally. https://worldjusticeproject.org/news/discrimination-getting-worse-globally (accessed March 31, 2025).

World Population Review. (2024a). Autocratic countries. https://worldpopulationreview.com/country-rankings/autocratic-countries (accessed March 31, 2025).

World Population Review. (2024b). Child death. https://worldpopulationreview.com/country-rankings/infant-mortality-rate-by-country (accessed March 31, 2025).

World Population Review. (2024c). Democracy countries. https://worldpopulationreview.com/country-rankings/democracy-countries (accessed March 31, 2025).

World Population Review. (2024d). Homelessness. https://worldpopulationreview.com/country-rankings/homelessness-by-country (accessed March 31, 2025).

World Wildlife Fund. (2024). What is the sixth mass extinction? https://www.worldwildlife.org/stories/what-is-the-sixth-mass-extinction-and-what-can-we-do-about-it (accessed March 31, 2025).

Zheng, L. (2022). The failure of the DEI industrial complex. *Harvard Business Review*. https://hbr.org/2022/12/the-failure-of-the-dei-industrial-complex (accessed March 31, 2025).

Zipoli, D. (2024). The human rights data revolution. Geneva Academy. Briefing 23. https://www.geneva-academy.ch/joomlatools-files/docman-files/Briefing%2023_web.pdf (accessed March 31, 2025).

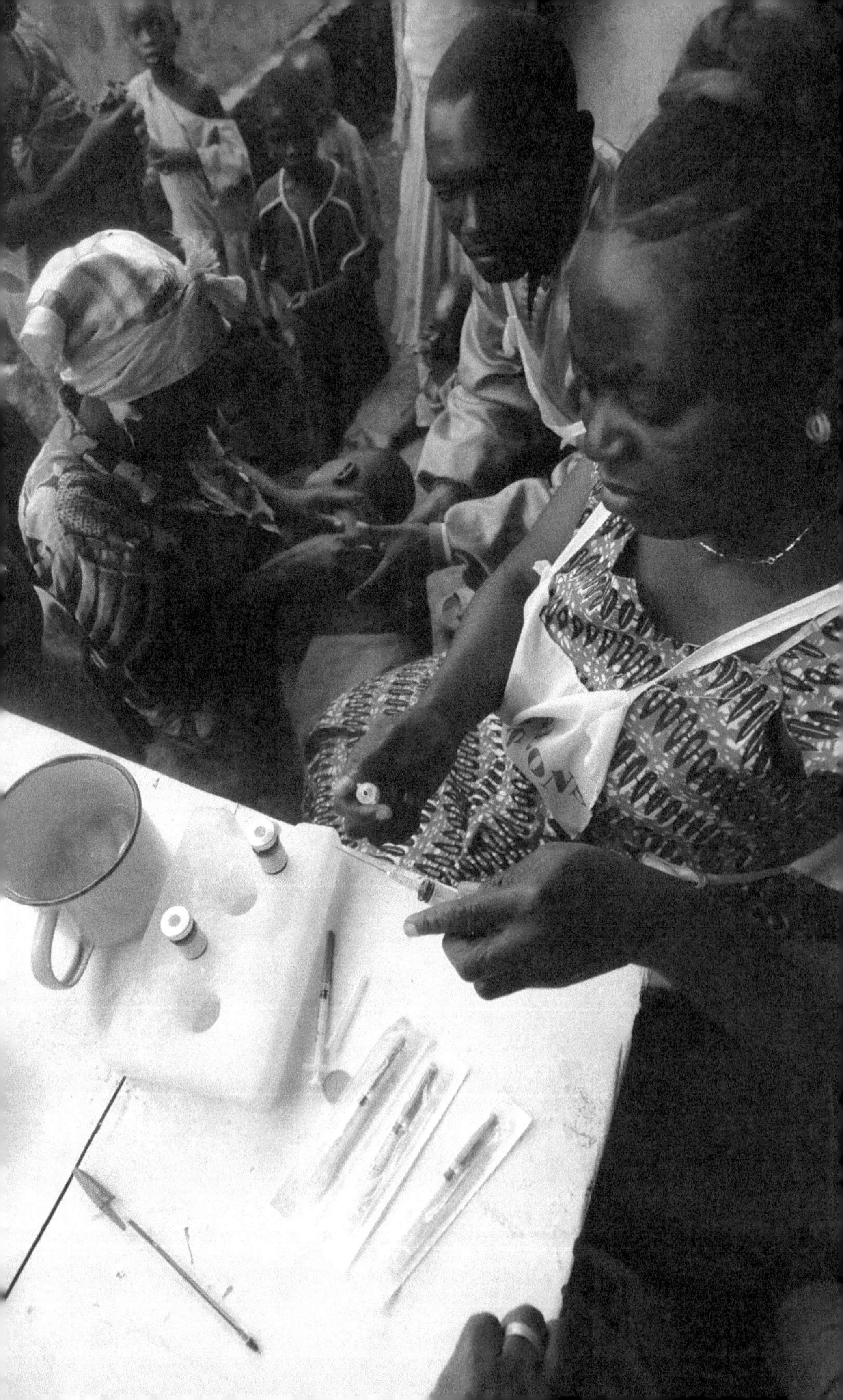

3

Perspectives

The study of human rights has developed over the years through the contributions of individual scholars whose combined works have created a strong foundation for our understanding of the field. In this chapter, renowned scholars and practitioners have submitted their thoughts about their contributions and the current status of human rights around the world. Theresa Harris discusses the importance of science in protecting human rights, and Steven Livingston writes about the eradication of trust that people feel toward each other and our fundamental social institutions. Jan Marie Fritz focuses her essay on challenges that older individuals face, while Jane Williams describes challenges that the youngest members of the global community confront. Laura Guerico describes her work protecting children in armed conflict around the world and the need for universal peace and justice.

Everyone Has the Right to Work … Except Many Older Adults

Jan Marie Fritz

Article 23 of the UDHR (1948) indicates, in part, that "Everyone has the right to work, to free choice of employment, to just and favourable conditions of work and to protection against unemployment." If you grow up in countries where you can generally choose to continue with paid employment, you may be very

---

An emergency measles vaccination effort in Rwanda in 2008, at the same location as a Red Cross and World Food Program food distribution. Distribution was interrupted by nearby gunfire. Essential humanitarian relief services are difficult to administer in areas of conflict and political instability. (Julien Harneis via Flickr, Creative Commons license CC-BY-SA-2.0)

surprised to learn that this is not the case for older adults in many countries. Many people face mandatory ages of retirement, and, in some countries, women must retire several years before men (Fritz 2022).

I first learned about this problem many years ago when a university professor from Sweden told me she was very angry that she was being forced to give up her academic position because of her age. I said I could not believe that a progressive country like Sweden would have this kind of rule. I then saw this problem again when I began working as a Distinguished Visiting Professor for the University of Johannesburg (South Africa). I saw faculty members who were much younger than me having to stop working because there was a rule that they must do this when they reached a certain age.

And there are personal stories. There is the woman who was a health administrator in Iceland and told the top executive that she thought she ought to write a report about a project that had just been completed. The executive said that was an excellent idea but also told her she should make sure to complete the report by the day before her birthday because on her birthday she will have to retire. There was the professor in South Africa who was worried about his mandatory retirement date. He had been using his savings to support his family members because of the huge unemployment rate in the country. He did not know how he was going to manage the situation when he would have to retire. And there is South Korea (Fritz 2024), a country with a developed economy where people are forced to retire because of mandatory retirement as well as being forced out earlier (involuntary retirement) than the mandatory retirement age because employers can then avoid paying an older employee an increased salary. The average "retirement" age is forty-nine and one survey noted that 76 percent of the respondents indicated that this early retirement was not voluntary. One older man indicated he was glad the government wanted to increase pensions in the future, but said that was not going to help him now. Households of only one older person had the highest poverty rate (71.5 percent) in the country.

I began to see that many people around the world were facing this issue. Some were happy to retire if they had excellent pensions and wanted to retire. However, even some of the people who didn't mind going through forced retirement thought the decision to retire generally should be made by the older adult and not by the government or one's employer. And then, of course, there are people who have worked their whole lives in low income jobs but never received a pension.

What needs to be considered? People in many countries are living much longer and so employees may be forced to retire many, many years before they will die; women, who often live longer than men, might be required to retire years before men have to retire; people who do not have sufficient pensions and savings can face a very difficult period as older adults; there may not be enough younger workers in a country to support the pensions for the aging population; and older adults can face discrimination/ageism because of their advanced age and rules like mandatory retirement. A blanket decision that older adults can't continue their paid employment when they reach a certain age is a structural factor that can support discrimination against older adults. And, if the right to work is a basic right, why should older adults not have that right?

Because aging is not dealt with in a specific way in any UN document, the United Nations General Assembly, in 2010, adopted Resolution 65/182, which established the "Open-Ended Working Group on Ageing for the Purpose of Strengthening the Human Rights of Older Persons." The Working Group's mandate was to review the existing international documents regarding the human rights of older adults, identify any possible problems, and present "at the earliest possible date" a proposal with "the main elements that should be included in an international legal instrument to promote and protect the rights and dignity of older persons" (UN General Assembly 2013, 3). Many human rights groups, non-governmental organizations and some Member States saw the need for a Convention on the Rights of Older Persons.

The United Nations Open-ended Working Group on Ageing was established in 2010 but there never has been a draft convention. The discussion in the eleventh yearly meeting of the Working Group, in 2021, indicated that "the existing international human rights instruments, the United Nations Principles for Older Persons, the Madrid International Plan of Action on Ageing and the 2030 Agenda contained very limited or no specific recognition of access to justice for older persons" (UN Open-ended Working Group 2021, 12). The 2021 meeting focused on the "Right to Work and Access to the Labour Market." While mandatory retirement is not mentioned in the report of that meeting, the report did include the following: "Delegations agreed on the need to address ageism at all levels. Several delegations shared national experiences of initiatives aimed at promoting the human right of access to work among older persons, including training programmes for employers and changes in retirement legislation to allow for more flexibility" (14).

During the 2024 session of the Open-ended Working Group on Ageing, the UN Member States adopted a decision by consensus (without voting). It identified gaps in the protection of human rights for older adults, specifically mentioned employment as well as training and recommended that UN Member States consider "an international legally binding instrument to promote, protect and ensure the recognition and realization, on an equal basis, of all human rights of older persons" (UN Open-ended Working Group 2024). In August 2024, the UN General Assembly decided that the Open-ended Working Group had completed its work.

In the fourteen years of its existence, the Working Group never developed a draft of a convention to protect the rights of older adults. The Global Alliance for the Rights of Older People (2024) has noted that this is an "exciting new phase" in the campaign to get a convention protecting the rights of older adults. The Alliance welcomes leaving behind the "highly political environment in New York where it was challenging to get governments to agree (on) concrete outcomes."

Both the Working Group's decision and the Alliance look to the UN's Human Rights Council in Geneva to move forward in developing a convention. I certainly hope that happens and that the convention deals in a strong way with the rights for older adults to continue with paid employment (if they wish to do so), receive training for new kinds of employment and be secure (e.g., financially, physically, emotionally) when they are retired.

Further Reading

Fritz, J. M. (2024). Mandatory retirement and involuntary retirement: Addressing a social justice issue. In J. Zajda and Y. Vissing (Eds.), *Globalisation, Cultural Diversity and Human Rights*(pp. 163–83). Springer.

Fritz, J. M. (2022). Mandatory retirement of older adults: Notes from Iceland. In J. Zajda, Y. Vissing and S. Majhanovich (Eds.), *Globalisation, Ideology and Social Justice Discourses*. Springer.

The Global Alliance for the Rights of Older People. (2024). Frequently asked questions. https://rightsofolderpeople.org/faq-strengthening-older-persons-rights-worldwide (accessed March 31, 2025).

United Nations. (1948). Universal Declaration of Human Rights. https://www.un.org/en/about-us/universal-declaration-of-human-rights (accessed March 31, 2025).

United Nations General Assembly. (2013). Towards a comprehensive and integral international legal instrument to promote and protect the rights and dignity of older persons. Resolution 67/139. Adopted on December 20, 2012.

United Nations General Assembly. (2010). Follow-up to the Second World Assembly on Ageing. Resolution 65/182.

United Nations Open-ended Working Group on Ageing. (2024). Draft decision by the chair of the Open-ended Working Group. AC.278/2024/L.1 May 14.

United Nations Open-ended Working Group on Ageing. (2021). Report of the Open-ended Working Group on Aging on its eleventh session. June 3.

Jan Marie Fritz is a Professor in the School of Planning (and affiliated with the Department of Women's Gender and Sexuality Studies and the Department of Sociology) at the University of Cincinnati as well as a Distinguished Visiting Professor in the Department of Sociology at the University of Johannesburg. She has been a professional mediator for twenty-five years and currently mediates cases for the city of Cincinnati's Law Department/ Prosecution Division. Dr. Fritz has been a Fulbright Scholar at the Hungarian Academy of Sciences; a Fulbright Distinguished Chair in Human Rights and International Studies at the Danish Institute of Human Rights in Copenhagen, Denmark; a Fulbright-National Science Foundation Arctic Scholar in Iceland; and a Woodrow Wilson Fellow at the Woodrow Wilson International Center for Scholars in Washington, DC. She has received many awards including the DAAP College Award (University of Cincinnati) for Outstanding Research and Creative Work; the American Sociological Association's Distinguished Career Award for the Practice of Sociology; the Ohio Mediation Association's Better World Award for a distinguished career in mediation as well as awards from the Association for Applied and Clinical Sociology and the practice division of the American Sociological Association. She is a past Vice-President of the International Sociological Association (ISA), a representative of the ISA to the United Nations, and a member of the ISA Executive Committee. She was the founder and convener of the Cincinnati for CEDAW Community Coalition (CCCC) that led to a gender study of Cincinnati's city administration and the establishment of the Mayor of Cincinnati's Gender Equality Task Force. She was appointed by the Mayor to be a member of the Task Force. Dr. Fritz also was appointed by the director of the US Environmental Protection Agency to be a member of two US EPA advisory councils. She just completed a six-year term as a member of NEJAC—the National Environmental Justice Advisory Council. She has written or edited more than 130 publications, including the award-winning International Clinical Sociology, *"Special Education Mediation in the United States," "Women, Peace, Security and the National Action Plans," "Addressing Environmental Racism," "Practicing Sociology: Clinical Sociology and Human Rights,"* Moving Toward a Just Peace: The Mediation Continuum, *the award-winning* Community Intervention: Clinical Sociology Perspectives *(with Jacques Rhéaume), and* Clinical Sociology for Southern Africa *(with Tina Uys). She edits Springer's Clinical Sociology book series and is a co-editor of the* Clinical Sociology Review.

Championing Children's Rights: A Moral Imperative

Laura Guercio

I am grateful for the opportunity to share my work about the plight of children in armed conflict. I have dedicated my professional life to the field of human rights, both as a lawyer and an academic. My journey has spanned advocacy, institutional frameworks, and the intricate intersections of law and policy. Through this work, I have arrived at a deep conviction: human rights should be the universal language—the *lingua franca*—of individuals and states alike.

Regrettably, this ideal remains far from reality. Time and again, we witness humanity losing its sense of respect and compassion, veering away from the foundational principles of human dignity. Why does this happen? Perhaps it stems from the darker facets of human nature, the shadows that cloud empathy and justice. Yet, amid this darkness, there is a radiant light: the innate human capacity to believe in and aspire to something greater. This capacity fuels the hope that human rights can transcend borders, ideologies, and conflicts. While the path may be fraught with challenges, the destination—a world where human rights truly unite us all—is one worth striving for.

In 2023, violence against children in armed conflict reached harrowing levels, with a 21 percent rise in grave violations. Children, the most vulnerable victims of war, bore the devastating consequences of profound disregard for their fundamental rights, particularly the right to life. The number of children killed and maimed surged by an alarming 35 percent. In the midst of crises in Israel and the Occupied Palestinian Territory, especially in Gaza, as well as in Burkina Faso, the Democratic Republic of the Congo, Myanmar, Somalia, Sudan, the Syrian Arab Republic, Ukraine, and numerous other regions, children endured unprecedented suffering (United Nations 2023).

The United Nations verified a total of 32,990 grave violations, 30,705 of which occurred in 2023, with 2,285 committed earlier but verified during the year. These violations affected 22,557 children—15,847 boys, 6,252 girls, and 458 of unknown sex—across twenty-five conflict situations and one regional monitoring arrangement covering the Lake Chad basin (United Nations General Assembly 2024).

Among the most appalling statistics were the killing (5,301) and maiming (6,348) of 11,649 children. Other significant violations included the recruitment and use of 8,655 children, the denial of humanitarian access in 5,205 verified incidents, and the abduction of 4,356 children. Additionally, 2,491 children were detained for alleged associations with armed groups, including those designated as terrorist organizations by the United Nations, or for reasons related to national security (United Nations General Assembly 2024).

Children are not just statistics; their lives are forever altered by the horrors of war. Their futures, hopes, and potential are tragically uprooted by violence, displacement, and trauma. Whether forced into child soldiering, deprived of education, subjected to physical and emotional abuse, or stripped of their safety, the impact of conflict on children is profound and enduring. Each violation reflects not only a tragedy, but a life irreparably harmed. This highlights the urgent need for swift, comprehensive action to safeguard children from the ravages of armed conflict, ensuring the protection of their rights, security, and dignity (United Nations Office for the Coordination of Humanitarian Affairs 2023).

We must actively foster and defend children's rights to ensure their protection and wellbeing in an increasingly complex world. Human rights are the bedrock of global justice and equity, enshrining the principles of dignity, freedom, and equality for all. These rights, codified in instruments like the UDHR (1948) and the United Nations CRC (1989), serve as guiding principles in the quest for inclusive, just societies. For children, the CRC offers a broad framework for their protection, guaranteeing access to education, healthcare, and safeguarding them from exploitation and abuse. However, the complexities of our modern world—from rapid technological advancements to the harsh realities of armed conflict—demand that we continuously refine our understanding and application of these rights.

Advocating for children in conflict zones necessitates a multifaceted approach, blending immediate relief efforts with long-term strategies that address the root causes of violence and instability. This requires engaging governments, civil society, and international organizations to prioritize the demilitarization of child soldiers, facilitate the reintegration of displaced children into safe environments, and establish resilient educational systems that can endure the disruptions caused by war. We must ensure that the voices of children are heard.

International efforts, such as those led by the Special Representative of the Secretary-General for Children and Armed Conflict, highlight children's violations, including recruitment, abduction, and attacks on schools and hospitals (United Nations 2023). Organizations like UNICEF emphasize the vital need for psychosocial support and educational opportunities to aid the recovery and future development of children impacted by war (UNICEF 2022).

These interventions reflect the enduring commitment of international actors to protect children, even in the most challenging circumstances.

What should we do to protect children? We must ensure legal protections for children in armed conflict exist, as described in the United Nations CRC (1989). Article 6 affirms every child's right to life and development, and Article 19 mandates the protection of children from all forms of violence, forming the bedrock of children's rights (United Nations 1989). Article 38 of the CRC requires states to take all feasible measures to ensure that children under fifteen are not recruited into hostilities and to provide special protections for those affected by conflict (United Nations 1989). The Optional Protocol to the CRC on the Involvement of Children in Armed Conflict (2000) strengthens these protections by raising the minimum age for direct participation in hostilities to eighteen and encouraging states to criminalize the recruitment of child soldiers (United Nations 2000). The Geneva Conventions (1949) and their Additional Protocols (1977) provide specific protections for children during armed conflict, ensuring their humane treatment, access to education, and protection from conscription (International Committee of the Red Cross 1949). The Rome Statute of the International Criminal Court (1998) further criminalizes war crimes involving children, such as the recruitment of child soldiers and attacks on schools and hospitals (International Criminal Court 1998). These legal instruments establish a comprehensive framework for protecting children's rights and holding violators accountable.

Advocacy efforts in these areas must strengthen local and international mechanisms to prevent the recruitment of child soldiers. Addressing root causes of child recruitment and implementing stronger legal frameworks and enforcement mechanisms to ensure that recruitment is prevented and perpetrators are held accountable are essential (United Nations 2019). For children already affected by armed conflict, comprehensive rehabilitation and reintegration programs are essential. These programs must include psychological care to address trauma, and educational/vocational training to help children rebuild their lives and reintegrate into society. Holding perpetrators of crimes against children accountable is critical to preventing future violations. Strengthening international justice systems, such as the International Criminal Court, is necessary to ensure that those responsible for crimes against children are brought to justice.

Every step taken—whether it is raising awareness, supporting humanitarian programs, or holding perpetrators accountable—brings us closer to a world where children can live free from the horrors of war, exploitation, and trauma. The path forward demands courage, innovation, and unwavering dedication. As we navigate an increasingly complex and interconnected world, the responsibility to champion the rights and wellbeing of children becomes ever more urgent. We must challenge systems of oppression and inequality, adapt our tools and frameworks to emerging challenges, and place children at the heart of our efforts. This journey is not only a moral imperative but a testament to our shared humanity.

Governments and international organizations have a duty to enforce policies that target root causes of inequality. Equitable access to education, healthcare, and social protection are pillars that give children the opportunity to thrive. UNESCO highlights that breaking the cycle of intergenerational poverty is intricately linked to providing equitable education (UNESCO 2023). Equally important is community empowerment. Transformative change begins at the grassroots level. When local communities are engaged in initiatives to combat harmful practices, such as child labour or early marriage, real progress is possible. We cannot overlook the need for global collaboration to address systemic oppression. Frameworks like the UN SDGs offer a shared vision and strategy to tackle global inequalities and promote peace.

We have a shared responsibility towards creating a just future. The plight of children affected by armed conflict demands our unwavering attention, compassion, and action. Their stories, etched in the statistics of tragedy and resilience, remind us that they are not just casualties of war but potential architects of the future. The scale of the challenges they face—from recruitment and exploitation to deprivation of education and healthcare—requires a collective response that transcends borders, disciplines, and ideologies.

Establishment of initiatives like the Universities Network for Children in Armed Conflict highlights the transformative potential of academic and grassroots partnerships. By integrating research, advocacy, and empowerment programs, such efforts pave the way for systemic change and enduring peace. The journey ahead is formidable, but the stakes are too high to falter. It is only by uniting as governments, organizations, and individuals that we can dismantle the barriers of inequality and injustice. Together, we can forge a world where every child is free to thrive, a testament to the enduring belief that even in the face of adversity, change is not just possible—it is inevitable. Let us recommit to this vision with purpose and resolve, striving toward a future defined by dignity, justice, and hope for all children.

Further Reading

Bronfenbrenner, U. (1979). *The Ecology of Human Development: Experiments by Nature and Design*. Harvard University Press.

Education Cannot Wait. (2022). *Annual results report*. https://educationcannotwait.org (accessed March 31, 2025).

Global Coalition to Protect Education from Attack. (2017). *Education Under Attack 2017*. GCPEA.

Hart, R. A. (1992). *Children's Participation: From Tokenism to Citizenship*. UNICEF.

International Committee of the Red Cross (ICRC). (1949). *Geneva Conventions of 1949 and their additional protocols*. https://www.icrc.org (accessed March 31, 2025).

International Committee of the Red Cross (ICRC). (2018). *International Humanitarian Law and the Protection of Children in Armed Cconflict*. ICRC.

International Criminal Court. (1998). *Rome Statute of the International Criminal Court*. https://www.icc-cpi.int (accessed March 31, 2025).

International Rescue Committee. (2023). *Protecting children in crisis*. https://rescue.org (accessed March 31, 2025).

UNESCO. (2023). *Education for all: Breaking the Poverty Cycle*. https://unesco.org (accessed March 31, 2025).

UNICEF. (2020). *The Importance of Child Participation in Policy-making*. UNICEF.

UNICEF. (2021). *The state of the world's children 2021: On my mind—Promoting, protecting and caring for children's mental health*. https://www.unicef.org/reports/state-worlds-children-2021 (accessed March 31, 2025).

UNICEF. (2021). *The climate crisis is a child rights crisis*. https://www.unicef.org/reports/climate-crisis-child-rights-crisis (accessed March 31, 2025).

UNICEF. (2022). *Children in armed conflict*. https://www.unicef.org/reporting-children-armed-conflict (accessed April 18, 2025).

United Nations. (1948). *Universal Declaration of Human Rights (UDHR)*. https://www.un.org/en/about-us/universal-declaration-of-human-rights (accessed April 18, 2025).

United Nations. (1989). *Convention on the Rights of the Child (UNCRC)*. https://www.ohchr.org/en/instruments-mechanisms/instruments/convention-rights-child (accessed April 18, 2025).

United Nations. (2000). *Optional Protocol to the Convention on the Rights of the Child on the Involvement of Children in Armed Conflict*. https://www.ohchr.org/en/instruments-mechanisms/instruments/optional-protocol-convention-rights-child-involvement-children (accessed April 18, 2025).

United Nations. (2019). *Children and Armed Conflict: Report of the Secretary-General*. United Nations.

United Nations. (2023). *Office of the Special Representative of the Secretary-General for Children and Armed Conflict*. https://childrenandarmedconflict.un.org (accessed March 31, 2025).

United Nations Office for the Coordination of Humanitarian Affairs (OCHA). (2023). *Humanitarian Impact on Children.*
United Nations General Assembly. (2024). Report of the Secretary-General on Children and Armed Conflict.

Laura Guercio is a Professor of Sociology of Human Rights and International Cooperation to Development at the University of Perugia and Professor of International Relations and Intelligence Systems at the University Cusano. She is a Member of the Council of the European Law Institute in Vienna; Expert of the Moscow Mechanism Osce, Consultant or Team Leader in International Projects and Missions in Africa, the Middle East, and Eastern Europe (supported and carried out by the European Union; OSCE; Italian Ministry of Foreign Affairs), and Coordinator of the Universities Network for Children in Armed Conflict since its establishment. She was Italian Agent of the MB of the EU Fundamental Rights Agency and SG of the Italian Inter ministerial committee. Her area of research includes Human Rights, International Justice, Sociology of Human Rights, and International Relations. She is author of articles and handbooks on sociological and international legal aspects on women and children's rights, international relations, and sociology of political systems. She has received the Pareto award for research activity in the Sociology field (2021), Perugia; the Victor Hugo award for Human Rights (2017), Lecce; and the Youth for Human Rights award (2017), New York.

How to Survive a Pandemic: The Right to Enjoy the Benefits of Scientific Progress and Its Applications

Theresa Harris

Human rights practitioners and scientists alike are often surprised to learn that the UDHR and the Convention on Economic, Social, and Cultural Rights include the right to enjoy the benefits of scientific progress and its applications (or "the right to science" in shorthand). In part, this lack of understanding is because the right to science is so tightly knitted within the human rights framework that at first, it does not appear to stand on its own. When the right to science does get noticed, it is usually in connection with the rights to education, healthcare, clean water, sanitation, and a healthy environment. For years, human rights advocates did not see how the right to science could be violated, so it was rarely included in civil society shadow reports or campaigns (Wyndham et al. 2017).

That perception changed during the COVID-19 pandemic, when governments around the world sealed borders, prohibited public gatherings, closed schools and other public buildings, and enacted new laws to protect public health. While scientists worked at breakneck pace to understand the virus and develop a vaccine, national, state, and local governments held daily briefings to inform the public on the latest research results and data on infection and death rates. These experiences during the pandemic help illustrate how the right to science is, in fact, unique from other human rights and at the same time indivisible from them.

For example, one of the right's core obligations is that governments must provide the public with accurate and timely scientific information. During the COVID-19 pandemic, people needed up-to-date and accurate public health information from trusted sources so they could make individualized risk assessments about what exposures might be safe for them, their workplaces, and their schools. While most governments saw the benefits of being transparent as knowledge about the virus evolved, some governments disseminated misinformation, and worse, intentional disinformation, about the virus, protective actions, and treatments (Porsdam 2023).

Once this misinformation and disinformation were disseminated by governments, it was inadvertently spread by people who lacked scientific knowledge. When misinformation is shared by trusted officials and influential celebrities, especially during a time of confusion and fear, it becomes difficult to figure out what advice to trust. This is why the right to enjoy the benefits of scientific progress and its applications requires an adequate, up-to-date education in science: so each individual in society is able to understand and apply scientific information. This ability is especially needed when scientific findings are evolving very quickly, as was the case during the COVID-19 pandemic. Unfortunately, when new scientific knowledge was shared, even by trusted public health officials, people who did not understand the scientific method concluded that the changes meant those officials had lied or that scientists simply could not be trusted at all. This became a dangerous situation for public health and for public health officials themselves, who became targets for threats and violence (Mello, Greene, and Sharfstein 2020).

During the pandemic, many schools moved classrooms online. This created significant disparities for children who do not have access to computers or broadband internet, either due to poverty or location. Virtual classrooms also negatively impacted many children with disabilities and students in unstable households. Many communities are still grappling with the long-term consequences of these disparities (Colucci-Gray 2022). When everyone has equal access to scientific education and the technologies necessary to fully participate in learning, regardless of their social status or geographic location, they will be better able to understand and analyze information that affect their lives, especially during an emergency when decisions need to be made every day with new research findings.

Scientific education opportunities need to go beyond the classroom, however. Fully enjoying the benefits of scientific progress and its applications requires governments to ensure that adults also have opportunities beyond formal education to stay informed about new scientific discoveries. For example, governments have cited their support for science programs on radio and television and at public science and technology centers as efforts consistent with the right to science (American Association for the Advancement of Science n.d.). These technologies and facilities, however, are not accessible to many people due to poverty, educational levels, government control of information, or geography.

The right to benefit from scientific progress and its applications also includes, and is grounded in, the right of everyone to participate in science (International Science Council 2024). That includes opportunities for identifying and framing research priorities for government funding. Everyone should also have the opportunity to contribute to scientific research, especially when the research directly impacts them and their community (Xanthaki 2024). Participation in science also means that careers in science are open to everyone without discrimination. Unfortunately, this is often not the case. As just one of many examples, women and persons with disabilities are sometimes prohibited from working in chemistry laboratories due to outdated concerns about safety (Kottmayer 2023). Without scientists from many backgrounds involved in the scientific enterprise, the way research is conducted is filled with gaps and blind spots. During the COVID-19 pandemic, one such gap became apparent when an important tool for identifying a COVID-19 infection, pulse oximeters, was documented to perform differently depending on skin color (Gottlieb et al. 2022). As was noted in this case, how technologies work across racial and ethnic groups may cause unintentional disparities in healthcare.

The drafters of the International Covenant on Economic, Social, and Cultural Rights included a very specific freedom within the right to science: international collaboration. Complex global challenges, like a novel infectious virus, require the global scientific community to share data, openly review and discuss new results to identify gaps or errors, and collaborate across the biological, physical, behavioral, social, and earth sciences. These collaborations and sharing were paramount for every country affected by the virus. Where countries did not share information, or refused to collaborate during the pandemic, information that could prevent the next pandemic remains inaccessible (UNESCO 2022).

The COVID-19 pandemic demonstrated many ways in which recognizing a human right to science is an essential component of the full human rights spectrum. Benefiting from science does not require an advanced degree, but it does require governments to ensure that everyone has access to accurate and timely scientific findings, the education that enables people to use that information, the freedom to participate in collaborative research, and the ability to conduct that research in partnerships across national borders. Strengthening the right to science is an important way governments and civil society can prevent the next pandemic.

Further Reading

American Association for the Advancement of Science. (n.d.). Right to science: State reports. https://www.aaas.org/programs/scientific-responsibility-human-rights-law/resources/state-reports (accessed March 31, 2025).

Colucci-Gray, L. (2022). Reviewing the impact of COVID-19 on children's rights to, in and through education. *The International Journal of Human Rights*, 27 (9–10): 1389–405. doi: 10.1080/13642987.2022.2057961.

Gottlieb, E. R., Ziegler, J., Morley, K., Rush, B., and Celi, L. A. (2022). Assessment of racial and ethnic differences in oxygen supplementation among patients in the intensive care unit. *JAMA Internal Medicine*, 182 (8): 849–58. doi:10.1001/jamainternmed.2022.2587.

International Science Council. (2024). The International Science Council's interpretation of the right to participate in and benefit from science. https://council.science/wp-content/uploads/2024/11/The-Right-to-Participate-in-and-Benefit-from-Science_ISC.pdf (accessed March 31, 2025).

Kottmayer, M. (2023). Exploring the interconnected world of gender equality, conflicts and science. EuChemS. https://www.magazine.euchems.eu/gwb-2023-2 (accessed March 31, 2025).

Mello, M. M., Greene, J. A., and Sharfstein, J. M. (2020). Attacks on public health officials during COVID-19. *Journal of the American Medical Association*, 324 (8): 741–2. doi: 10.1001/jama.2020.14423.

Porsdam, H. (2023). Countering science-related populist speech. *Frontiers in Sociology*, 8. doi: 10.3389/fsoc.2023.1275384.

UNESCO. 2022. Brief on the Right to Science and COVID-19. https://unesdoc.unesco.org/ark:/48223/pf0000381186 (accessed March 31, 2025).

Wyndham J. M., Vitullo, M. W., Kraska, K., Sianko, N., Carbajales, P., Nuñez-Eddy, C., and Platts, E. (2017). Giving Meaning to the Right to Science: A Global and Multidisciplinary Approach. AAAS Science and Human Rights Commission. doi: 10.1126/srhrl.aao4380.

Xanthaki, Alexandra. (2024). The Right to Participate in Science, Report of the Special Rapporteur in the field of cultural rights. United Nations General Assembly A/HRC/55/44.

Theresa Harris directs the Center for Scientific Responsibility and Justice at the American Association for the Advancement of Science (AAAS). At AAAS, she leads projects on science and human rights, including On-call Scientists, a volunteer referral service that provides technical support for human rights organizations. She also serves as coordinator of the AAAS Science and Human Rights Coalition, a network of scientific, engineering, and health associations that recognize the role of science and technology in human rights. Prior to joining AAAS, Ms. Harris represented survivors of human rights violations before United States courts, the Inter-American human rights system, and United Nations human rights mechanisms. She has served on the Board of Directors of Amnesty International USA and is a member of the governing body of the World Organization Against Torture (OMCT).

Explaining the Origins of Democratic Backsliding

Steven Livingston

Few democracies in recent decades have suffered a sudden bloody death in a coup d'état (Cebotari et al. 2024). Rather, they have died slow, almost imperceptible deaths of institutional decay (Levitsky and Ziblatt 2018). This observation is our jumping-off point in this brief essay. First, we review evidence of the decades long erosion of core democratic institutions in the United States. We then note what might be the most common contemporary explanation for backsliding—the idea that social media are responsible for the erosion of institutional legitimacy. This understanding is partially correct but dangerously incomplete. As a consequence, it invites poorly thought-out solutions. An alternative explanation understands democratic decay to be the result of deeply inequitable socioeconomic conditions and elite mismanagement of the public trust. Given the limited space, we restrain our ambition to only noting the arguments and directing the reader to additional resources.

Trust in America

There are plenty of disquieting signs of institutional distress in the United States. According to the Pew Research Center, trust in government in the United States has been on a six-decade slide. In 1958, about 75 percent of Americans trusted the government to "do the right thing almost always or most of the time." This apex of trust began falling precipitously in the late 1960s, with the moving average hitting 50 percent in 1970. By 1980 it had fallen to 27 percent. While levels of trust would fluctuate in coming decades, by the end of 2024 it hovered at a little over 20 percent (Pew Research Center 2024). (The running average climbed to about 50 percent following the 9/11 attacks on New York and Washington.)

Measurements of public attitudes concerning specific institutions brings the severity of crisis into sharper focus. For example, a 2024 Gallup survey found that only 35 percent of Americans express faith in the federal courts (Saad 2024). Congress is trusted even less. In 2022, only 5 percent of Republicans and 10 percent of Democrats reported having a great deal or quite a lot of confidence in Congress (Jones 2022). Except for the military and police, other government institutions generally fared little better.

The crisis of trust has not been limited to government institutions. A 2023 Gallup poll found that only a third of Americans trusted the US privatized health system, down ten points from 2021 during the COVID-19 crisis (Saad 2023). On the same measurement scale, public schools stood at 26 percent; organized labor 25 percent; newspapers 18 percent; big business 14 percent; large tech companies 26 percent; and television news 14 percent (Saad 2023).

The steep decline in trust in institutions is also associated with a *decline* in trust of other people (Pew Research Center 2019). Not only do Americans not trust institutions, but they are also less likely to trust one another. This can be thought of as declining social capital—understood as the "connections between people, and the norms of trust and reciprocity that arise from those connections" (Putnam 2000). According to the results of a comparative global analysis done in 2024, the United States was ranked 118th out of 191 countries in levels of social capital (Solability 2024).

Clearly, the foundational ideas and institutions upon which liberal democracy and human rights rests have weakened substantially in the United States over the last half-century. In fact, there is jarring evidence that something more menacing than distrust has emerged. A 2024 Pew Research Center survey found that 38 percent of Americans under-thirty expressed support for *authoritarianism* (Silver and Fetterolf 2024). Other surveys have captured similar sentiments. For example, relying on a slightly provocative yet long-established "authoritarian personality" scale, a 2024 PRRI survey found that four in ten Americans show an inclination toward authoritarianism (Public Religion Research Institute 2024). This same survey also found that about one-third of Americans agree that "because things have gotten so far off track in this country, we need a leader who is willing to break some rules if that's what it takes to set things right." Republican Trump supporters are more than twice as likely to agree with this statement than are non-supporters (55 percent vs. 26 percent). The same PRRI survey found that a third of the country, and a majority of Republicans, embrace not only authoritarianism but also the use of political violence. In a country with as many as 400 million guns, this is alarming, especially when Donald Trump said during the 2024 campaign that if he weren't re-elected "there would be a bloodbath" (Kinnard and Colvin 2024; Mackie and Ramirez 2024). How do we explain these alarming trends?

Explanations

We will briefly touch on two commonly offered explanations. The first points to the destabilizing effects of social media; the second looks to the effects of concentrations of social and economic power.

Since the 2016 presidential election and the Brexit vote in the United Kingdom, many observers have held social media responsible for democratic backsliding (Mounk 2018; Tucker et al. 2018). The argument follows a fairly straightforward logic. Because the social media behemoths prioritize financial growth and market dominance over social and civic responsibility, they have little compunction designing algorithms that amplify the sort of extremist content that holds user attention (Heffner 2019; Zuboff 2019). As a result, individual users are drawn deeper into motivated reasoning—the human tendency to uncritically embrace information that is aligned with prior beliefs while holding at arm's length information, no matter how sound, that undermines them (Porter and Wood 2019; Taber and Lodge 2006). In this way citizens are pulled ever deeper into proverbial rabbit holes (Iyengar and Westwood 2015; Mason 2018; Rawlings 2022). As people uncritically take in dubious information, they become more polarized. And as they become more polarized, they are more receptive to dubious information.

As commonsensical as this explanation seems, it rests on a cognitive science-inspired political science literature that is in crisis. Key findings of some of the foundational claims made by cognitive and political scientists have not been reproduceable in subsequent attempts (Ellis 2022; Lillenfeld 2017; Maxwell, Lau, and Howard 2015). Even foundational ideas, including the precise nature of motivation, the core concept of motivated reasoning remain undertheorized and ambiguous (Livingston 2023; Livingston and Miller 2024). And simple common sense calls into question the explanatory power of the social media for a trend—weakening trust in institutions—that began in the 1960s.

Yet most problematic is the way the cognitive science understanding of political polarization, anger, and alienation is framed. Because politics exists solely in the mind, as the cognitive science explanation implies, alienation and anger are understood as the result of unfortunate human information processing tendencies. Solutions to a problem so understood involve technical solutions involving fact checking and better crafted corrections designed to counter the tendency toward motivated reasoning. This is a solution that falls short of the problem.

Elided from view is the possibility that political anger and alienation arise from lived experience. Philosopher Charles Taylor puts the counterpoint this way. Democracy is an ongoing project that requires continuous care and the proper conditions to flourish. The neoliberal era, beginning in the 1980s but reaching full fruition in the 1990s, has been marked by an undermining of these conditions as a result of a withdrawal of democratic control of markets (Slobodian 2018) and the wholesale privatization of state provisioning of public goods (i.e., the elimination of the social safety net). This has created levels of inequality that "saps democratic unity." The high levels of social solidarity once present during the more equal New Deal era "has been bled away to a remarkable degree" (Tayler 2023). Taylor goes on to say that neoliberalism has been accompanied by an idea that his fellow philosopher Michael Sandel refers to as the "tyranny of merit" (Sandel 2020). The tyranny of merit is the belief that succeeding in hypercompetitive late capitalism must be attributed to one's special talents. Conversely, if one fails, it must be because one doesn't have what it takes. This belief overlooks the role of chance and contingency in success and failure. Yet the tyranny of merit destroys any sense of the common good. It leads us to believe that we owe nothing to anyone, and no one owes anything to us (Calhoun, Gaonkar, and Taylor 2022). Wealth inequality and economic stagnation have exacerbated political divisions, but the bigger problem is the fraying of the civic solidarity that knits citizens together across lines of difference.

This is an extraordinarily different understanding of democratic backsliding, one that puts the burden of decline in social trust on an economic and political system rather than on the foibles of the human brain. It calls for wholesale change, not better messaging. At a time when three persons own as much as the bottom 170 million Americans, it seems worthy of our consideration.

Further Reading

Calhoun, C., Gaonkar, D. P., and Taylor, C. (2022). *Degenerations of Democracy.* Cambridge University Press.

Cebotari, A., Chueca-Montuenga, E., Diallo, Y., Ma, Y., Turk, R. A., Xin, W., and Zavarce, H. (2024). Political fragility: Coups d'état and their drivers. International Monetary Fund Working Papers. https://www.imf.org/en/Publications/WP/Issues/2024/02/16/Political-Fragility-Coups-dtat-and-Their-Drivers-544943 (accessed March 31, 2025).

Ellis, R. J. (2022). Questionable research practices, low statistical power, and other obstacles to replicability: Why preclinical neuroscience research would benefit from registered reports. *eNeuro* 4 (July-August). doi: 10.1523/ENEURO.0017-22.2022.

Heffner, A. (2019). Greed is to blame for the radicalization of social media. *Wired*, August 8, 2019. https://www.wired.com/story/greed-is-to-blame-for-the-radicalization-of-social-media (accessed March 31, 2025).

Iyengar, S., and Westwood, S. J. (2015). Fear and loathing across party lines: New evidence on group polarization. *American Journal of Political Science*, 59 (3): 690–707. doi: 10.1111/ajps.12152.

Jones, J. M. (2022). Confidence in U.S. institutions down; Average at new low. Gallup, July 5, 2022. https://news.gallup.com/poll/394283/confidence-institutions-down-average-new-low.aspx (accessed March 31, 2025).

Kinnard, M., and Colvin, J. (2024). Trump warns of "bloodbath" if he isn't reelected at Ohio rally for Senate candidate Moreno. PBS News. May 17, 2024. https://www.pbs.org/newshour/politics/trump-warns-of-bloodbath-if-he-isnt-reelected-at-ohio-rally-for-senate-candidate-moreno (accessed March 31, 2025).

Levitsky, S., and Ziblatt, D. (2018). *How Democracies Die.* Crown.

Lillenfeld, S. O. (2017). Psychology's replication crisis and the grant culture: Righting the ship. *Perspectives on Psychological Science*, 12 (4). https://journals.sagepub.com/doi/full/10.1177/1745691616687745 (accessed March 31, 2025).

Livingston, S. (2023). The nature of beliefs. An exploration of cognitive science and sociological approaches to the crisis of democracy. SCRIPTS Working Paper No. 31, Berlin. Cluster of Excellence 2055 "Contestations of the Liberal Script (SCRIPTS)."

Livingston, S., and Miller, M. (2024). Considering the assumptions of the technocentric model of democratic flourishing and decay. *Journal of Illiberalism Studies*, 4 (3): 139–60. doi: 10.53483/XCQZ3584.

Mackie, J., and Ramirez, A., JD. (2024). How many guns are in the US?: Ownership breakdown. Consumer Shield. October 31, 2024. https://www.consumershield.com/articles/how-many-guns-us (accessed March 31, 2025).

Mason, L. (2018). *Uncivil Agreement: How Politics Became our Identity.* University of Chicago Press. doi: 10.7208/chicago/9780226524689.001.0001.

Maxwell, S. E., Lau, M. Y., and Howard, G. S. (2015). Is psychology suffering from a replication crisis? What does "failure to replicate" really mean? *The American Psychologist*, 70 (6): 487–98. doi:10.1037/a0039400.

Mounk, Y. (2018). Can liberal democracy survive social media? *New York Review of Books*. April 30, 2018. https://www.nybooks.com/daily/2018/04/30/can-liberal-democracy-survive-social-media (accessed March 31, 2025).

Pew Research Center (2019). The state of personal trust. July 22, 2019. https://www.pewresearch.org/politics/2019/07/22/the-state-of-personal-trust (accessed March 31, 2025).

Pew Research Center. (2024). Public trust in government: 1958-2024. June 24, 2024. https://www.pewresearch.org/politics/2024/06/24/public-trust-in-government-1958-2024 (accessed March 31, 2025).

Porter, E., and Wood, T. J. (2019). *False Alarm: The Truth About Political Mistruths in the Trump era*. Cambridge University Press. doi: 10.1017/9781108688338.

Public Religion Research Institute. (2024). Survey: Four in ten Americans are susceptible to authoritarianism, but most still reject political violence. September 10, 2024. https://www.prri.org/press-release/survey-four-in-ten-americans-are-susceptible-to-authoritarianism-but-most-still-reject-political-violence (accessed March 31, 2025).

Putnam, R. D. (2000). *Bowling Alone: The Collapse and Revival of American Community*. Simon & Schuster.

Rawlings, C. M. (2022). Becoming an ideologue: Social sorting and the microfoundations of polarization. *Sociological Science*, 9: 313–45. doi: 10.15195/v9.a13.

Saad, L. (2023). Historically low faith in U.S. institutions continue. Gallup. July 6, 2023. https://news.gallup.com/poll/508169/historically-low-faith-institutions-continues.aspx (accessed March 31, 2025).

Saad, L. (2024). Americans pass judgement on their courts. Gallup. December 17, 2024. https://news.gallup.com/poll/653897/americans-pass-judgment-courts.aspx (accessed March 31, 2025).

Sandel, M. (2020). *The Tyranny of Merit: Can we Find the Common Good?* Farrar, Straus and Giroux.

Silver, L., and Fetterolf, J. (2024). Who likes authoritarianism, and how do they want to change their government? Pew Research Center. February 28, 2024. https://www.pewresearch.org/short-reads/2024/02/28/who-likes-authoritarianism-and-how-do-they-want-to-change-their-government (accessed March 31, 2025).

Slobodian, Q. (2018). *Globalists: The end of Empire and the Birth of Neoliberalism*. Harvard University Press.

Solability. (2024). Social capital index. https://solability.com/the-global-sustainable-competitiveness-index/social-capital (accessed March 31, 2025).

Taber, C. S., and Lodge, M. (2006). Motivated skepticism in the evaluation of political beliefs. *American Journal of Political Science*, 50 (3): 755–69. doi: 10.1111/j.1540-5907.2006.00214.x.

Taylor, C. (2023). Hedgehog noontime discussion with Charles Taylor. Institute for Advanced Studies in Culture. January 11, 2023. https://www.youtube.com/watch?v=31ktLt8suxg&t=545s (accessed March 31, 2025).

Tucker, J. A., Guess, A., Barberá, P., Vaccari, C., Siegel, A., Sanovich, S., Stukal, D., and Nyhan, B. (2018). Social media, political polarization, and political disinformation: A review of the scientific literature. William and Flora Hewlett Foundation. Technical report, March 19, 2018. https://hewlett.org/wp-content/uploads/2018/03/Social-Media-Political-Polarization-and-Political-Disinformation-Literature-Review.pdf (accessed March 31, 2025).

Zuboff, Shoshana. (2019). The age of surveillance capitalism: The fight for a human future at the new frontier of power, Kindle edition. PublicAffairs.

Steven Livingston is Professor of Media and Public Affairs and the Founding Director of the Institute for Data, Democracy, and Politics, holds an appointment in the Elliott School of International Affairs, and is a senior fellow in the Illiberal Studies Program in the Elliott School. Livingston also founded the Public Diplomacy Institute at George Washington University. He has had appointments at the Brookings Institution, Harvard Kennedy School, Fulbright awards in Finland and Lebanon, and appointments in the United States, New Zealand, United Kingdon, Europe, the Middle East, and others. His books include The Terrorism Spectacle, The Nature of Beliefs, The Disinformation Age *(with W. Lance Bennett),* When the Press Fails *(with W. Lance Bennett and Regina G. Lawrence),* Connective Action and the Rise of the Far Right *(with Michael Miller), and* Bits of Atoms *(with Gregor Walter-Drop).*

A Thousand Words on Children's Rights

Jane Williams

I am a professor of law who at the time of writing is soon to retire from Swansea University. Over the past twenty-five years, with others in and outside the university, I set up a Children's Legal Centre for Wales. We have had some successes in influencing child rights-oriented change in law and practice in Wales, the UK and beyond.

It is said that children's rights are emblematic of devolution in Wales (Rees 2010). The country boasts several firsts in the field: the first of the UK's four Children's Commissioners, the first legislative reference to the CRC in UK law, the first general legislative measure of implementation of the CRC and numerous firsts in sectoral reforms drawing the CRC into the exercise of public functions (Williams 2013; 2024).

The Children's Legal Centre and a wider Observatory on Human Rights (Observatory n.d.) in their university home contributed to this process, in the way that higher education institutions can: providing expertise, reflective space, research, learning, teaching and what the industry terms "impact" on policy and practice. The Observatory supported change elsewhere too, including in Scotland and the Channel Islands.

Scotland now has very strong legislation on children's rights, since its parliament passed the United Nations Convention on the Rights of the Child (Incorporation) (Scotland) Act 2024. This Act is stronger than anything yet enacted in Wales, with provisions that compel all public authorities to act compatibly with the CRC, that confer strike down powers on courts where legislation is incompatible, impose reporting and scrutiny requirements on government and provide for individual legal remedies for violation of rights (Adamson 2025).

This Scottish law comes a century after Eglantyne Jebb penned her Declaration on the Rights of the Child and managed, through her tireless campaigning, persuasion and perseverance plus, it might be added, a rolodex of personal, political and intellectual contacts, to get the League of Nations to adopt it in 1924. It was Jebb's experience of trying to raise funds for children afflicted by the ravages of war and disease that led to her conviction that safeguarding children must be done on "constructive rather than on charitable lines" and that the key to achieving this would be to "claim certain rights for children and labour for their universal recognition" (Mulley 2009: 304). In 1989 the adoption of the CRC by the UN General Assembly delivered the internationally agreed list of those "certain rights," together with the beginnings of a constructive framework in which that labor could bear fruit. In Scotland, to a lesser extent in Wales, and in many other jurisdictions, that fruit can be seen in the form of legal integration in each country's domestic law: in law reform, policy changes, practice guidance and multiple modalities deployed by civil society to hold governments to account for children's rights (Lundy et al. 2012).

For all these labors, changes and reforms, what has changed for the world's children? Giving the Observatory's annual lecture in November 2024, Bruce Adamson, Children and Young People's Commissioner Scotland from 2017–2023 and Chair of the European Network of Ombudspersons for Children

2019–2022, reflected on the century of children's rights and spoke of children's rights as a "rainbow against the dark clouds": dark clouds which include war, preventable disease, climate change, violence, exploitation, poverty, inequality, forced displacement, and the sinister side of digital technologies. UNICEF Innocenti's 2023 Global Outlook for Children describes a "polycrisis" of global events, shocks and trends impacting adversely on children now, most harshly on those in most vulnerable situations, and threatening the future lives of children everywhere (UNICEF 2023).

The numbers are stark and horrifying. In December 2024, UNICEF declared that the impact of armed conflicts had reached "devastating and likely record levels" in 2024, making it the worst year since the establishment of UNICEF itself (UNICEF 2024). Some 19 percent of the world's children were living in areas of conflict, up from 10 percent in the 1990s. This equates to 473 million children, with over 47 million displaced. It is hard to make an accurate comparison, but in numerical terms the suffering of children afflicted by armed conflict in the world is far greater now than when Eglantyne Jebb strode across Europe demanding rights for children a century ago. The need for a massive collaborative effort to address the plight of suffering children is ever more pressing. UNICEF Innocenti's 2023 Global Outlook concludes with a call that mirrors, in more modern language, Jebb's call for a constructive approach among nations and institutions (UNICEF 2023: 50).

Back closer to home, the Children's Legal Centre Wales, working constructively with a variety of governmental, NGO and professional stakeholders, identifies, and campaigns on multiple issues in child rights implementation: in education (especially for children with additional learning needs), for children affected by school exclusions or involved in the youth justice system, children in care, refugee and asylum seeking children, among others (Children's Legal Centre Wales 2024).

It is in this constructive approach that Adamson (2025) finds his rainbow against the dark clouds. It is right to acknowledge the progress that has been made. Sovereign states across the world, except the USA, have agreed to be bound in international law by the CRC, and they do participate in its monitoring and reporting process, and many have changed laws and practices to give further effect to its requirements. We have, in multiple countries, structures to support children's rights: children's commissioners, ombudspersons, youth parliaments, local mechanisms for children's participation in governance, and opportunities for complaints and redress.

The question remains, however, what use any of this is to the millions of children in extreme need. How do we, witnessing that need, make the connection between what they are suffering and these structures of children's rights? How do we compel authority to do so? How does the hungry, injured, destitute or displaced child know that what is happening to them is a violation of their rights? And if they or we make the connection, what can be done within these structures for child rights to bring relief?

For the child in extremis, two things matter: first, justiciability of rights, meaning an accessible, local legal route to redress; and second, guidance and support through that route. Scotland has made significant steps forward on both these, conferring a legal remedy for violation and at the same time strengthening the power of the Children's Commissioner to act for and intervene on behalf of children in court. Returning to where I began, the ambition of the Children's Legal Centre Wales is to grow capacity among children, carers and practitioners to use what remedies are available as well as press for more. In common with myriad similar organizations across the world, this work for children's rights remains, as in Jebb's day, dependent on charity. Only when that ceases to be the case will we really be able to say that the labor for recognition of children's rights has truly borne fruit.

Further Reading

Adamson, B. (2025). UNCRC incorporation in Scotland: The how, the why and looking ahead. *Family Law*, 65: 258–81.

Children's Legal Centre Wales. (2024). Child Rights and the Law Report. https://childrenslegalcentre.wales/wp-content/uploads/2024/12/Childrens-Rights-and-Law-Event-Report-FINAL.pdf (accessed April 1, 2025).

Lundy, L., Kilkelly, U., Byrne, B., and Kang, J. (20122012). The UN Convention on the Rights of the Child: a study of legal implementation in twelve countries. https://www.unicef.org.uk/publications/child-rights-convention-2012-report (accessed February 6, 2025).

Mulley, C. (2009). *The Woman who Saved the Children*. Oneworld Publications.

Observatory. (n.d.). Swansea University. https://www.swansea.ac.uk/law/observatory (accessed February 6, 2025).

Rees, O. (2010). Dealing with Individual Cases: An Essential Role for National Human Rights Institutions for Children?. *The International Journal of Children's Rights*, 18 (3): 417–36.

UNICEF. (2023). Prospects for children in the polycrisis: Global outlook, 2023. https://www.unicef.org/innocenti/media/651/file/UNICEF-Innocenti-Prospects-for-Children-Global-Outlook-2023.pdf (accessed April 1, 2025).

UNICEF. (2024). One of the worst years in history for children in conflict. UN News Global Perspective Human Stories. https://news.un.org/en/story/2024/12/1158561 (accessed April 1, 2025).

Williams, J. (2013). *The United Nations Convention on the Rights of the Child in Wales.* University of Wales Press.

Williams, J. (2024). The impact of children's rights in Wales. *Transactions of the Honourable Society of the Cymmrodorion*, 30: 111–30.

Jane Williams's career spans private practice at the Bar of England and Wales, UK and Welsh Government legal work and professional training, prior to joining Swansea University in 2000. Her academic work features extensive public and policy engagement. She founded and edited the Wales Journal of Law and Public Policy *(2001–2006) and was pivotally involved in civil society efforts to secure legislation on the rights of the child in Wales and the establishment of the Welsh Youth Parliament. She co-founded the Observatory on Human Rights of Children and secured grant funding to establish the Children's Legal Centre Wales. From 2014 to 2020, Williams led successive grant-funded projects developing human rights approaches to empowering children as researchers and agents of change. Her innovations in teaching include the introduction of modules on Street Law and Human Rights Approaches to Research with Children. Her academic publications are in the fields of devolution, child law and children's rights.*

4

Profiles

Many different people and organizations have contributed to the development of human rights as we know them. This chapter provides a brief introduction to some of the main individuals and groups that have influenced our understanding of human rights around the world. The further reading points to works that provide more information on how individuals and organizations have contributed to making the world a more rights respecting place.

Individuals

Thomas Aquinas (1225–74)

Thomas Aquinas was an Italian priest who studied the Greek philosopher Aristotle's work on natural law and integrated it into early Christianity as a fundamental concept. This concept can be seen in the faith's mandate to do good and avoid evil. It became the foundation for his study of natural law, which became a dominant precept in the building of a human rights focus. Aquinas's work on natural law acknowledged that rights are a universal aspect of a person's human essence. It laid the foundation for political rights as well. His doctrine of natural law was described in his writing of the *Summa Theologiae*. It laid a foundation for the later works by Hobbes, Descartes, Locke, Voltaire, and Jean-Jacques Rousseau.

Abolitionist and women's rights advocate Sojourner Truth, c. 1863. (Liljenquist Family Collection of Civil War Photographs, Library of Congress)

Muhammad Ali (1942–2016)

Muhammad Ali, born Cassius Clay, had a successful boxing career but ultimately became a human rights advocate, particularly around race and religion. Clay converted to Islam in 1964. In 1966 he argued that the Vietnam War was against the dictates in the Qur'an. A conscientious objector, he refused to be inducted into the armed forces when drafted and was subsequently stripped of his boxing title by the World Boxing Association, sentenced to five years in prison, banned from boxing for three years, and fined $10,000. The court's ruling against Ali in *Clay v. The United States* was overturned in 1971 by the Supreme Court of the United States. In 2005, he founded the Muhammad Ali Center in Louisville, Kentucky, to promote human rights. The Ali Center provides training, civic engagement activities, conferences, and humanitarian awards to support the knowledge of the importance of civil and human rights.

Kofi Annan (1938–2018)

Kofi Annan of Ghana was the Secretary-General of the United Nations from 1997 to 2006 and a co-recipient with it of the Nobel Peace Prize in 2001 for reforms to make the UN more effective and for his work on advancing human rights. A student of economics and international studies, he began his career with the UN as a budget officer for the World Health Organization. A constant advocate for human rights, Annan worked to protect people from war crimes and helped to create a UN counterterrorism strategy, among other efforts. He was instrumental in creating the UN's Global Fund to Fight AIDS, Tuberculosis, and Malaria. He was also the founder and chair of the Kofi Annan Foundation, and chair of The Elders, an international organization founded by South African leader Nelson Mandela. He advocated that protecting the human rights of one individual would promote the protection of the human rights of others and increase the chances for peace of all humanity.

Susan B. Anthony (1820–1906)

Susan Anthony was an American Quaker, and her faith inspired her belief in equality for all. Women did not have equal rights when she was young, and she believed that the US Constitution was not created just to support men or white people. She became an abolitionist and women's rights activist in the 1800s and played a major role, along with Elizabeth Cady Stanton, in promoting both racial and gender justice. They worked together during the Civil War to collect 400,000 signatures in support of abolishing slavery. They founded the Women's Loyal National League, the American Equal Rights Association, and the National Woman Suffrage Association. They also published a women's rights newspaper, *The Revolution*. Her activism contributed to the American Anti-Slavery Society and the American Equal Rights Association. Her fight for women to have the right to vote did not pass during her lifetime but eventually resulted in ratification of the Nineteenth Amendment to the US Constitution in 1920.

Michelle Bachelet (1951–)

Verónica Michelle Bachelet Jeria is a politician and activist for social justice and women's health human rights in Chile. Born into a politically active family that was imprisoned and tortured, she ultimately became the UN High Commissioner for Human Rights from 2018 to 2022. She worked to establish the National Institute for Human Rights, the Museum of Memory and Human Rights, and the Ministry of Women and Gender Equality. She also approved the Civil Union Act legislation, which granted rights to same-sex couples. Bachelet ran for president as a member of the Socialist Party. Her campaign endorsed the support of women's rights, aid to the poor, and making reforms to Chile's pension system. She became the president of Chile (2006–10 and 2014–18), making her the first woman to hold the position of president in that country. She was also the first president to be re-elected in Chile since 1932, and she won the majority of the popular vote.

Raif (Raef) bin Muhammed Badawi (1948–)

Raif Badawi, born in Al Khobar, Saudi Arabia, is a human rights activist and blogger on Free Saudi Liberals or the Saudi Liberal Network. He advocated for the end of religious influence in public life and was sentenced to 600 lashes and seven years in prison in 2013 for insulting Islam through electronic channels. Flogging is a common penalty in his country, and he advocated against it as being inhumane. He did not see the world from just a religious viewpoint and was inspired by the work of writers who advocated for a more just, open, secular, tolerant, and liberal society. He attempted to educate other Saudi citizens about human rights and their own rights and responsibilities. Badawi was released from jail in 2022. He has been the recipient of a variety of awards and honors, including the Courage Award from the Geneva Summit for Human Rights and Democracy in 2015, the Günter Wallraff Prize for journalism in 2019, and the International Laïcité Award and the Daniel Pearl Award in 2018. He was also nominated for the Nobel Peace Prize in 2015 and 2016. The Canadian-based Raoul Wallenberg Center for Human Rights has served as his legal counsel.

Ralph Bunche (1904–71)

Ralph Johnson Bunche was a political scientist and diplomat. He was the first Black individual to receive the Nobel Peace Prize (1950) for his mediation in Israel of a ceasefire with four Arab nations. He advocated for mediation to help solve conflict in his work both at the United Nations and in the United States. Bunche graduated from both the University of California Los Angeles and Howard University in political science. He was the first African American to gain a PhD in political science from an American university and taught at Howard University and conducted research at a variety of academic institutions in both the United States and internationally. He was actively involved in the US civil rights movement. He worked at the United States State Department and the United Nations.

Helen Caldicott (1938–)

Helen Mary Caldicott is an Australian-born American physician and activist. She is a former Harvard professor whose advocacy focused on the medical and environmental hazards of nuclear weapons. An MD, she saw a keen relationship between health and social actions, particularly war and weapons of mass destruction. Caldicott is regarded as a premier leader who advocates for the prevention of war. She founded Physicians for Social Responsibility and the Nuclear Policy Research Institute and was nominated for the Nobel Peace Prize. She regards war and nuclear weapons to be antithetical to the protection of the human rights of survival and good health. Her work was critically important in demonstrating the relationship between health and war interventions and that physicians would be unable to adequately address the harms that would result from a nuclear war. Her role in the film, *The Last Epidemic* (1980) highlights medical consequences of what would happen in a nuclear war or with the use of nuclear weapons.

Jimmy Carter (1924–2024)

James Earl (Jimmy) Carter Jr. was president of the United States from 1977 to 1981 and promised to lead the United States in the promotion of human rights. Carter was born and died in Plains, Georgia. During his childhood his home had no running water or electricity. His early years of financial challenge had lifelong impacts on his support of civil rights and assistance for those in poverty. A peanut farmer and businessman, he became the Governor of Georgia and later ran as a dark-horse candidate for president. A one-term president, his foreign policy agenda was centered on human rights principles. During his presidency, his human rights emphasis was clear. He pardoned all Vietnam draft dodgers, those who evaded being drafted into fighting in the war. He developed an international presence, including the Panama Canal treaties, creating diplomatic relations with China, conducting Strategic Arms Limitation talks, and other foreign policy agreements. He established a national Department of Education, viewing education as essential to the preservation of democracy. An environmental conservationist, he created the Department of Energy and advocated for the use of new technologies. He also passed into law the Mental Health Systems (MHSA) Act in order to make mental health services more available to individuals and community organizations. His post-presidency has been regarded as one of the most successful in history. In 1982, he founded the nonprofit Carter Center, working to resolve conflicts, promote democratic ideas, advance economic development, and prevent disease with the aim of addressing human rights issues around the world. He also worked extensively supporting Habitat for Humanity, which works to build or improve housing for people in need.

Cesar Chavez (1927–93)

Cesario Estrada Chavez was an American farm worker, labor leader, and civil rights activist. Born in Arizona to Mexican-American parents, he went into the Navy and afterwards relocated to California where he worked with the Community Service Organization (CSO) to register laborers to vote. He later became the national CSO director. Along with Dolores Huerta and Gilbert Padilla,, he co-founded the National Farm Workers Association, which later merged with the Agricultural Workers Organizing Committee to become the United Farm Workers (UFW) labor union. The efforts of these organizations succeeded in improving wages and working conditions, as well as securing other protections, for agricultural workers. His many awards include the Jefferson Award for Greatest Public Service Benefiting the Disadvantaged (1973), and in 1994 he was given the Presidential Medal of Freedom. He is a member of the California Hall of Fame and had Asteroid 6982 named for him. The National Chavez Center in California honors him and his work with the UFW.

Cyrus the Great (600–500 BCE)

Cyrus II of Persia, better known as Cyrus the Great, was a military strategist who founded the Achaemenid Empire. Known for his diplomatic acumen, military prowess, and commitment to justice and tolerance, he conquered the Neo-Babylonian Empire in 539 BCE. His Persian forces captured the city of Babylon without bloodshed. His policies advanced religious and cultural tolerance by allowing conquered peoples to retain their customs, languages, and religious practices. He is known for overcoming the Median Empire and bringing a variety of states together throughout west and central Asia to become the largest polity. He was recognized for his work in human rights. The Cyrus Cylinder, or Cyrus Charter, is a sixth century BCE object associated with his reign. It is a clay cylinder on which was written cuneiform text that portrays Cyrus as having been chosen by the Babylonian god Marduk to bring peace and order, and to care for the people and repair the region. The cylinder, which is now housed at the British Museum in London, has been declared by the United Nations as an ancient declaration of human rights.

14th Dali Lama (1935–)

Tenzin Gyatso is the 14th Dalai Lama and spiritual leader of Tibetan Buddhism. The Dalai Lamas are said to be the manifestations of the Bodhisattva of Compassion, who chose to reincarnate to promote the welfare of people. Born in a barn on a straw mat in rural Tibet to a farming family, he lived in an atmosphere of political, religious, and geographic tensions between Tibet and China. He attempted to protect the Tibetan people and preserve their culture and religion in the face of Chinese oppression. However, external pressures forced him to become exiled to India in 1959. He continues to support not just Tibet but all people in their nonviolent struggle for human rights and freedom. He has been given many human rights awards, including the Ramon Magsaysay Award, which is Asia's version of a Nobel Prize, as well as the Nobel Prize in

1989. He has received an Honorary Citizenship by the Governor of Canada, among other honors for his message of love, compassion, understanding, hope, and nonviolence.

F. W. de Klerk (1936–2021)

F. W. de Klerk was president of South Africa from 1989 to 1994, when the apartheid system of racial segregation in South Africa was brought to an end. He worked to negotiate a transition to majority rule of Black citizens instead of the historic white rule. De Klerk is remembered for defending the South African Constitution and supporting its transformation into a society that respects and incorporates racial equality. His work for reconciliation, national unity, and mutual understanding was foundational in helping move the nation away from its segregated history into one of political equality. He helped Nelson Mandela to assume his leadership role in the transformation of South Africa, and the two men worked closely together to create this world renowned social change. He and Mandela jointly received the 1993 Nobel Prize for Peace for their collaboration to establish nonracial democracy in South Africa.

Patrick Dodson (1948–)

Patrick Lionel Djargun Dodson is a member of the Yawuru people of Western Australia and a renowned Australian Indigenous leader. He is known as the "Father of Reconciliation" for his work as the founding chairperson of the Council for Aboriginal Reconciliation. The Council's goal is to promote reconciliation between the Aboriginal and Torres Strait Islander peoples and the rest of Australia's community. Its efforts include public awareness campaigns to develop appreciation for Indigenous cultures and achievements and to encourage cooperation in addressing disadvantages faced by these groups. Dodson was also a senator for Western Australia, representing the Australian Labor Party. He was awarded the 2008 Sydney Peace Prize. In 2009 he was given the John Curti Medal.

W. E. B. Du Bois (1868–1963)

William Edward Burghardt (W. E. B.) Du Bois was the first Black American to earn a PhD from Harvard University (1895) and attended the Friedrich Wilhelm University in Berlin. He was a leader of a Black civil rights activist group called the

Niagra Movement, which demanded full civil rights and political representation. He was part of an African American intellectual elite in his time, and felt as a member of "the talented tenth" that this group could uplift the chances for their advanced education and leadership. This, he felt, could improve opportunity, respect, and equality for all Black individuals. Du Bois was a founding member of the National Association for the Advancement of Colored People (NAACP). He used his NAACP position to promote national attention to rights and justice issues. A professor at Atlantic University, he was regarded as a socialist and targeted by the Federal Bureau of Investigation. He moved to Ghana in the latter years of his life after a career of attacking racism through polemics. His publications include *The Souls of Black Folk*, an analysis of the complex identity of African Americans in their struggle for justice and equality. He also protested against discrimination in education and employment, and advocated for legal changes to prevent lynching and the establishment of Jim Crow laws.

Abdul Sattar Edhi (1928–2016)

Abdul Sattar Edhi was a Pakistani humanitarian and philanthropist. He was born into a Memon Muslim family in India and felt that action was more important than professing godly rhetoric. While not for or against religion, he advocated that being a humanitarian was the way to demonstrate one's faith and service to God. He was known as an ascetic, owned few clothes, had no salary, and lived in simple accommodations. He founded the Edhi Foundation, which is the world's largest ambulance network (18,000 ambulances), providing emergency medical care to millions of people. His foundation trains emergency personnel, runs welfare centers across Pakistan, and has established orphanages and rehabilitation facilities. The Edhi Foundation is reportedly the largest welfare organization in Pakistan with 350 centers that provide food, shelter, clinics, and other services. It has rehabilitated over 50,000 orphans, rescued 20,000 abandoned babies, and trained over 40,000 nurses. He is known as Pakistan's Angel of Mercy and regarded as one of the world's greatest humanitarians.

Nancy Flowers (1940–)

Nancy Flowers is a writer and human rights education expert. She developed Amnesty International's education program and is a founding member of Human Rights Educators USA.

Flowers has consulted with a variety of groups on how to promote human rights, including governmental organizations, nonprofit organizations, and United Nations agencies. Her work includes developing curriculum materials and training human rights defenders and professionals in a variety of roles in both the United States and around the world. She has been honored with a lifetime achievement award from HRE USA in recognition of her decades of work in the field to advance human rights education. Her books include *Towards a Just Society: The Personal Journeys of Human Rights Educators; Human Rights. YES! Action and Advocacy for the Rights of Persons with Disabilities; Acting for Indigenous Rights;* and *Local Action/Global Change: A Handbook on Women's Human Rights.*

Marielle Franco (1979–2018)

Marielle Franco, born Marielle Francisco da Silva, was a sociologist from Brazil. A human rights activist, she was also a feminist and socialist. She served as a Rio de Janeiro city councillor for the Socialism and Liberty Party and advocated for Afro-Brazilians, the poor, the LGBTQ community, and women. A Black, bisexual single mother, she was a minority in Brazilian politics. Franco was an outspoken critic of President Michel Temer and the city's police brutality and extrajudicial killings. She was assassinated by two police officers in 2018 in what is regarded as a retaliation for her political positions. Over 100,000 people protested her murder in Rio, and demonstrations in her honor were held around the world. Both the United Nations and Amnesty International demanded an investigation into her assassination.

Betty Friedan (1921–2006)

Betty Goldstein Friedan, a journalist, was a major contributor to the advancement of women's rights in the 1960s. She became the co-founder of the National Organization for Women and was an active proponent for the Equal Rights Amendment to the Constitution of the United States. Her book *The Feminine Mystique* (1963) raised awareness of the issues of gender roles and gender equality and is sometimes credited with prompting the second wave of feminism in the United States. She helped the US National Association for the Repeal of Abortion Laws in 1969 and organized the Women's Strike for Equality in 1970. Freidan worked with other feminists to encourage the role of women in national politics, with the creation of the National Women's Political Caucus.

Mahatma Gandhi (1869–1948)

Mohandas Karamchand Gandhi was an attorney who advocated for the use of nonviolent civil disobedience in India in its quest to obtain independence from British rule. In 1893, he went to South Africa to work as a lawyer, fighting for Indian rights there. During his years in South Africa, he studied Satyagraha, the power of truth as a form of political resistance. "Mahatma" is an honorary word meaning "great soul" and was given to him in South Africa, and later widely adopted, to acknowledge his courage and peaceful, selfless humility. In 1930, he led the 240-mile Salt March in India, as a form of civil disobedience to protest the British salt monopoly. India gained its independence in 1947, but Gandhi did not participate in official Independence Day celebrations, as he was fasting to protest religious violence that erupted between Hindus, Muslims, and Sikhs after the partitioning of India and Pakistan by the British. He was assassinated the following year by a Hindu nationalist who opposed his inclusive vision for India.

Hugo Grotius (1583–1645)

Hugo Grotius was a seventeenth century jurist in the Netherlands who advocated for universal rights. He developed a theory of human rights in his writing, *De Jure Belli ac Paci* (On the Law of War and Peace), that led to the development of approaches that became central to law, both criminal and protections pertaining to individuals' private lives. Grotius also wrote an edict of toleration and addressed the strained relationship between church and state. His work was deemed controversial, and he was imprisoned but escaped in a box of books that had been brought to him for reading. Grotius made contributions to the development of international law based on respect for humanity. He was one of the first to promote the idea that natural rights were a higher order than man-made laws and that nations were bound by natural law. He believed that war was only justified if it served a right. His ideas regarding the freedom of the seas underpinned modern maritime laws.

Deb Haaland (1960–)

Deb Haaland, a member of the Pueblo of Laguna tribe, was one of the first two Native American women elected to the House of Representatives. She was the first Native American appointed as Cabinet Secretary of the United States Department of the Interior, which oversees the Bureau of Indian Affairs serving 574 tribes and 55 million areas of land trust. Haaland has worked diligently to increase trial decision-making of issues that impact the lives of Indigenous communities and their lands. She has worked to improve relations between the United States and tribal governments and made progress in addressing the bureau's past ill treatment of Indigenous peoples. She has supported government policies that endorse Medicare for All as well as supporting environmental policies of the Green New Deal.

Befaqadu (Befekadu) Hailu (1980–)

Befaqadu Hailu is co-founder of Ethiopia's Center for the Advancement of Rights and Democracy and is a writer, poet, and activist. He started a blog in 2011 to share his thoughts about human rights and democracy in Ethiopia that grew to showcase the need for social and governmental change. His blog, *The Q Perspective*, was met with censorship by the government, and he was jailed for alleged terrorism. Hailu was arrested and released more than once because of his blogging activity. His work indicates that the biggest threats to Ethiopia's democracy are foundering institutions, weak civic engagement, coordinated systems of disinformation, and toxicity of the Ethiopian political system. In 2015, he and other bloggers were awarded the International Press Freedom Award.

Michael Harrington (1928–89)

Edward Michael Harrington was a political scientist, professor at Queens College in New York, and radio commentator. He was a founding member of the Democratic Socialists of America. He published sixteen books and is associated with coining the term "neoconservatism." He was regarded as "the man who discovered poverty" in the United States after he published *The Other America*, which described the economic disparity in the nation between the "haves" and "have nots." The book shaped national policy and continues to be foundational to understanding poverty as a human rights issue. The City University of New York honored Harrington by establishing the Michael Harrington Center for Democratic Values and Social Change at Queens College.

Nancy Herz (1996–)

Nancy Herz is a writer, human rights advocate, and the State Secretary of the Ministry of Labour and Social Inclusion in Norway. She is a leader of the Young People's Freedom of Expression Council and is an activist with Amnesty International. Coauthor of *Shameless*, Herz and other activists started the #Shameless movement, which seeks to confront a culture of shame as social control. Herz is a fierce advocate for social justice, gender equality, feminism, women's rights, gender roles, and diversity. Her work is designed to inspire females to free themselves from constrictive gender roles. She is the 2016 recipient of the Freedom of Expression Tribute award.

Hin-mah-too-yah-lat-kekt (Chief Joseph) (1840–1904)

Chief Joseph was the leader of the Nez Percé tribe in northeastern Oregon who led his followers to Canada in a dramatic effort to escape exploitation by white settlements. The Nez Percé were being forcibly removed from their ancestral land by the US federal government, and Chief Joseph led 800 members of the tribe to find political asylum with the Lakota people under the leadership of Sitting Bull in Canada. The Nez Percé War resulted, and the tribal members conducted themselves in a manner that earned the admiration of others. Chief Joseph surrendered to the US army on the condition that his people would be allowed to return to a reservation in Idaho, but this agreement was violated by the military. His advocacy for Native Americans who were confronted with discrimination and oppression is part of the American story of the fight for Indigenous human rights. Chief Joseph is renowned as a humanitarian, peacemaker, and passionate, principal resistor to injustice.

Jose Ramos Horta (1949–)

Jose Manuel Ramos Horta was a political activist in Portuguese Timor, which resulted in his being exiled for two years in 1970–1 to Portuguese East Africa. At age twenty-five he was given the position of Foreign Minister in the Democratic Republic of East Timor government. Indonesian troops were threatening to invade East Timor, so Horta traveled to New York to speak at the UN Security Council and urge them to take action in the face of the Indonesian occupation.

The people of East Timor were awarded the Rafto Prize in 1993, and in 1996 Horta was awarded the Nobel Peace Prize with fellow Timorese Bishop Ximenes Belo in honor of their sustained efforts to hinder the oppression of a small people. The hope was that the award would inspire efforts to find a diplomatic solution to the conflict of East Timor based on the people's right to self determination and reduced poverty. Horta became the president of Timor Leste and was appointed head of the United Nations Integrated Peacebuilding Office in Guinea-Bissau (UNIOGBIS).

Hilaria Supa Huamán (1957–)

Hilaria Supa Huamán is an Indigenous human rights advocate in Peru. She has supported Indigenous rights, anti-colonialism, and fought against the Peruvian government's forced sterilization of Indigenous women. She is a strong advocate against women's abuse and cultural exploitation. In 1980 she worked with other Indigenous women to create a community program to give free meals to poor children. Her activism increased to protecting land rights and founding the Women's Federation of Anta, which supported literacy programs, traditional medicine, and improving other health issues, such as reducing the use of pesticides. She was a Congresswoman in Cusco as a member of the Ollanta Humala's Partido Nacionalista Peruano party and was elected president of the Education Commission of the Peruvian Congress as well as Representative of Gana Perú's Andean Parliament.

Eglantyne Jebb (1876–1928)

Eglantyne Jebb of Britain was foundational to promoting the idea that children were entitled to human rights. She helped found the organization Save the Children, and helped draft the document that became the Declaration for the Rights of Children. She began her career working with the Charity Organisation Society, which exposed her to how urban conditions impacted the lives of children. She began publishing her research, which led to her being appointed to the Education Committee of Cambridge, the League for Physical Education and Improvement, and the Boys Employment Registry. Through work with the Macedonian Relief Fund, she learned that life for children in war-torn countries was worse than what the government propaganda had led the public to believe. She engaged in a series of social activism endeavors that ultimately led to the

Save the Children Fund. This in turn led to the Declaration of the Rights of the Child, or the Declaration of Geneva, which was adopted by the League of Nations in 1924. Ultimately, it influenced the creation of the United Nations CRC decades later.

Martin Luther King, Jr. (1929–68)

Martin Luther King Jr. was a minister at the Ebenezer Baptist Church in Atlanta who became a central figure promoting the civil rights movement in the United States during the 1960s. He was awarded the Nobel Peace Prize for his promotion of nonviolent resistance in seeking equal rights for Black Americans. He helped found the Southern Christian Leadership Conference, which promotes nonviolent protest strategies to combat discrimination. He was involved in a series of anti-racial segregation efforts in the United States, including the Montgomery bus boycott, Atlanta sit-in (including one at a restaurant), the Albany movement, Birmingham arrest and imprisonment, and a huge march on Washington, where he gave his famous "I Have a Dream" speech in 1963. He spoke around the country in support of desegregation, including New York, Florida, Maine, Chicago, and at the Selma, Alabama "Bloody Sunday" attack in 1965. King was active in the Poor People's Campaign and advocated for economic justice for all people. He was opposed to the Vietnam War and was investigated by the CIA. King also was supportive of Indigenous rights and the fair treatment for Native Americans. He was assassinated for his activism, and his legacy has inspired people from around the world to fight for justice, peace, and equality. To honor him, the United States has made Martin Luther King, Jr. Day a national holiday, and many monuments and awards attempt to keep his contributions to justice alive in the public's awareness. He was awarded over fifty honorary degrees from institutions of higher education, as well as the 1964 Nobel Peace Prize.

Maggie Kuhn (1905–95)

Margaret Elliza "Maggie" Kuhn was a social activist who is best known as a founding member of the Gray Panthers, which advocated for human rights for people who are older. She fought to advance the idea that maltreatment of aging people is a human rights concern that societies are obligated to address. Kuhn was a staunch supporter of human rights, including peace, economic justice, mental health, social supports, healthcare, disability rights, and rights for people with challenges of all sorts. She encouraged the inclusion and integration of all people, and especially those who had been marginalized. She advocated that older people were a huge untapped and undervalued human energy source that had much to contribute, pointing out that they were often unable to do so because of socially structured inequality and systems of organizational and policy oppression. She was a vocal advocate for the rights of older people, which gained her national attention in the public sector and in the rising media of television.

John Lewis (1940–2020)

John Robert Lewis was an American civil rights leader who actively participated in racial desegregation efforts in the 1960s. These included the March on Washington, Nashville sit ins, Freedom Rides, and the "bloody Sunday" Selma March, during which he led marchers across the Edmund Pettus Bridge where state troopers attacked them. He was considered one of the main civil rights leaders in the United States. He was elected to the US House of Representatives as a Democrat and served seventeen terms in office. Lewis was awarded the Presidential Medal of Freedom in 2012 along with many other honors.

Laura Lundy (1955–)

Laura Lundy is a major international children's human rights legal scholar. She is a professor and director of the Centre for Children's Rights at Queens University in Belfast, Ireland. She is the editor of the *International Journal of Children's Rights* and author of many publications. World renowned, she does significant consulting, especially in the area of youth participation. She developed the Lundy Model, which conceptualizes children's right to participation, as identified in Article 12 of the UN CRC.

Nelson Mandela (1918–2013)

Nelson Rolihlahla Mandela of South Africa is regarded as the father of that nation. A lawyer by training, he fought against apartheid and was jailed for twenty-seven years for challenging the state's racial laws before being released.

While jailed, concerns over a possible racial civil war in the nation grew. Government leaders were faced with domestic and international pressure to prevent it. President F. W. de Klerk released Mandela from prison in 1990, and Mandela and de Klerk worked together collaboratively to lead negotiations to end apartheid. Mandela became the nation's first Black head of state and the first Black elected president of the African National Congress. He was elected in the nation's first fully representative democratic election. Under his administration, apartheid was dismantled. He encouraged racial reconciliation and sought peace and justice. His work as an advocate for justice, peace, education, and democracy was universally respected.

Thurgood Marshall (1908–93)

Thoroughgood (Thurgood) Marshall was an attorney who became highly respected during the US civil rights era. He attended Howard University and worked at the NAACP. He was the first African American to serve as a Supreme Court justice. His legal decisions helped the nation through the 1960s civil rights movement. In particular, his liberal decisions on the court cases of *Brown v. Board of Education* (1954), *Murray v. Maryland* (1936), and *Missouri ex rel Gaines v. Canada* helped embed human rights into the Constitution. He was data driven in his decisions, and relied upon scholarly sociological data to help him see trends that were in the public's best interests. He opposed the death penalty, viewing it as a form of cruel and unusual punishment. He supported abortion rights in *Roe v Wade*. Marshall's time on the bench helped create a culture of human rights support in the 1960s that lasted decades.

Rigoberta Menchú (1959–)

Rigoberta Menchú Tum of Guatemala is an Indigenous peoples' rights advocate. Her early work as a labor rights advocate for farm workers eventually led to her becoming the Guatemalan federal government's goodwill ambassador for the National Peace Accords. She was awarded the Nobel Peace Prize in 1992, Peace Abbey Courage of Conscience Award in 1996, and Peace Abbey Courage of Conscience Award in 1988. As a UNESCO Goodwill Ambassador, she received the Prince of Asturias Award in 1998. She founded Guatemala's first Indigenous political party, Winaq.

Alexei Anatolyevich Navalny (1976–2024)

Alexei Anatolyevich Navalny was a lawyer, anti-corruption activist, and human rights activist in Russia. He received his law degree from Russia's People's Friendship University in 1998 and received a scholarship to the Yale World Fellows Program to study political science and world affairs at Yale University. He worked as a corporate lawyer for several Russian companies but decided to join the Russian United Democratic Party, Yabloko, where he became its leader. His political activism increased as he organized anti-government demonstrations and ran for political office. He later became involved with a centrist political party called The People's Alliance, which promoted democratic policies. He ran for mayor of Moscow, and his presence in the election proved to be controversial for the state. Due to increased popular support, Navalny announced he would run for president. This was met with significant challenge by Russian authorities, who created reasons to arrest and imprison him repeatedly. While campaigning in Siberia in 2020, he was poisoned, allegedly by Russian authorities, and almost died. He was evacuated to Berlin, where he recovered and chose to return to Russia to fight for his country. Arrested as a political prisoner, and seen as an enemy of Vladimir Putin, Navalny died under suspect circumstances at a remote Russian prison shortly before he anticipated a release. He was the founder of the Anti-Corruption Foundation (FBK) and was recognized as a prisoner of conscience by Amnesty International. He was awarded the Sakharov Prize for his work in human rights. His wife is carrying on his political mission.

Tran Minh Nhat (1988–)

Tran Mihn Nhat is a Vietnamese journalist and activist who promotes economic, social, and cultural rights in Vietnam. He worked for the Vietnam Redemptorist News, which promoted the protection of social, economic, and cultural rights for people in the nation. His writings supported free speech and a pluralist political system. He was accused of carrying out activities that would overthrow the government administration under article 79 of Vietnam's criminal code. He was imprisoned for his human rights support, but he continues to speak out against injustices and to fight for human rights. The organization Human Rights Watch and other international diplomatic and human rights organizations have sought to support Nhat, who states he is in fear for his life because of his activism.

Audrey Osler (1950–)

Audrey Osler is Editor-in-Chief of the scholarly journal *Human Rights Education Review* and Co-Chair of the International Association for Human Rights Education. She teaches in both England and Norway as well as in Hong Kong, Europe, the United States, and other countries around the world about the importance of human rights education (HRE). She publishes extensively about HRE and global democratic citizenship. Osler's background is in sociology, legal scholarship, and political science. She examines child participation and the importance of how marginalized and minority groups construct notions of their identity. Honors bestowed upon her come from the Council of Europe General Rapporteur: Human Rights and Democracy in Action as well as the American Educational Research.

Rosa Parks (1913–2005)

Rosa Louise McCauley Parks was part of the NAACP and was a 1960s civil rights activist. Inspired by the experience of teenager Claudette Colvin in refusing to give up her seat on a bus to a white person, Parks was recruited to do the same in order to create a court challenge banning segregation laws in Alabama. Parks has gone down in history as the mother of the freedom or civil rights movement in the United States as a result. The NAACP worked with her to engage in civil disobedience for violating Alabama segregation laws on the bus. Her refusal to give up her seat to a white person became a symbol of resistance, and it inspired further support for desegregation. She remained politically active for the remainder of her life and was given awards such as the NAACP's 1979 Spingarn Medal, the Presidential Medal of Freedom, and the Congressional Gold Medal. After her death a statue in her honor was placed in the United States Capitol's National Statuary Hall.

Alice Paul (1885–1977)

Alice Stokes Paul was an activist for women's rights in the United States. A Quaker, she joined forces with other suffragettes to strategize how to move the government forward to create a constitutional amendment in support of women's rights. They mobilized events such as the Silent Sentinels and Woman Suffrage Procession. These women were often attacked by men and police officers. Suffering extensive physical abuse and police brutality, she always responded with courage and nonviolence. Paul was put into jail in deplorable conditions for her resolution to support women's rights. She spent fifty years as the leader of the National Women's Party and helped write and fought for the Equal Rights Amendment, which has not been recognized as a formal constitutional amendment. However, her work did protect women as a group from discrimination in the 1964 Civil Rights Act.

Ed Roberts (1939–95)

Edward Verne Roberts is known as a pioneer for disability human rights advocacy. He contracted polio as a youth, which resulted in paralysis from his neck down. He lived in an iron lung for years and could only move a few fingers and toes. He was denied access to education and jobs and fought to challenge these structural obstacles. At first his education was via phone, and his mother fought for him to be able to attend school. Fearful of being stared at and ridiculed, Ed decided to think of himself as a star instead of being helpless. He was going to be denied a high school diploma because he couldn't take physical education classes, which triggered his activism. He eventually was admitted to the University of California at Berkeley, where he became the first student to use a wheelchair. Throughout his education there, Ed demanded access to classes, housing, and resources that allowed him, and other students with disabilities, to be treated in the typical way that other students were treated. He worked to create the Physically Disabled Student's Program, which is the first student-led disability services program in the United States. He became known as the Father of the Independent Living movement. He became the director of the California Department of Vocational Rehabilitation, where he facilitated the establishment of independent living centers throughout the state, and he fought to pass Section 504 of the Rehabilitation Act of 1973, which prohibits discrimination on the basis of disability in federally funded programs. He also helped found the World Institute on Disability with Judith E. Heumann and Joan Leo, which is known internationally for its disability activism.

Eleanor Roosevelt (1884–1962)

Anna Eleanor Roosevelt was the wife of President Franklin D. Roosevelt. She became regarded as a premiere human and civil rights advocate. She is perhaps best known as a central figure in the creation of the UDHR. She worked to advance child and youth rights and supported the creation of the American Youth Congress, which sought to involve youth in political decision-making and employment. The Roosevelts introduced the American Youth Bill of Rights to Congress, which inspired the development of the National Youth Administration. She advocated for social reform for all people and was keenly involved in supporting racial and gender human rights. Her activism was beloved by many, but it was also a source of controversy within a politically conservative segment of the population. She was opposed to the harms created by war that were inflicted upon innocent people, which helped advance her work with the UDHR as well as her support of New Deal initiatives. She was actively involved in the United Nations and was awarded the US Presidential Medal of Freedom. Eleanor was the first chair of the Presidential Commission on the Status of Women. President Harry Truman reported that she was the "First Lady of the World" because of her international human rights activism and since her death has been highly honored for her human rights advocacy.

Jean-Jacques Rousseau (1712–78)

Philosopher Jean-Jacques Rousseau lived during the time known as the Enlightenment. It was a time of social change that endorsed the development of intellectual thought and social action that would benefit individuals. In his writings, such as his *Discourse on Inequality*, *The Social Contract*, and *Emile* (On Education), Rousseau argued that society needed to create a new social contract that would support the wellbeing of the masses. The French Revolution influenced his thought regarding how political and social orders could benefit individuals and societies. He viewed private property as the source of inequality. His ideas of a social contract shaped modern political and social thought, as well as the importance of education. He was concerned about how social systems can positively or negatively impact a person's inherent goodness.

Bertrand Russell (1872–1970)

Bertrand Russell of Wales was a philosopher, logician, mathematician, epistemologist, social reformer, and peace advocate. Known as the founder of analytic philosophy, his article "On Denoting" is considered to be a paradigm of philosophic thought. He was a pacifist who went to prison for his views during World War I. During World War II he described war as the lesser of two evils, he opposed Russian totalitarianism, condemned the Vietnam War, and supported nuclear disarmament. Russell was awarded the Nobel Prize for Literature in 1950 for his works campaigning for peace, social reform, political reform, and the support of moral subjects. The recipient of the De Morgan medal, Sylvester medal, Kalinga prize, and Jerusalem prize, he was honored for championing humanitarian ideas and supporting freedom of thought.

Andrei Sakharov (1921–89)

Andrei Dmitrievich Sakharov was a Soviet physicist and human rights activist whose contributions have been credited for preventing a third world war. He worked in the Soviet program developing nuclear and thermonuclear weapons. He is associated with the development of the hydrogen bomb. Sakharov was a political activist for individual freedom and civil liberties and advocated for reforms in the Soviet Union. He worked to develop a partnership between the USSR and the United States to prevent a nuclear war. He demanded an end to nuclear testing after realizing the weapons' potential devasting impact. He was awarded a Nobel Peace Prize, but because he was labeled as a political dissident, he was not given permission by his government to travel to Oslo to receive it. He experienced other persecutions by the Soviet government in opposition to his dedication to freedom and human rights activism.

Alexya Salvador (1980–)

Alexya Lucas Evangelista Salvador is transgender and a Brazilian advocate for LGBTQ+ rights. She wanted to be a priest and joined a seminary but found that the Catholic church was not supportive of LGBTQ+ individuals. She became a public school teacher and married Roberto. They were married as gay men, adopted children, and continued to attend church. Salvador is now a pastor at the Metropolitan Community Church in Sao Paulo. She is also the vice president of the Brazilian Association of Homotransaffective Families. She uses her platform to speak about adoption, different family formations, and education.

Óscar Arias Sánchez (1940–)

Óscar Arias Sánchez studied economics and law in Costa Rica as well as in the United Kingdom and the United States and obtained a doctorate in economics. He was a member of the Social Democratic Party and became politically active. In 1986, he was elected President of Costa Rica during a time when there was civil discord in Nicaragua. As president he devised a strategy to end civil wars that were plaguing countries in the Central America region. In 1987 the plan was approved by his country as well as El Salvador, Guatemala, Nicaragua, and Honduras. His plan was focused on ending foreign interference in political affairs of the countries. It also promoted free elections and a variety of safeguards for people's human rights protections. He stood firm in his defense of his regional peace strategy despite opposition and challenges on multiple fronts. The peace accord was signed later that year, and he was awarded the 1987 Nobel Peace Prize for his proposal to remove foreign powers from Central America. While his plan was not officially adopted, it was reflected in future actions. He was awarded the Albert Schweitzer Prize for Humanitarianism, a trustee of Economists for Peace and Security, and elected to the International Criminal Court's Trust Fund for Victims.

Oskar Schindler (1908–74)

Oskar Schindler was a German industrialist who became concerned for his Polish workforce when Nazi Germany occupied the land and persecuted Jewish people during World War II. Schindler was a corporal in the Czechoslovak army and worked with the German military intelligence unit. He ultimately joined the Nazi Party collecting data on railways and troop movements. Many of Schindler's employees were Jewish and were likely to be killed at the Auschwitz gas chambers, so he compiled lists of names and was able to move people to avoid their being identified and killed. He spent much of his own fortune on Nazi police bribes and supplies for his workers. He is credited with having rescued over 1,200 people from concentration camps. Schindler's list has been the topic of books and films, as well as other forms of recognition. After the war he moved to West Germany and later to Argentina. He died in Germany and was honored to be "Righteous Among the Nations" by the Israeli government for his protection of Jewish people.

Albert Schweitzer (1875–1965)

Ludwig Philipp Albert Schweitzer was an Alsatian-German physician, musician, and philosopher who missioned in equatorial Africa. As a theologian and Lutheran minister, his views of Jesus and Christianity were sometimes regarded as controversial. As a physician, he went to Gabon in Africa and founded the Hospital Albert Schweitzer in what was then called Lambarene French Equatorial Africa. He received the 1952 Nobel Prize for Peace for his efforts on behalf of the Brotherhood of Nations and for his philosophy of the reverence for life. He demonstrated how human rights are interdependent, and how social rights can impact the health and lives of people everywhere.

Hugh Starkey (1954–)

Hugh Starkey is an emeritus professor of Citizenship and Human Rights Education at the University of London whose research focuses on education for democratic citizenship and human rights education from an intercultural perspective. He recognizes that in today's world, people move around and may have multiple citizenship alignments and families in many different geographic parts of the world. He is a consultant on human rights education for the Council of Europe, UNESCO, and the British Council. He was editor of the *London Review of Education* and *Human Rights Education Review* and is co-director of the World Educational Research Association's International Research Network on Human Rights Education.

Greta Thunberg (2003–)

Greta Tintin Eleonora Ernman Thunberg is a young environmental activist who has inspired youth around the world to be concerned about the environment and climate change as a human rights issue. She held a *Skolstrejk för klimatet* (School Strike for Climate) protest outside of the Swedish parliament in 2018, which inspired youth engagement around the world. She was age fifteen when she began skipping school to protest outside the Swedish parliament to demand stronger action for the nation to address climate change. She addressed the United Nations Climate Change Conference in 2018 and worked with others to hold city protests around the world, in which over a million youth participated.

As an example of how human rights issues are interdependent, her activism now includes anti-war efforts, especially in Ukraine, Palestine, Armenia, and Sahara regions. She was named *Time Magazine*'s Person of the Year in 2019, included in the *Forbes* list of the World's Most Powerful Women, and was nominated for a Nobel Peace Prize.

Arnold Toynbee (1852–83)

Arnold Joseph Toynbee was an English economist and social reformer whose writings influenced the study of work during the Industrial Revolution. He examined labor's impact on poor and working class people and encouraged the development of trade unions as ways to support workers. He was a professor at the London School of Economics and Kings College London and was considered an expert in international affairs. As the director of studies at Chatham House, he wrote over thirty-four volumes of work that became considered the bible for international studies, including the 12-volume *A Study of History*. He was concerned with how communities and civilizations organize themselves. He was also interested in what he called creative minorities. These were not leaders but people who had the ability to think creatively and encourage transformative social change. Many such leaders exemplified human rights, such as Florence Nightingale and Mahatma Gandhi.

Sojourner Truth (1797–1883)

Isabella Baumfree was an African American woman who was born into slavery and escaped into freedom in 1826. She sought court assistance to recover her son, and this was the first time a Black woman won a court case against a white man. An abolitionist and activist for women's rights, civil rights, and alcohol temperance, she renamed herself Sojourner Truth in 1843 after feeling God wanted her to use her voice to advocate for justice for those who were oppressed. She began speaking around the country, and her 1851 speech at the Ohio Women's Rights Convention became known as the "Ain't I a Woman" speech. During the Civil War she recruited Black soldiers to fight for the Union army. Later she tried to secure land grants for Black individuals under the government's promise to provide forty acres and a mule to people who would work the land. She challenged social norms about both women and Black individuals. A bust of her is now found in Emancipation Hall of the US Capitol, making her the first

Black woman to have a statue there. She is regarded by the Smithsonian as one of the 100 most influential Americans of all time.

Desmond Tutu (1931–2021)

Desmond Tutu was an Anglican bishop and theologian in Johannesburg and Cape Town in South Africa. His advocacy for human rights gained him a visible role in the nation's religious, political, and social institutions. He was an anti-apartheid activist who promoted racial justice and equality. Tutu was also opposed to war and the use of violence as a problem solving strategy. He was forthright in his support for women to be clergy members and in his support for gay rights at a time and place where their equal rights were seen as controversial. He became General-Secretary of the South African Council of Churches (SACC) and advocated for the SACC to become South Africa's most visible human rights organization. He became chair of the Truth and Reconciliation Commission to promote anti-apartheid action in the nation. He worked with Nelson Mandela to facilitate a smooth transition in post-apartheid South Africa. Tutu and Mandela were regarded as national leaders in the development of a transformed nation. Tutu was nominated for the Nobel Prize several times and was finally given that award in 1984 for his work in opposing apartheid in South Africa.

Lech Wałęsa (1943–)

Lech Wałęsa is a shipyard electrician and labor activist who helped form and lead Poland's first independent trade union, Solidarity. He was regarded as a charismatic leader of Polish workers and later became the first democratically elected President of Poland (1990–5). During his presidency he helped Poland transition from a socialistic state into a free-market capitalist democracy. He was awarded the Nobel Prize for Peace in 1983. He has also been awarded hundreds of honors, including being named the 1981 *Time* Person of the Year and one of the 100 most important people of the twentieth century, honorary degrees from Harvard University, and having the nation's airport named for him.

Ida B. Wells-Barnett (1862–1931)

Ida Bell Wells-Barnett was an African American investigative journalist born into slavery in Mississippi. She was freed by the Emancipation Proclamation.

Her early life was full of challenges, which inspired her journalistic writings to give voice to the voiceless. She worked for several publications and wrote many articles and public presentations to defend women and Black people during the US civil rights movement. She documented lynching and analyzed how it was being used to terrorize African Americans in the southern states. Her writings debunked the stereotype of Black people being dangerous or criminal. Her critique of the oppression and discrimination inflicted upon them led to her being a co-founder of the NAACP. She was honored after her death with a Pulitzer Prize for her courageous reporting of the violence that African Americans faced during the early part of the twentieth century.

Eliezer "Elie" Wiesel (1928–2016)

Elie Wisel was a Holocaust survivor, writer, and professor. Born in Romania and growing up in Hungary, his Jewish family was sent by Nazi soldiers to the Auschwitz concentration camp during World War II. His mother and sister were killed in the gas chambers, while he and his father were ordered to do hard labor. He survived the Holocaust and moved to Paris and studied at the Sorbonne where he heard lectures from philosophers such as Jean-Paul Sarte, Franz Kafka, Martin Buber, Thomas Mann, and Fyodor Dostoevsky. Wiesel became a good writer, and while he initially did not want to write about the horrors he had experienced as a child, he was encouraged by mentors that he should write about them so the world would understand what had happened to people in the camps. He chronicled the horror of the Nazi regime, especially in the concentration camps, in his book *Night*, as well as fifty-six other books. He continued to be a strong advocate for human rights and to chronicle the oppression that others faced in South Africa, the Sudan, Argentina, Ethiopia, Armenia, and other nations. He was awarded the Nobel Peace Prize in 1986 for his humanitarianism. Wiesel was also a founder of the New York Human Rights Foundation and the recipient of many other awards.

Roy Wilkins (1901–81)

Roy Ottoway Wilkins was a journalist who published writings at the *Minnesota Daily*, *The Appeal*, *The Call*, and *The Crisis*, which was the official magazine of the NAACP. He later became the director of the NAACP. An advocate for civil rights, he challenged Jim Crow laws, helped organize the March on Washington and the Selma (Alabama) march as well as other civil rights activism. As director of the NAACP, he was central in court actions such as the *Brown v. the Topeka Board of Education* lawsuit and the Voting Rights Act.

Liu Xiaobo (1955–2017)

Liu Xiaobo was an advocate for political reform, democracy, and human rights who challenged the authoritarian policies of the Chinese Communist Party. He became internationally regarded as a literary critic, became president of the Independent Chinese PEN Center and president of the magazine *Minzhu Zhongguo* (*Democratic China*), and worked at several universities. Advocating for greater freedom of expression and political openness, he helped draft Charter 08, a manifesto calling for political reform and the protection of basic human rights in China. He supported the Tiananmen Square protests. He was arrested and imprisoned several times for his support for democracy and human rights. He was awarded the 2010 Nobel Peace Prize for his political reform, democracy, and human rights efforts but was denied the right to have a representative collect the prize for him. His legacy of nonviolent resistance against what he regarded as an oppressive political regime in China continues to bring him honor.

Malala Yousafzai (1997–)

Malala Yousafzai is a Pakistani global education and women's rights advocate who in 2014 became the youngest person ever to be awarded a Nobel Peace Prize. At age eleven, when her school was overtaken by the Taliban, she chronicled her experience for a BBC blog. Her outspokenness put her at risk even though she received positive affirmation for her support of democracy. For instance, she received Pakistan's first National Youth Peace Prize, was given an internship supporting education at the Swat Relief Initiative, and was nominated for the International Children's Peace Prize by Desmond Tuto. Her actions resulted in a 2012 assassination attempt in which she was struck in the head by a bullet while riding the bus after taking an exam. She survived thanks to international supports and good medical care. Since then, she has graduated from Oxford University and founded the Malala Fund to assist every girl to access education and have the opportunity to choose their own futures.

Muhammad Yunus (1940–)

Muhammad Yunus of India is best known as a Bangladeshi economist. However, he is also a politician, civil servant, and entrepreneur. He was the chief advisor of the Interim Government of Bangladesh and founder of the Grameen Bank, which provided microcredit or small loans to poor people. This action helped to establish creditworthiness and financial self-sufficiency for people who otherwise would not have been able to do so. Yunus and Grameen received the 2006 Nobel Prize for Peace for their efforts to provide economic justice and opportunity to marginalized individuals. Yunus was also awarded the US Presidential Medal of Freedom (2009). A university professor, he is author of a variety of publications and books related to his microeconomics approach. In 2024 he was listed as one of the 500 most influential Muslims in the world.

Ofelia Zepeda (1952–)

Ofelia Zepeda is an American Indian human rights activist and leader of the American Indian Language Development Institute, an organization dedicated to revitalizing Indigenous language use across new generations. She is Regents' Professor of Tohono O'odham language and linguistics at the University of Arizona where she is also the editor for Sun Tracks, a book series that focuses on the work of Native American artists and writers. Zepeda put together a textbook of American Indian languages so that the language and culture could be maintained and transmitted to new generations. She is the recipient of a Genius grant from the MacArthur Fellowship to preserve American Indian languages.

Organizations

American Association for the Advancement of Science Human Rights Council

The American Association for the Advancement of Science is the premier international organization to protect the role of scientists in their pursuit of research, education, and development of scientific inquiry. They have established a human rights council that brings together scholars from around the world to advocate for human rights principles to be incorporated into the study and practice of all forms of science. The council also supports the human rights of scholars and researchers in their work of being a human rights lens. This is particularly important during a time when science is under attack by some political and religious organizations.

American Civil Liberties Union

The American Civil Liberties Union (ACLU) is an American nonprofit human rights organization that has been in existence since 1920. The organization strives to defend and preserve the rights and freedoms of every person in the country. The ACLU's origins began after World War I when the United States observed civil liberties being compromised. Attorney General Mitchell Palmer arrested and deported thousands of so-called radicals without warrants. These individuals were not allowed constitutional protections and were treated with brutality and thrown into deplorable imprisonments. Observers decided to do something to help them, which resulted in the creation of the ACLU. The organization stepped forward during the 1925 Scopes Trial in Tennessee, which concerned biology teacher John Scopes teaching evolution, a practice banned in the state. The ACLU and attorney Clarence Darrow came to his defense. The organization also challenged the mandatory teaching of creationism in Arkansas in 1981 and the teaching of religion in the classroom as a violation of church and state. Other monumental ACLU assistance was provided in the 1942 fight against the government putting over 110,000 Japanese Americans into concentration camps, and the 1954 *Brown v. the Board of Education* Supreme Court case that declared racially segregated schools violated the 14th Amendment of the Constitution. The ACLU has actively protected free speech, such as in landmark cases such as *Tinker v. Des Moines*, involving students' rights in protesting the Vietnam War; a case in Skokie, Illinois, in which the ACLU controversially defended the rights of Nazis to march; and a 1997 internet free speech case. The organization has worked to protect reproductive rights, including through involvement in the abortion rights case *Roe v. Wade*. It supported the Defense of Marriage Act and has fought against discrimination in all forms, including against women, racial minorities, and LGBTQ+ individuals.

Amnesty International

Amnesty International was founded in 1961 by British lawyer Peter Benenson in response to the imprisonment of two Portuguese students who were jailed for raising their glasses in a toast to freedom. It conducts detailed research to fight abuses of human rights worldwide, including bringing torturers to justice, changing discriminatory and oppressive laws, and protecting people's freedom of voice and action. Amnesty International works to support human rights involving topics that include armed conflict, climate change, freedom of expression, anti-violence, women's rights, LGBTQ+ rights, refugee and migrant rights, reproductive rights, corporate responsibility, detention, gun violence, Indigenous people's protections, police violence, racial justice, online violence, torture, and the abolition of the death penalty.

Anti-Slavery International

Slavery is not a thing of the past; over 50 million people worldwide are entrapped in some form of slavery. Anti-Slavery International seeks to eliminate all forms of slavery. Poverty and weak laws are primarily responsible for the existence of slavery, which takes forms such as domestic servitude, trafficking, forced labor, debt bondage, child slavery, child marriage, and cases where people are born into slavery. The organization reports that a quarter of slaves today are children. It works with the UN Economic and Social Council and International Labor Organization campaign and other organizations to educate people about the existence of slavery and to enforce human rights treaty articles.

The Board on Children, Youth, and Families

The Board on Children, Youth, and Families is a nongovernmental, scientific body that relies upon multidisciplinary scholars to research critical issues that face children and families. It is a unit within the National Academies of Sciences, Engineering, and Medicine and is part of the Health and Medicine Division. It analyzes both social science, behavioral health, and biological research to better understand challenges that face families and youth and to identify a set of best practices. Its reliance upon quality data, scientific analysis of facts, and independent external peer reviews help to promote recommendations that will benefit their public health.

Center for Excellence in Child and Adolescent Health Research

The Center for Excellence in Child and Adolescent Health Research is a scholarly collaboration between the Children's Hospital of Pittsburgh and the University of Pittsburgh Clinical and Translational Science Institute that is designed to promote the health and wellbeing of young people. Through analysis of data from a multidisciplinary team of reporters that includes participants, families, researchers, healthcare providers, and the community, the organization provides insights that may promote the improved health of children and youth. Use of advanced, meaningful, and innovative clinical research has been found to significantly improve the lives and wellbeing of children and youth.

Centre for Sport and Human Rights

The Centre for Sport and Human Rights is a new international center that focuses on the multiplicity if ways that human rights may be violated or defended on and off the playing field. Relying on good data and scholarship, it uses a broad ecosystem approach that shows how individuals, families, teams, schools, communities, businesses, nations, and multinational corporations have made contributions that influence whether rights are defended. This includes players, spectators, vendors, workers, corporations, and communities at large from all different types of sports and sport organizations. Its human rights emphasis is documenting improvements at events such as the World Cup, professional sports teams, youth sports, and community sporting.

Civil Rights Defenders

Civil Rights Defenders was established in 1982 in Sweden to defend civil and political rights of people and empower human rights defenders at risk around the world. There are countless defenders of human rights around the world and this organization helps to provide them support in their actions, many of which are dangerous, putting defenders into life-threatening situations. The organization collaborates with 200 local partners around the world to create positive, sustainable change to promote justice, freedom, and the defense of people's human rights.

Cultural Survival

Cultural Survival is a nonprofit organization located in Cambridge, Massachusetts that is dedicated to defending the human rights of Indigenous peoples throughout the world. Founded in 1972, the organization has worked with Indigenous communities around the world to honor and protect their culture, lands, languages, arts, and spiritual traditions. It assists them in their right to self governance and self determination. An activist organization, it provides educational materials, resources, and updates on events. It has a subscription unit to disseminate information.

Doctors Without Borders

Doctors Without Borders is also known as Médecins Sans Frontières. In 1971, a famine in Biafra, Nigeria, was resulting in the morbidity and mortality of countless people, and emergency care was desperately needed. French physicians and journalists mobilized together to deliver humanitarian and medical aid there, founding the organization. Since then, thousands of volunteers have joined together in seventy countries to provide assistance, including doctors, nurses, researchers, social services, and logistics experts. Doctors Without Borders provides care to all people irrespective of their gender, race, nationality, religion, and political or other affiliations. The organization was awarded the 1999 Nobel Peace Prize for their work.

Equitas

Equitas is an international human rights training organization located in Montreal, Canada. It supports values of non-discrimination, respect for diversity, gender equality, inclusion, and solidarity by providing leaders with skills to influence decision makers and to hold governments accountable for their human rights actions. Human rights educational programs range from preschool and K-12, through higher education. It also offers a summer-long international human rights training program so that people can become rights implementers and defenders. It involves leaders from a variety of human rights organizations and the United Nations in its state-of-the art programs.

European Centre for Minority Issues

The European Centre for Minority Issues (ECMI) is based on the Germany–Denmark border and was founded in 1996. It is an international human rights organization that conducts policy research, consultation, and information sharing related to national minorities in Europe. ECMI serves European governments and closely cooperates with the academic community and general public to facilitate diversity in all aspects of society. Its mission is to provide new knowledge, education, and tool kits to help organizations and governments to build a more peaceful, inclusive, and diverse Europe. The ECMI is research based and regarded as Europe's leading institution in implementing minority protection and empowerment guidelines.

Every Human Has Rights

The Every Human Has Rights (EHHR) campaign was launched in 2007 on the sixtieth anniversary of the UDHR in Cape Town, South Africa. It works in partnership with a diverse group of global nongovernmental organizations, nonprofit organizations, civil society organizations, and businesses to promote UDHR principles, such as the right to health, women's rights, and freedom of expression.

Everytown USA

Everytown USA is the largest gun violence protection organization in the United States and has the goal to reduce gun violence in America. It conducts research, collects data, makes reports, and sets up initiatives that include voting, electing candidates that support gun control, demanding safety action from elected officials, and changing the narrative about how people think about guns. This grassroots organization states it has over 10 million members working to conduct research, change laws, and advocate for greater gun controls. Promoting education and awareness of gun violence is hoped to result in greater safety for everyone.

The Global Network for Human Rights and the Environment

The Global Network for Human Rights and the Environment (GNHRE) consists of a community of scholars, activists, practitioners, defenders, researchers, and policy makers working at the intersection of human rights and the environment. The GNHRE encourages collaboration, learning, and resistant reimagining to learn from world-leading environmental scholarship and practice from all over the world. Its current main projects include conferencing that created the Escazú Agreement, a Climate Litigation in the Global South Project, their

GNHRE-UNEP School for Human Rights and the Environment, and the publication of the Environmental Rights Review.

Global Rights

Global Rights is an international human rights nongovernmental organization established in 1978 in Washington. It moved its location to Nigeria in 2014 in partnership with activists in over twenty countries in Africa, Asia, and Latin America to build the grassroot capacities of underserved and marginalized populations. The NGO encourages the development of greater platforms for participatory governance. Its policy reforms include access to justice, women's rights, disability rights, security, and natural resource governance. Current initiatives include a national summit on mass atrocities, national business and human rights roundtables, and programs about how rape is a crime, election interference, and mining host community concerns.

Habitat for Humanity

Habitat for Humanity is an independent, nonprofit organization started in 1976 that specializes in building houses and settlements in 117 nations in five different continents. It views housing as a fundamental human rights issue, along with access to clean water, sanitation, and social services. In creating a sustainable habitat, the organization hopes to create a livable planet for everyone. It has served about 60 million people, enabling them to live in more affordable and safe homes. Its programs include home construction, helping underserved populations, helping older people to age in place, neighborhood revitalization, housing finance and education programs, avoiding homelessness, disaster responses, and other services.

Hope for Children CRC Policy Center

Located in Cyprus, the Hope for Children CRC Policy Center brings together scholars from universities around the world who study children's human rights. They have an innovative set of programs in youth participation, child sexual abuse prevention, and working with homeless and unaccompanied youth. Their policy chairs conduct research on child rights and work to improve understanding through greater awareness of the humanitarian crises that children may face.

They research, publish their works, make professional presentations, and support the Hope for Children center in Cyprus that provides care to abused and homeless children.

Human Rights Educators USA

Human Rights Educators USA is a network of teachers and practitioners who specialize in instructional techniques and materials that support the dissemination of information about human rights. While they focus on K-12 education, they also provide resources for higher education and community human rights education. They provide training, curriculum materials, and podcasts, and share access to human rights events and award opportunities. It is an international organization, despite its name, promoting a training-in-action series, supplying curriculum materials, and sponsoring conferences and events. It has a regional representatives program to disseminate human rights education materials.

Human Rights Measurement Initiative

The HRMI is a research tool that enables investigators to track the human rights progress of different countries. It is an independent, nonprofit that measures human rights as defined by international laws. Providing online tools and databases that assist researchers with analysis and action endeavors, it is easy to use and has robust data that anyone can use to push for improvements in human rights at both governmental and local community levels. HRMI focuses on five economic and social rights and eight civil and political rights. This data can be used for global social improvement by individuals and nations.

Human Rights Watch

Human Rights Watch is an international nongovernmental organization headquartered in New York. It was founded in 1978 as Helsinki Watch to investigate human rights abuses as outlined in the Helsinki Accords. The organization conducts research and investigates abuses such as massacres, genocides, government take-overs, discrimination of vulnerable groups (including women, minority, and LGBTQ+ individuals), war crimes, refugees, children, people with disabilities, deportation of immigrants, illegal arrests, political prisoners, and more. They work around the world in over seventy nations and champion justice at national and international courts. The organization uses research to encourage governments, policymakers, companies, and individuals to denounce abuse and increase greater respect human rights. Human Rights Watch shared the Nobel Peace Prize in 1997 as a founding member of the International Campaign to Ban Landmines. The organization was instrumental in the 2008 treaty banning cluster munitions.

Human Rights Without Frontiers

Human Rights Without Frontiers (HRWF) is an international nonprofit organization founded in 2001 in Belgium. Its mission is to promote respect for human rights around the globe. It also advocates for democracy, social justice, and the rule of law. HRWF is an active rights organization, focusing primarily on promoting human rights in European Union institutions and designing policies in Europe towards human rights. Its main activities include advocacy and publishing research, particularly through *Bitter Winter*, a magazine focusing on religious liberty and human rights in China that is published by the Center for Studies on New Religions. HRWF spreads human rights education, organizes public events, and advocates for governmental support of international human rights treaties. It also monitors human rights issues and maintains a global database of freedom of religion/belief.

International Committee of the Red Cross and the Red Crescent

The Red Cross and Red Crescent are interlocked international humanitarian organizations whose mission is to provide aid to people in distressed areas. In 1859, Henry (or Jean-Henri) Dunant was overwhelmed when he witnessed the suffering of soldiers at the Battle of Solferino in Italy and the lack of healthcare they received. He attempted to organize people in the local area to help them. When he returned to Geneva, Switzerland, he chronicled his experiences in a book he published (*A Memory of Solferino*) and brought together four colleagues in 1863 to discuss what would ultimately become the International Committee of the Red Cross and support the signing of the Geneva Convention. Over time the organization expanded to include the Red Crescent and to assist more people around the world. The organizations require that their staff and volunteers are impartial, neutral, and work to protect the dignity of victims and provide them assistance. They are guided by universal human rights principles. The Red Cross and Dunant were awarded the first Nobel Prize in 1901.

International Criminal Court

The International Criminal Court (ICC) was founded in 1919 at the Paris Peace Accord after World War I. It was the first, and remains the only, permanent international court. Its mission is to prosecute those who are responsible for genocide, war crimes, crimes against humanity, and other acts of aggression. It investigates crimes that are of gravest concern to the global community and seeks to establish justice. While the International Court of Justice hears disputes between states, the ICC has more power but typically requires that lower courts hear the dispute cases first. The ICC was restructured to have more power in 2002 in accordance with the multilateral Rome Statute. Its presence is important as it is the only vehicle to uphold international law.

KidsRights

KidsRights is an international nongovernmental organization founded in 2003. Its mission is to promote the participation and wellbeing of children across the world. It advocates to advance children's rights and encourage child participation through three pillars: advocacy, research, and action. It also gives out an annual International Children's Peace Prize and other awards to youth who are engaged in social activism to promote human and child rights. The organization houses a KidsRights Index, which is the only global ranking that annually measures how children's rights, based on the UN CRC, are respected worldwide. This data is supported by the KidsRights Foundation, the Erasmus School of Economics, and the International Institute of Social Studies. Its index identifies progress on the UN's SDGs and found that only one in three of the SDG indicators (protecting only one in four children) have been met.

Leading for Kids

Leading for Kids hosts a website that contains a variety of international resources about what other countries are doing to support children's human rights and ensure their wellbeing. It contains resources from Scotland, Australia, New

Zealand, and stimulates ideas about what other countries can do to become leaders in the defense of comprehensive wellbeing. It was founded by pediatrician and children's human rights advocate, David Alexander.

Musicians for Human Rights

The mission of Musicians for Human Rights (MFHR) is to foster a culture of humanism through music worldwide, in support of the UDHR Founded in 2009 by horn player Alessio Allegrini and a group of musicians and humanists active on four continents, Musicians for Human Rights encourages professional musicians, audiences, and secondary school and university students musicians to take action to advance the wellbeing of people living at the margins. With a home base in Italy and an association in Switzerland, it supports refugees, children, and democratization through eighteen organizations in thirteen countries.

Norwegian Refugee Council

The Norwegian Refugee Council (NRC) is a humanitarian, nongovernmental organization that was developed after World War II. The war left Europe in ruins and people needed assistance to rebuild their communities. Displaced and refugee families were in terrible distress—a situation that continues worldwide today. The NRC focuses on assisting people that are displaced and forced to flee their homes and homelands because of conflict, violence, climate change, natural disasters, or human rights violations. The NRC is independent with no political or religious alignments. It assists people not just in Norway and Europe, but also in twenty countries in Africa, Asia, the Middle East, and South America.

Office of the High Commissioner for Human Rights

The Office of the High Commissioner for Human Rights oversees all of the human rights programs, conventions, and activities that are under the umbrella of the United Nations. It set policies and standards for how to protect the rights of all people that are guaranteed in the UDHR. This office was created in 1993 and sets activities via the United Nations Human Rights Council. It is based on Articles 1, 13, and 55 of the Charter of the United Nations. Its mission is to be an international leader in supporting human rights, to promote international cooperation to that end, to provide human rights education assistance, and to promote the creation of national rights structures and infrastructures.

Oxfam

Oxfam was originally founded in 1942 in Oxford, England, as the Oxford Committee for Famine Relief by a group of Quakers and academics to address hunger and poverty that resulted because of World War II. The first international partner was Canada, and in 1965 the organization changed its name to Oxfam. Since that time, it has grown to be a global movement that fights inequality to end poverty and injustice so all people can survive and thrive. It works with people, communities, partners, and allies in seventy-nine countries, guided by a vision of a just and sustainable world. Oxfam offers lifesaving support to people and regions in crisis, and advocates for economic justice, gender equality, and climate action. It is regarded as a global leader in providing water sanitation to people in impoverished and war-torn areas, as well as providing mental health support, food, and other forms of humanitarian assistance to people in war or in disaster areas.

Physicians for Human Rights

Physicians for Human Rights is a United States based nonprofit organization that relies upon physicians, science, and the field of medicine to investigate and document human rights violations around the world. Founded in 1986, it employs medical and scientific tools to identify human rights abuses and mass atrocities. Physicians, nurses, scientists, and other medical professionals investigate and document human rights violations that include mass atrocities, torture, and persecution. They seek to hold perpetrators accountable. Their work focuses on psychological and physical effects of sexual violence, executions, chemical weapons, identification of mass graves, incidents of torture, use of force on civilians, and creating forensic documentation that can be used in legal proceedings. The organization has done work in Iraq, Bosnia, Colombia, Honduras, Rwanda, Mexico, Peru, Libya, Sierra Leone, and other nations. They have a forensics training institute and program to help them in their task. The organization shared the 1997 Nobel Peace Prize for its role in the International Campaign to Ban Landmines.

Protection International

Protection International is an international nonprofit organization that is dedicated to the protection of human rights defenders. Human rights defenders are often subject to threats and danger. This organization was founded in 1998 as the European Peace Brigades International and became Protection International in 2007. With headquarters in Brussels, Belgium, Protection International works with thirty countries, including the Democratic Republic of the Congo, Guatemala, Colombia, Kenya, and Thailand. It views its actions as proactive rather than reactive. Its mission is to enhance the security and the protection of civil rights activists through nonviolent means. It provides training and protection measures to human rights defenders that include both individuals and organizations.

Refugees International

Refugees International is an independent humanitarian organization that was started in 1979 as a grassroots movement to help people fleeing from Vietnam, Laos, and Cambodia. This was during a time of conflict in Southeast Asia when people were displaced due to war, invasion, poverty, and fear for their lives. Refugees International accepts no government funding and relies on partners to investigate challenges that displaced people face and to identify ways to help them. It provides lifesaving assistance and protection to displaced people as they seek to find solutions for displacement crises. The organization helps both refugees as well as internally displaced and stateless people

Save the Children

Save the Children is an international charitable organization that is active today in over 100 countries. It was founded in 1919 by British child rights advocate Eglantyne Jebb to improve the lives of children around the world. Its mission is to take measures that will ensure that all children have basic human rights, such as the right to grow up healthy, be educated, and be safe from harm. Save the Children accepts donations to fund education, healthcare, safety, and economic programs. It actively enters communities that are in crisis to focus on making sure that children are safe and receive resources necessary for their survival, health, education, and wellbeing. The organization has been awarded a general consultative status in the United Nations Economic and Social Council and has been found to significantly improve the health, safety, and wellbeing of children around the world.

Southern Poverty Law Center

The SPLC is a US nonprofit organization that monitors and exposes hate groups and advocates for civil rights and social justice. It provides educational material, advocates for people's wellbeing, and contains detailed maps and resources about the rise of hate groups. It was founded in 1971 in Alabama and has fought racial segregation, discrimination, the Ku Klux Clan, prison and detention maltreatment, mistreatment of immigrants, poverty, violence, and the unconstitutional mixing of church and state. As a legal center, the SPLC was founded by civil rights leaders such as Morris Dees, Joseph Levin, and Julian Bond. It continues to fight racism but has expanded its work to analyze a variety of hate groups and has created a map of hate groups across the nation. Many of these hate groups are promoting white supremacy, evangelical Christianity over other faiths, and opposition to LGBTQ+ individuals. The SPLC has published the magazine *Teaching Tolerance* for decades to distribute educational materials, especially to K-12 teachers. It recently changed the magazine's name to *Learning for Justice* to reflect its broader mission.

UNICEF

The United Nations International Children's Emergency Fund is more commonly known as UNICEF. It is an agency of the United Nations, and it is responsible for providing humanitarian and developmental aid to children worldwide. Founded in 1946, it sought to protect children after World War II, declaring that it made no difference what country children were from because all children had the same human rights and the same potential for goodness as social change agents. The organization makes available food, water, shelter, medical care, education, and resources that are essential to children's survival and their ability to develop and thrive.

Universities Network for Children in Armed Conflict

The Universities Network for Children in Armed Conflict was launched in 2020 with the support of the Italian Ministry of Foreign Affairs and International

Cooperation. This organization consists of scholars from around the world and is the first International Academic Network for the Protection of Children in Armed Conflict in the world. Its aim is to utilize the skills of the academic communities to provide education to government leaders, nongovernment organizations, and others who are engaged in the protection of children, directly and indirectly, in armed conflict. It works with countries in Africa, the Middle East, Europe, and Asia in the pursuit of preventing armed conflict in the first instance and helping young children who are soldiers or victims of violence to recover.

University of Minnesota Human Rights Library

The University of Minnesota has created an online library that contains one of the richest central depositories of human rights information in the world. It contains information about all of the different human rights treaties, as well as a country-by-country list of whether they have signed and ratified each of the treaties. This is an easy-to-use library that contains hundreds of treaties and documents for researchers, policymakers, as well as human rights educators.

Further Reading

Ali, Muhammad. (1975). *The Greatest.* Random House.

Badawi, Raif, and Schreiber, Constantin. (2015). *1000 Lashes: Because I say What I think.* Greystone Books.

Befaqadu Hailu. (2013). *Children of the Parents.* Freedom Press.

Caldicott, Helen. (1982). The final epidemic. *The Sciences.* https://nyaspubs.onlinelibrary.wiley.com/doi/10.1002/j.2326-1951.1982.tb02051.x (accessed April1, 2025).

Caldicott, Helen. (2017). *Sleepwalking to Armageddon: The Threat of Nuclear Annihilation.* New Press.

Clark, Nancy, and Worger, William. (2022). *South Africa: The Rise and Fall of Apartheid.* Routledge.

14th Dalai Lama. (1991). *Freedom in Exile.* Harper.

Du Bois, W. E. B. (1903). The Talented Tenth. In *The Negro Problem: A Series of Articles by Representative American Negroes of To-Day* (pp. 31–75). James Pott & Co.

Friedan, Betty. (1963). *The Feminine Mystique.* Norton.

Harrington, Michael. (1962). *The Other America.* Simon and Schuster.

History. (2024). The fight for women's suffrage. History.com. https://www.history.com/topics/womens-history/the-fight-for-womens-suffrage (accessed April 1, 2025).

Keneally, Thomas. (1982). *Schindler's Ark*. Hodder and Stoughton.

Knight, Russell. (2024). *The Untold Story of President Jimmy Carter: The Humble Humanitarian who Changed the World*. Kindall.

Lisska, Anthony J. (1997). *Aquinas's Theory of Natural Law: An Analytic Reconstruction*. Oxford. doi: 10.1093/acprof:oso/9780198269670.003.0009.

Myrdal, Gunnar. (1944). *An American Dilemma: The Negro Problem and Modern Democracy*. Harper and Brothers.

Schweitzer, Albert. (1971). *Reverence for Life*. Hallmark. https://ia801003.us.archive.org/2/items/reverence-for-life-schweitzer/Reverence%20for%20Life%20-%20Albert%20Schweitzer.pdf (accessed April 1, 2025).

Shapiro, Joseph. (1993). *No Pity: People with Disabilities Forging a new Civil Rights Movement*. Random House.

Tutu, D., and Abrams, D. C. (2016). *The Book of Joy: Lasting Happiness in a Changing World*. Random House

Wiesel, Elie, and Marion Wiesel. (2006). *Night*. Penguin Books.

Yousafzai, M., and Lamb, C. (2014). *I am Malala*. Weidenfeld & Nicolson.

Zepeda, O. (2017). *Where Clouds are Formed*. University of Arizona Press.

epp
EPP

5

Documents

Many documents, reports, speeches, and materials have been created over the years that have shaped our understanding of human rights. This chapter contains the contents of the US Bill of Rights, the UN UDHR, the UN CRC, and testimonies from three individuals that pertain to the rise of autocracy, Russia's invasion of Ukraine and Belarus, and the growth of white supremacy in the United States.

US Bill of Rights (1791)

The US Constitution and its Bill of Rights provide an example of how rights are often built upon concepts that were influenced by previous documents and modified over time. These influences include the 1215 Magna Carta, the English Bill of Rights, the Toleration Act of 1689, the 1776 Declaration of Rights, and the Articles of Confederation. There was significant disagreement about what the new country's Constitution should contain. Issues of states' rights, representation, and slavery were key points of contention. There was also disagreement about whether delegates from small and large states should have the same representation in the new Congress or representation proportional to the size of each state's population. The result was a Constitution that contained seven articles pertaining to legislative and procedural powers including, in Article 1, a House of Representatives and a Senate, term limits, taxation, interstate commerce, and criteria for impeachment. Article 2 and 3 identified the executive and judiciary branches and the courts.

Belarusian opposition leader Sviatlana Tsikhanouskaya speaks at the European People's Party (EPP) Congress in Rotterdam, 2022. (European People's Party via Flickr, Creative Commons license CC-BY-2.0)

Article 4 started to address citizen privileges, and Article 5 focused on how to amend the Constitution. Article 6 prohibited religious tests for office holders and issues of public debt, and Article 7 stipulated that nine states needed to ratify the Constitution for it to be actionable.

In 1791, ten amendments to the new US Constitution were ratified and became known as the Bill of Rights. These appear in the following document. Since that time, additional Constitutional amendments have passed, with the total now at twenty-seven. These include the 13th Amendment, which outlaws slavery; the 14th Amendment, which grants citizenship and equal civil and legal rights to African Americans and former enslaved people; the 15th Amendment, which guarantees that the right to vote cannot be denied on the basis of race, color, or previous servitude; the 16th Amendment, which calls for a federal income tax; the 18th Amendment, prohibiting alcohol (later repealed in the 21st Amendment); the 19th Amendment, which gave women the right to vote (some fifty years after it was given to formerly enslaved men), and the 26th Amendment, which gave voting rights to citizens age eighteen or older. The last amendment passed was in 1992. There have been over 10,000 proposed amendments to the US Constitution, but most have failed, including an Equal Rights Amendment for women, an amendment ensuring that child labor protections are in place, and an amendment providing protections for people with disabilities.

Amendment I: Congress shall make no law respecting an establishment of religion, or prohibiting the free exercise thereof; or abridging the freedom of speech, or of the press; or the right of the people peaceably to assemble, and to petition the Government for a redress of grievances.

Amendment II: A well regulated Militia, being necessary to the security of a free State, the right of the people to keep and bear Arms, shall not be infringed.

Amendment III: No Soldier shall, in time of peace be quartered in any house, without the consent of the Owner, nor in time of war, but in a manner to be prescribed by law.

Amendment IV: The right of the people to be secure in their persons, houses, papers, and effects, against unreasonable searches and seizures, shall not be violated, and no Warrants shall issue, but upon probable cause, supported by Oath or affirmation, and particularly describing the place to be searched, and the persons or things to be seized.

Amendment V: No person shall be held to answer for a capital, or otherwise infamous crime, unless on a presentment or indictment of a Grand Jury, except in cases arising in the land or naval forces, or in the Militia, when in actual service in time of War or public danger; nor shall any person be subject for the same offence to be twice put in jeopardy of life or limb; nor shall be compelled in any criminal case to be a witness against himself, nor be deprived of life, liberty, or property, without due process of law; nor shall private property be taken for public use, without just compensation.

Amendment VI: In all criminal prosecutions, the accused shall enjoy the right to a speedy and public trial, by an impartial jury of the State and district wherein the crime shall have been committed, which district shall have been previously ascertained by law, and to be informed of the nature and cause of the accusation; to be confronted with the witnesses against him; to have compulsory process for obtaining witnesses in his favor, and to have the Assistance of Counsel for his defence.

Amendment VII: In Suits at common law, where the value in controversy shall exceed twenty dollars, the right of trial by jury shall be preserved, and no fact tried by a jury, shall be otherwise re-examined in any Court of the United States, than according to the rules of the common law.

Amendment VIII: Excessive bail shall not be required, nor excessive fines imposed, nor cruel and unusual punishments inflicted.

Amendment IX: The enumeration in the Constitution, of certain rights, shall not be construed to deny or disparage others retained by the people.

Amendment X: The powers not delegated to the United States by the Constitution, nor prohibited by it to the States, are reserved to the States respectively, or to the people.

Source: US Bill of Rights. 1791. National Archives. https://www.archives.gov/founding-docs/bill-of-rights-transcript.

Universal Declaration of Human Rights, United Nations (1948)

Regarded as the foundational document establishing human rights, the Universal Declaration of Human Rights is the most translated document in the world, available in 562 languages from Abkhaz to Zulu. Created in 1948 after World War II, it was designed to increase respect for human rights with the hope that future wars and conflicts would cease to exist. The declaration in its entirety follows.

Preamble

Whereas recognition of the inherent dignity and of the equal and inalienable rights of all members of the human family is the foundation of freedom, justice and peace in the world,

Whereas disregard and contempt for human rights have resulted in barbarous acts which have outraged the conscience of mankind, and the advent of a world in which human beings shall enjoy freedom of speech and belief and freedom from fear and want has been proclaimed as the highest aspiration of the common people,

Whereas it is essential, if man is not to be compelled to have recourse, as a last resort, to rebellion against tyranny and oppression, that human rights should be protected by the rule of law,

Whereas it is essential to promote the development of friendly relations between nations,

Whereas the peoples of the United Nations have in the Charter reaffirmed their faith in fundamental human rights, in the dignity and worth of the human person and in the equal rights of men and women and have determined to promote social progress and better standards of life in larger freedom,

Whereas Member States have pledged themselves to achieve, in cooperation with the United Nations, the promotion of universal respect for and observance of human rights and fundamental freedoms,

Whereas a common understanding of these rights and freedoms is of the greatest importance for the full realization of this pledge,

Now, therefore,

The General Assembly,

Proclaims this Universal Declaration of Human Rights as a common standard of achievement for all peoples and all nations, to the end that every individual and every organ of society, keeping this Declaration constantly in mind, shall strive by teaching and education to promote respect for these rights and freedoms and by progressive measures, national and international, to secure their universal and effective recognition and observance, both among the peoples of Member States themselves and among the peoples of territories under their jurisdiction.

Article 1: All human beings are born free and equal in dignity and rights. They are endowed with reason and conscience and should act towards one another in a spirit of brotherhood.

Article 2: Everyone is entitled to all the rights and freedoms set forth in this Declaration, without distinction of any kind, such as race, colour, sex, language, religion, political or other opinion, national or social origin, property, birth or other status. Furthermore, no distinction shall be made on the basis of the political, jurisdictional or international status of the country or territory to which a person belongs, whether it be independent, trust, non-self-governing or under any other limitation of sovereignty.

Article 3: Everyone has the right to life, liberty and the security of person.

Article 4: No one shall be held in slavery or servitude; slavery and the slave trade shall be prohibited in all their forms.

Article 5: No one shall be subjected to torture or to cruel, inhuman or degrading treatment or punishment.

Article 6: Everyone has the right to recognition everywhere as a person before the law.

Article 7: All are equal before the law and are entitled without any discrimination to equal protection of the law. All are entitled to equal protection against any discrimination in violation of this Declaration and against any incitement to such discrimination.

Article 8: Everyone has the right to an effective remedy by the competent national tribunals for acts violating the fundamental rights granted him by the constitution or by law.

Article 9: No one shall be subjected to arbitrary arrest, detention or exile.

Article 10: Everyone is entitled in full equality to a fair and public hearing by an independent and impartial tribunal, in the determination of his rights and obligations and of any criminal charge against him.

Article 11: Everyone charged with a penal offence has the right to be presumed innocent until proved guilty according to law in a public trial at which he has had all the guarantees necessary for his defence. No one shall be held guilty of any penal offence on account of any act or omission which did not constitute a penal offence, under national or international law, at the time when it was committed. Nor shall a heavier penalty be imposed than the one that was applicable at the time the penal offence was committed.

Article 12: No one shall be subjected to arbitrary interference with his privacy, family, home or correspondence, nor to attacks upon his honour and reputation. Everyone has the right to the protection of the law against such interference or attacks.

Article 13: Everyone has the right to freedom of movement and residence within the borders of each State. Everyone has the right to leave any country, including his own, and to return to his country.

Article 14: Everyone has the right to seek and to enjoy in other countries asylum from persecution. This right may not be invoked in the case of prosecutions genuinely arising from non-political crimes or from acts contrary to the purposes and principles of the United Nations.

Article 15: Everyone has the right to a nationality. No one shall be arbitrarily deprived of his nationality nor denied the right to change his nationality.

Article 16: Men and women of full age, without any limitation due to race, nationality or religion, have the right to marry and to found a family. They are entitled to equal rights as to marriage, during marriage and at its dissolution. Marriage shall be entered into only with the free and full consent of the intending spouses. The family is the natural and fundamental group unit of society and is entitled to protection by society and the State.

Article 17: Everyone has the right to own property alone as well as in association with others. No one shall be arbitrarily deprived of his property.

Article 18: Everyone has the right to freedom of thought, conscience and religion; this right includes freedom to change his religion or belief, and freedom, either alone or in community with others and in public or private, to manifest his religion or belief in teaching, practice, worship and observance.

Article 19: Everyone has the right to freedom of opinion and expression; this right includes freedom to hold opinions without interference and to seek, receive and impart information and ideas through any media and regardless of frontiers.

Article 20: Everyone has the right to freedom of peaceful assembly and association. No one may be compelled to belong to an association.

Article 21: Everyone has the right to take part in the government of his country, directly or through freely chosen representatives. Everyone has the right of equal access to public service in his country. The will of the people shall be the basis of the authority of government; this will shall be expressed in periodic and genuine elections which shall be by universal and equal suffrage and shall be held by secret vote or by equivalent free voting procedures.

Article 22: Everyone, as a member of society, has the right to social security and is entitled to realization, through national effort and international co-operation and in accordance with the organization and resources of each State, of the economic, social and cultural rights indispensable for his dignity and the free development of his personality.

Article 23: Everyone has the right to work, to free choice of employment, to just and favourable conditions of work and to protection against unemployment. Everyone, without any discrimination, has the right to equal pay for equal work. Everyone who works has the right to just and favourable remuneration ensuring for himself and his family an existence worthy of human dignity, and supplemented, if necessary, by other means of social protection. Everyone has the right to form and to join trade unions for the protection of his interests.

Article 24: Everyone has the right to rest and leisure, including reasonable limitation of working hours and periodic holidays with pay.

Article 25: Everyone has the right to a standard of living adequate for the health and well-being of himself and of his family, including food, clothing, housing and medical care and necessary social services, and the right to security in the event of unemployment, sickness, disability, widowhood, old age or other lack of livelihood in circumstances beyond his control. Motherhood and childhood are entitled to special care and assistance. All children, whether born in or out of wedlock, shall enjoy the same social protection.

Article 26: Everyone has the right to education. Education shall be free, at least in the elementary and fundamental stages. Elementary education shall be compulsory. Technical and professional education shall be made generally available and higher education shall be equally accessible to all on the basis of merit. Education shall be directed to the full development of the human personality and to the strengthening of respect for human rights and fundamental freedoms. It shall promote understanding, tolerance and friendship among all nations, racial or religious groups, and shall further the activities of the United Nations for the maintenance of peace. Parents have a prior right to choose the kind of education that shall be given to their children.

Article 27: Everyone has the right freely to participate in the cultural life of the community, to enjoy the arts and to share in scientific advancement and its benefits. Everyone has the right to the protection of the moral and material interests resulting from any scientific, literary or artistic production of which he is the author.

Article 28: Everyone is entitled to a social and international order in which the rights and freedoms set forth in this Declaration can be fully realized.

Article 29: Everyone has duties to the community in which alone the free and full development of his personality is possible. In the exercise of his rights and freedoms, everyone shall be subject only to such limitations as are determined by law solely for the purpose of securing due recognition and respect for the rights and freedoms of others and of meeting the just requirements of morality, public order and the general welfare in a democratic society. These rights and freedoms may in no case be exercised contrary to the purposes and principles of the United Nations.

Article 30: Nothing in this Declaration may be interpreted as implying for any State, group or person any right to engage in any activity or to perform any act aimed at the destruction of any of the rights and freedoms set forth herein.

Source: United Nations. 1948. Universal Declaration of Human Rights. https://www.ohchr.org/en/human-rights/universal-declaration/universal-declaration-human-rights.

Convention on the Rights of the Child, United Nations (1989)

The 1989 United Nations Convention on the Rights of the Child is the most supported human rights treaty in the history of the world. It was ratified by all UN member countries except one—the United States. The document identifies rights that are in the "best interest of the child" no matter who they are or where they live.

Preamble

The States Parties to the present Convention, Considering that, in accordance with the principles proclaimed in the Charter of the United Nations, recognition of the inherent dignity and of the equal and inalienable rights of all members of the human family is the foundation of freedom, justice and peace in the world, Bearing in mind that the peoples of the United Nations have, in the Charter, reaffirmed their faith in fundamental human rights and in the dignity and worth of the human person, and have determined to promote social progress and better standards of life in larger freedom, Recognizing that the United Nations has, in the Universal Declaration of Human Rights and in the International Covenants on Human Rights, proclaimed and agreed that everyone is entitled to all the rights and freedoms set forth therein, without distinction of any kind, such as race, colour, sex, language, religion, political or other opinion, national or social origin, property, birth or other status,

Recalling that, in the Universal Declaration of Human Rights, the United Nations has proclaimed that childhood is entitled to special care and assistance, Convinced that the family, as the fundamental group of society and the natural environment for the growth and wellbeing of all its members and particularly children, should be afforded the necessary protection and assistance so that it can fully assume its responsibilities within the community, Recognizing that the child, for the full and harmonious development of his or her personality, should grow up in a family environment, in an atmosphere of happiness, love and understanding, Considering that the child should be fully prepared to live an individual life in society, and brought up in the spirit of the ideals proclaimed in the Charter of the United Nations, and in particular in the spirit of peace, dignity, tolerance, freedom, equality and solidarity, Bearing in mind that the need to extend particular care to the child has been stated in the Geneva Declaration of the Rights of the Child of 1924 and in the Declaration of the Rights of the Child adopted by the General Assembly on November 20, 1959 and recognized in the Universal Declaration of Human Rights, in the International Covenant on Civil and Political Rights (in particular in articles 23 and 24), in the International Covenant on Economic, Social and Cultural Rights (in particular in article 10) and in the statutes and relevant instruments of specialized agencies and international organizations concerned with the welfare of children, Bearing in mind that, as indicated in the Declaration of the Rights of the Child, "the child, by reason of his physical and mental immaturity, needs special safeguards and care, including appropriate legal protection, before as well as after birth", Recalling the provisions of the Declaration on Social and Legal Principles relating to the Protection and Welfare of Children, with Special Reference to Foster Placement and Adoption Nationally and Internationally; the United Nations Standard Minimum Rules for the Administration of Juvenile Justice (The Beijing Rules); and the Declaration on the Protection of Women and Children in Emergency and Armed Conflict, Recognizing that, in all countries in the world, there are children living in exceptionally difficult conditions, and that such children need special consideration, Taking due account of the importance of the traditions and cultural values of each people for the protection and harmonious development of the child, Recognizing the importance of international co-operation for improving the living conditions of children in every country, in particular in the developing countries, Have agreed as follows:

1. A child is defined as any person under the age of 18.
2. No discrimination is allowed. Children should not be treated unfairly for any reason. All children have all these rights, no matter where they live, who they are, what they look like, what language they speak, what their religion is, what their socio-economic status is, who their parents are, what they think, if they are a boy or girl, whether they have a disability, or what their parents or families believe or do.
3. The best interest of the child is a primary consideration of any decision that governments make that may affect children and their lives, and that all parents and adults should do what is best for children of any age. This includes making sure that parents, caregivers, and organizations do a good job in caring for children.
4. Governments are responsible for ensuring that every child can enjoy all the rights in the CRC.
5. Children need guidance as they develop so they can learn to use their rights in the best way and are able to grow more responsible and independent as they age.
6. All children have the right to be alive so governments and adults are to make decisions to ensure children's survival and give children opportunities to positively develop healthy bodies, minds, spirits, and use their gifts and talents.
7. All children are to be given a name and be recognized by the government to which they belong. If possible, children should know who are their parents and be cared for by them.
8. Children are not property; they have the right to their own identity and have a protected official record of who they are and where they come from.
9. Children should not be separated from their parents unless their parents are not keeping them safe and not looking after them properly or meeting their needs. When parents do not live together children have a right to have a relationship with both of them.
10. If a child lives in a different country than their parents, the child and parent must be allowed to travel so that they can stay in build a relationship with each other.
11. Children must be protected from kidnapping or being taken out of the country when this is against the law.

12. Respect for children's views must be honored since children have the right to give their opinions freely on issues that affect them and adults should listen and take children seriously.
13. Children have agency and ideas and have the right to share freely with others what they learn, think and feel, by talking, drawing, writing or in any other way—unless it harms other people.
14. Freedom of thought and religion is a right for children, just as for adults. They should be allowed to have their own thoughts, opinions and religion. Parents can guide children to explore ideas and faith.
15. Children can join or set up groups or organisations so they can meet and interact with others, but must do so in ways that do not harm other people.
16. Children have the right to privacy, with laws protecting children's privacy, family, home, communications and reputation from attack.
17. Access to information is a child's right. They have the right to get information from the media, Internet, radio, television, newspapers, books and other resources. Adults should make sure the information children access is not harmful or put them at risk. Information should be in a form that children can access and understand, and in their own languages.
18. Parents have the main responsibility of bringing up a child so they need to do so in a child rights respecting manner. If a child has two parents, both need to be responsible for good caregiving. If their parents are unavailable, unable, or unwilling to do so, governments should help them to have a guardian who will do this.
19. Governments must protect children from violence, abuse and being neglected by anyone who looks after them.
20. Children without families have the right to be well cared for by others who will respect their culture, religion, language and other aspects of their life.
21. Children who are adopted must be properly cared for by others, either in their own community, country, or in another country.
22. Children who travel from their home country to another country in order to be safe; they may be known as refugees and are entitled to help and protection and because they have the same rights as children born in that country.
23. Children may have a disability and if so measures should be taken to ensure that they enjoy the best life possible. Governments should remove

all obstacles for children with disabilities so they can become independent and actively participate in their community.

24. Children have a right to be healthy, which means they need access to clean water, nutritious food, healthcare, and a safe, sustainable environment.
25. When children are placed somewhere away from their home their situation should be reviewed regularly to make certain that all of their care needs are met and if not, changes may be needed to ensure their wellbeing.
26. Children have a right to social and economic help, including government support for money or other help, especially for impoverished families.
27. Governments should help parents and children access their right to food, appropriate clothing, and a safe place to live as these are essential to their heathy growth and development. so they can develop in the best possible way.
28. All children have the right to a free primary education; secondary and higher education should be available to every child. School discipline should respect children's rights and school officials should never use violence.
29. Children should be encouraged to go as far as they can in school, and education should help them fully develop their personalities, talents and abilities. This includes teaching them to understand their own rights, and to respect other people's rights, cultures and differences so that everyone can live peacefully. Protecting the environment is also a right they should learn to respect.
30. Children have the right to use their own language, culture and religion, no matter who they are or where they live, even if these are not shared by most people in the country where they live.
31. Rest, play, and taking part in cultural, artistic, and creative activities are also children's rights.
32. Protection from harmful work is important; children have the right to be protected from doing work that is dangerous or bad for their education, health or development. If children work, they have the right to be safe and paid fairly. Work should not interfere with their education.
33. Governments must protect children from taking, making, carrying or selling harmful drugs.
34. The government should protect children from sexual exploitation and sexual abuse. This includes people forcing children to have sex for money, or make sexual pictures or films of them.

35. Governments must make sure that children are not kidnapped, sold, or taken to other countries or places where they may hurt or exploited.
36. Children have the right to be protected from all other kinds of exploitation even if these are not specifically mentioned in this Convention.
37. Children who are accused of breaking the law should be treated respectfully and entitled to legal help and contact with their family. They should not be killed, tortured, treated cruelly, put in prison forever, or put in prison with adults. Prison should always be the last choice and only for the shortest possible time.
38. War is not in the best interest of the child, and children have the right to be protected during war. No child under 15 can join the army or take part in war in any way.
39. For children who have been impacted or involved with war, they have the right to timely recovery and reintegration into their community so they can regain their heath and dignity.
40. Children who break the law or accused of it have the right to legal help and fair treatment. There should be lots of solutions to help these children become good members of their communities. Jail or prison should only be the last choice.
41. Best law for children applies, so if a country's laws protect children's rights better than this Convention, then those are the laws that should be used.
42. Everyone must know children's rights. This means that human rights education is required by all governments to actively tell children and adults about this Convention so that everyone knows what human rights are and that children are entitled to them.

43 to 54. How the Convention works are explained in the remainder of the CRC Articles.

Source: United Nations. Convention on the Rights of the Child. 1989. https://www.ohchr.org/sites/default/files/Documents/ProfessionalInterest/crc.pdf.

Testimony of Leopoldo Lopez to US Senate Foreign Relations Committee (2023)

This document is the testimony of a Venezuelan freedom activist who was imprisoned because of his support of democratic views. His testimony to the US

Senate Foreign Relations Committee outlines the growth of autocratic governments around the world and the importance of international intervention to stop them before it is too late.

In February of 2014, after calling for non violent protests against the corrupt and autocratic regime of Nicolás Maduro, I was arrested, sent to a military prison, kept in solitary confinement for almost four years, and sentenced to 14 years of prison after a manipulated trial concluded I was guilty of inciting violence through subliminal messages during my public speeches. In 2017, I was sent to house arrest until I escaped in April of 2019 to seek refuge at the Spanish Embassy in Caracas, where I stayed until late 2020 when I escaped Venezuela to meet my family that had been in Spain since 2019. My struggle against the regime has now spanned decades. I was elected mayor of Chacao in Caracas in 2000, reelected in 2004, and since then I was banned from running for office and became the target of widespread attacks that included two murder attempts. My story is one of many; I have not been alone in this struggle. Hundreds of activists, social leaders, journalists, union leaders, business people, students, military officers, and common citizens have been the targets of the Maduro regime. After being in exile and learning first hand the testimonies of hundreds of democracy defenders, I now know that far from being an isolated case, this is the story of millions of individuals willing to stand up and fight for freedom around the world.

Last November, we launched the World Liberty Congress to gather pro-democracy leaders from more than 40 autocratic countries. The first day, we heard 40 delegations. It was eye opening that for hours we heard the same story repeating itself in different contexts and voices, the stories at the frontlines. It is from that perspective that I speak to you today, from the viewpoint of men and women who are willing to risk their freedom and lives to achieve freedom and democracy. The WLC is a non-ideological action oriented alliance of democracy defenders and freedom activists. We seek to provide pro-democracy movements with political, legal, financial, and strategic assistance to enhance their effectiveness. The idea of the WLC was initially spearheaded by Masih Alinejad of Iran, Garry Kasparov of Russia, and myself, but today counts among its membership hundreds of activists from across the planet.

According to Freedom House, 2023 marked the 17th consecutive year of democratic recession. This rise of autocracy has reached a level where 70% of the world population now live under some type of autocratic regime (according to V-Dem). However, this should not be confused with the will of the people; global polling reflects that 80% of the world's population wants to be free and live in a democracy. The recent and surprising protests in Iran, China, and Cuba to mention just a few, show that despite the efforts of dictators and despots, the will to be free remains consistent. However, it is also true that these movements have become less successful given the capacity of autocracies to repress and contain the transition to democracy through civil protests. Nonviolent pro-democracy movements went from a 60% success rate in transition to democracy in the 1990s to less than 5% today according to a recent study from Harvard University.

I am often asked how a dictator like Maduro can hold on to power even when his government and that of his predecessor, Hugo Chávez, have plundered the country and caused living standards to fall to the lowest of any nation in Latin America or the Caribbean. There are many ways to answer this question. Some say it is because of the government's access to natural resources, in particular oil, and the support from the military. Some even say it is because of divisions within the Venezuelan opposition. But in my view, there is one reason that stands above the rest: Maduro gets support from autocratic regimes throughout the world. These regimes provide funding, technology, military supplies, and know-how—all of which are ruthlessly deployed against those who are campaigning for human rights, democracy and freedom. In my conversations with freedom fighters living under other autocratic regimes, they tell the same tale of governments propped up by like-minded autocrats. Autocracies have aligned their efforts to support each other in a non-ideological but very pragmatic alliance to learn from and support each other. This concept, called "Autocracy Inc." by Anne Applebaum, is a complex web of transnational corruption and criminal affiliations. Twenty days before the Russian invasion of Ukraine, Putin was in Beijing solidifying his partnership with the Chinese regime, and both states released a joint statement declaring their alliance in international relations. These partnerships are a critical component of the resilience of these regimes. Russian oligarchs, anxious to prevent democratization in Latin America, routinely send delegations to Havana, Caracas, and Managua to discuss mutual "security." The most recent visit was that of Nikolai Patrushev, a Russian General, intelligence officer, and orchestrator of war crimes in Ukraine. The topic of discussion was the suppression of "color revolutions." Disguised as a diplomatic mission, this was a blatant Russian intervention in Latin America with the specific purpose of sharing methods of repression to terrorize and intimidate any possible dissenters. Putin, often considered to be a traditionalist, nationalist, and right-winger, has thrown massive support behind Nicaragua's Daniel Ortega, who styles himself as a socialist and a hardline left-winger. It's important to realize that these despots' "ideologies" are actually a thin facade for transnational corruption and the exportation of human rights violations. Putin will face no domestic backlash for his ideologically incomprehensible support of Ortega; Russian support is not rooted in admiration for Sandinismo in Nicaragua. It is merely a strategy to make the world less safe for those who respect human rights, the rule of law, and democracy.

Democracy is in retreat. Whether we want to accept it or not, there is a global battle being waged against liberal democracy by the forces of autocracy. Dictators recognize that their enemy is the system of democracy itself, because where it exists and thrives, it provides indisputable proof that the corrupt and decrepit ideals of autocracy are hollow and inferior. However, I want to stress that the fight against liberal democracy is also a fight against the United States, who is the principal defender and proponent of democracy on the global stage. This is why Chinese communists, Russian nationalists, and Iranian theocrats have wholeheartedly embraced one another. They are not tied together by ideology or principles. They are united merely by a fear of popular grassroots mobilization which is the primary challenge to their illegitimate rule, as well as a desire to undermine US influence across the world. They are thus willing to support each other unconditionally, because they recognize that they face an existential threat. If there is one purpose of my visit to this chamber today, it is to convince you, and freedom loving nations everywhere, that the political developments in Caracas or Khartoum or Hong Kong have direct implications for the security of the United States. We, too, face an existential threat.

There can be no delusion that sitting out of this fight is an option. A passive United States which is content to do business with dictators, and which shies away from doing everything possible to embolden and empower freedom fighters is making the world safer for human rights violators and kleptocrats. With or without the participation of the US, this battle is being fought. It must be understood that losing a square inch to autocracy outside of the US is a square inch closer to autocracy inside of the US. Those who seek to spread autocracy and undermine democracy are not short of funds or weapons. They have found new ways to protect their interests, exchanging resources, intelligence, military support, and methods of repression regardless of their supposed ideologies. This is why the US must take an active role in leading the creation of a parallel alliance, which is held together by a shared commitment to protect the values which we in this chamber hold dear. Imposing sanctions on human rights violators is logical and necessary, but because of the criminal transnational support between dictatorships, there must be a comprehensive re-examination of the policy tools available. Most importantly, we must realize that we don't have the luxury of "losing patience," or giving these grotesque regimes even a shred of legitimacy on the international stage. To do so not only condemns the people trapped inside to live in poverty and persecution in perpetuity, but it also makes the world safer for those who seek to replicate the Venezuelan tragedy, and I can say to you that there is no shortage of these people around the world.

It must also be spoken out loud and plainly; the United Nations has allowed some of the world's most rampant human rights violators to masquerade as statesmen and honest members of the international community. Last week, I testified at the UN Human Rights Council, where the fact finding mission stated that Maduro is responsible for committing crimes against humanity. It was striking to hear the chorus of autocratic nations defending the Maduro regime. Once again, irrespective of ideology, human rights violators align to present themselves as legitimate governments and vote to protect each other's interests. The resolution to expel the Iranian regime from the UN Women's Rights Commission, for example, faced stiff resistance. Those who voted against the resolution included: Bolivia, China, Kazakhstan, Nicaragua, Nigeria, Oman, Russia, and Zimbabwe. Journalist Hillel Neuer dubbed this group the "Axis of Shame." I will note that Venezuela does not vote on these matters since it is not up to date with its dues payments to the UN, but we can say with certainty that if it could, it would be a part of this cohort.

Authoritarianism is a hollow and decrepit ideal. It is incompatible with the human spirit, which innately yearns for freedom. Dictators intensely fear bottom-up popular mobilization, which is why they invest so heavily in suppressing it. By definition, authoritarianism centers itself around the suppression of basic human rights, such as freedom of expression, assembly, thought, and religion. This means that authoritarians will always have enemies, both within and beyond their borders. Dictators must always direct most of their energy, funds, and influence into terrifying and suppressing the will of their people, or their grip on power will slip. We have spoken of the advantages autocrats have over democrats. This, however, is an inescapable disadvantage of the dictators. They rely on terror, extortion, and the steady flow of funds and weapons to remain in power. Their opponents, however, are motivated by much more powerful, incorruptible ideals. Victims of authoritarianism have had their basic humanity stolen from them. This is why across the world, pro-democracy demonstrators are willing to take to the streets week after week, willing to be shot at, beaten, imprisoned, and tortured. In many places, dictators are finding that their habit of abusing and humiliating their populations creates a determined, and with the help of free nations, increasingly organized and well funded resistance. Even after 7 months, the people of Iran continue to fill the streets. When we see the images of Iranian women resisting a brutal theocracy, I ask you; what could be a better use of US influence and leadership, than to embolden these people? What is a better demonstration of the American ideals of democracy and liberty than the Iranian, or indeed the Cuban, Hong Kongese, Sudanese, or Venezuelan people at this moment.

Policy Recommendations

Recommendation #1: Secure Bipartisan Support for Global Democracy Assistance. It is critical that the issues of human rights and democracy not become caught up in partisan politics. For the US to lead a sustained multinational effort to confront this issue, it is essential that within all elements of the US government, there be a unified front and commitment to preserve freedom and democracy at the global level. This includes law enforcement agencies, the presidential administration, congress, and the judicial system. Facilitating the conditions for people to elect their own leaders and to not be subjected to human rights violations should not be partisan. The US must speak with one voice on this issue.

Recommendation # 2: Support Civil Resistance and Democracy Initiatives. Research shows that the most effective engines to transition to democracy are nonviolent popular grassroots movements. External pressure is necessary, but should be viewed as complementary to pro-democracy and civil resistance movements. It's key to understand that internal pressure requires the mobilization of large numbers of people, either protesting or voting. We need to find innovative ways to provide resources, strategies, and coordination assistance to make these movements more effective. The US and its allies should assist civil society initiatives which participate in community organizing and provide training in nonviolent methods of resistance. These kinds of initiatives are critical in not only getting people on the streets but also increasing their effectiveness.

Recommendation #3: Declare Democracy a Central Foreign Policy Focus. The United States Government should make supporting organic, localized pro-democracy movements a central focus in its foreign policy. In other words, irrespective of political denominations, the US should seek to identify pre-existing movements who are struggling for democratic change and provide them with technical and financial support. All foreign policy decisions should take into account potential consequences for human rights and democracy. It is necessary to coordinate efforts within and beyond the US government. Different US departments and agencies should be working in conjunction toward the same goal. Simultaneously, coordination with civil society and NGOs is critical in expanding the reach of pro-democracy policies.

Recommendation #4: Incorporate the Private Sector. The struggle for freedom and democracy should also include the private sector. We have seen the consequences of tying the economies of free nations to autocratic ones like Russia and China. The war in Ukraine demonstrated the danger of many European governments' dependence on Russian oil. We have also seen how guided investment in the ESG framework (Environment, Social, and Governance) has generated trillions of dollars into more conscious investors.

However, the SDG (Sustainable Development Goals), which are the 17 goals approved by the UN in 2015 on which ESG is based, makes no mention of human rights, freedom, democracy, and has only one mention of transparency. This is because the UN framework for SDG was discussed and approved with the vote of many autocratic regimes. The issues of human rights, democracy, and freedom are absent from the ESG framework, and we therefore propose the inclusion of the "F" for freedom in the ESG. This will guide investment and promote incentives for different initiatives that would promote freedom in different areas, such as communications, secure internet, and access to financial services.

Simultaneously, it's important to make consumers aware that the goods and services they are consuming are manufactured or extracted in autocratic regimes. For example in Xinjiang, the slave labor of Uyghurs is widespread in the production of consumer goods. Corporations which operate in autocratic countries should be exposed as being complicit in these human rights violations. Their economic activity is instrumental in propping up the regime of Xi Jingping, and US consumers and investors should be confronted with this reality.

Recommendation #5: Consistency in Denying Legitimacy to Dictators. The US should not send any financial or military assistance to regimes who are anti-democratic and commit human rights violations. For example, the US enjoys a beneficial military partnership with Uganda's Yoweri Museveni, who is the world's longest installed dictator, ruling the country with an iron fist since 1986. If the US is to credibly stand up for democratic ideals on the world stage, there can be no double standard or deviation for the sake of US interests. All dictatorships are incompatible with human rights, and the US should make it clear that it opposes dictatorships everywhere. Similarly, the US should use its influence with the European Union to adopt a similar stance. The US cannot democratize the world alone; the full cooperation of free nations is critical if the authoritarian threat is to be countered.

Recommendation #6: Massive Access to Internet, Smartphones. Autocratic systems are closed societies. Dictators spend much effort restricting outside information to prevent any challenges to the official narrative of the regime. Dictatorship is far more difficult to maintain with a well informed populace. Restrictions on the free flow of information constitutes an enormous challenge for democracy advocates within autocratic nations. To successfully mobilize large numbers of people for demonstrations and acts of civil disobedience, activist leaders need uncensored and widespread methods of communication which circumvent the control of autocrats. A program to distribute smartphones en masse in autocratic countries is a practical way to do this. It would assist not only in effective communications and combating misinformation, but also for access to different innovations and services that could be provided directly. There are also new technologies such as Starlink which can gravely undermine autocrats' controls on access to information.

Recommendation #7: Support for Exiles. As the US repositions its foreign policy to prioritize pro-democracy and pro-human rights work, it should simultaneously take into account the lives of activists who have been subjected to arbitrary detention, torture, disappearances, and assassination attempts. The US has traditionally offered asylum to many of these people, but the process must be expedited. The circumstances on the ground often change rapidly, and the US needs a process which rapidly assists human rights defenders who will face arrest if they are not quickly removed from the country. Bureaucratic steps in the visa granting process must be removed. Another way to assist democracy defenders is with stable migration status. There are thousands of exiles in the US who have a fragile status, which restricts their ability to travel. One of the main challenges we have is to coordinate the efforts of those who are exiled and those who are still in the country. Political refugees in the US should be able to move freely to coordinate pro-democracy efforts with their colleagues who are still inside the dictatorship.

Recommendation #8: Support and Visibility for Political Prisoners. The Department of State estimates that there are over one million political prisoners around the world. These people are not afforded legal protections and are regularly subjected to heinous forms of physical and psychological torture. They are not allowed visitation or the right to appeal, and are frequently unaware of what they have been charged with. We should elevate the voices of these people whenever possible. The US should apply diplomatic, economic, and political pressure to countries who have political prisoners. It should also highlight their names and facilitate international awareness of their plight. These brave people cannot be forgotten or allowed to rot away in prison cells for speaking out against dictatorship. Additionally, the US can also provide legal support to the families of political prisoners for them to advocate and communicate on their behalf more effectively.

Recommendation #9: Support International Enforcement Mechanisms like the ICC. The US and other democracies should explore ways to make international institutions more effective. The supposed mission of the United Nations of promoting global peace and protecting human rights is gravely undermined when countries like Russia and China exercise such massive influence in UN decision making. The potential for international enforcement mechanisms is immeasurable, but needs to be re-evaluated. The US should support the international institutions which identify, investigate, and punish crimes committed by autocrats. Organizations like the ICC are critical in the prosecution of these crimes, as we have seen in the recent decision by the ICC to issue a warrant for the arrest of Vladimir Putin to be tried for war crimes. It also initiated an investigation against Nicolás Maduro for crimes against humanity. I will also reiterate that the fact finding mission of the UN Human Rights Council also identified Maduro as having committed crimes against humanity. It's critical that the US and allied countries support these institutions so they can be more effective in their work.

Recommendation #10: Rethink Sanctions and empower Magnitsky legislation. The imposition of sanctions has been a consistent tool for democracies to prosecute authoritarians for human rights violations. The US should lead the way in pioneering new forms of targeted sanctions for corrupt officials in countries such as Venezuela. Magnitsky legislation has been a breakthrough on this front, denying Russian oligarchs or Venezuelan regime officials the ability to purchase properties or move with their families to live in free nations. Kleptocracy is not about ideology; it is about the theft of funds for private gain. By finding new ways to deny corrupt officials the ability to spend their ill-gotten monies, the appeal of transnational corruption is lessened. The Venezuelan regime pedals the lie that sanctions are the cause of the humanitarian catastrophe in Venezuela, which we know to be untrue. In 2019, before the imposition of sanctions, the Venezuelan economy had collapsed by more than 60%, and 4 million people had already fled the country. Let's be clear; the situation in Venezuela is the result of government mismanagement and corruption. Sanctions are one of the few peaceful diplomatic tools which can be used to consequence regimes which violate human rights. Without them, the autocrat has no reason to restrain his behavior. To increase the effectiveness of sanctions, we should take into account the transnational systems of corruption which prop up these regimes. They should confront the enablers—the individuals and companies which continue to do business with autocrats. Simply sanctioning regime officials will be insufficient in orchestrating political change.

Recommendation #11: Respond Effectively to Transnational Repression. Transnational repression is the attempt by autocrats to commit crimes against their opponents outside of their borders. This is an extremely common occurrence, and methods can include kidnapping, murder, extortion, unlawful deportations, coercion by proxy, or assault. Within our activist network at the World Liberty Congress, Masih Alinejad was subjected to an assassination attempt in New York earlier this year. Paul Rusesabagina, who we are glad to report was released from prison this week, was kidnapped in 2020 by the Rwandan government, boarding a plane he believed would take him to Burundi, but instead flew him to Kigali where he would be imprisoned. Another case within our network is that of Palestinian activist Fadi Elsalameen, who has been subjected to assassination attempts by the Palestinian Authority despite being a US citizen and living in Washington. US security and intelligence services should find effective methods to protect human rights defenders whose lives are threatened by dictators. There should be efforts to pre-empt attacks, and also to provide consequences for dictators when they send their agents to commit crimes against people in other countries.

Recommendation #12: Use of FinTech and Bitcoin/Lightning to overcome the obstacles of autocracies to bring financial support. We must use new technologies to move resources inside autocratic regimes without the surveillance of dictators. This includes using FinTech and Bitcoin/Lightning to transfer resources to activists. We have seen in recent periods that autocratic regimes seek to limit the access of NGOs by controlling their ability to use external financing. Providing reliable financial support is critical for democratic movements' success, so new methods of financing which circumvent the financial systems of autocrats are required.

Recommendation #13: An Alliance for Freedom. The cooperation of autocrats has been spoken about extensively. The central thesis of the World Liberty Congress is the need to articulate a global alliance of activist leaders who not only advocate for freedom internationally, but are willing to risk their lives inside their countries to achieve a democratic transition. We seek to identify concrete ways in which we can empower one another and cooperate to make our own movements more effective. By pooling together our experiences, resources, and strategies, we form a much more formidable threat to dictators. The membership of the WLC is extremely diverse-religiously, culturally, ethnically, geographically, and ideologically. However, because we have all faced the same brutal methods of repression and are all advocating for democratic transition, we are able to form a cohesive front. This is an excellent starting point, but is insufficient without the backing of a multinational alliance of sympathetic governments. The US should empower activist movements like the WLC and cooperate with our initiatives to advocate for the liberation of political prisoners, coordinate sanctions against kleptocratic networks, and train activists in nonviolent resistance. It should also use its global influence to enlist other governments who value freedom to do the same. Uniting freedom movements who are committed to fair elections, the rule of law, respect for human rights, and the restoration of democracy is essential in this fight, and the US has an enormous leadership role to play in making this a reality.

Source: Lopez, Leopoldo. 2023. Testimony to US Senate Foreign Relations Committee. March 28, 2023. https://www.foreign.senate.gov/imo/media/doc/45179b35-ff38-bb09-829a-641cb1d81a84/032823_Lopez_Testimony2.pdf.

Testimony of Sviatlana Tsikhanouskaya to US Senate Foreign Relations Committee (2023)

The following document is a testimonial by the president-elect of Belarus to the US Senate Foreign Relations Committee concerning the encroachment of Russia into countries such as Belarus and Ukraine. It outlines how Russia is using its autocracy to take over the lands and peoples of independent nations, and why it is essential for the democratic nations of the world to stop it.

Chairman Menendez, Ranking Member Risch, distinguished members of the committee: thank you for the opportunity to speak with you about the dire situation of democracy and human rights in Belarus and its implications for regional security and global interests. I will provide brief remarks while I would like to ask Chairman Menendez to accept my full testimony for the public record.

In 2020, Belarusians voted out incumbent Aliaksandr Lukashenka and protested against his refusal to step down. The illegitimate regime responded with lawless crackdown against political forces, civil society, and the media. Systemic repressions affected literally all strata of the society: women and men, children and seniors, workers and teachers, athletes and lawyers, medics and religious communities. Arrests are accompanied by violence, torture and degrading treatment amounting to crimes against humanity, as it was repeatedly recognized by the international community, including in the reports by the UN and OSCE experts. Repressions led to 60 thousand administrative arrests and criminal cases, at least 5 thousand political prisoners, and hundreds of thousands of Belarusians fleeing their country. Prison terms are extremely long, for example my husband Siarhei Tsikhanouski received 20 years, my own term is 15 years.

We cannot wait till these terms expire, we must do everything to end the regime and to free people. Names of many political prisoners became symbols of courage and dignity—Ihar Losik, Maria Kalesnikava, Pavel Sevyarynets, Mikalai Statkevich, even Nobel Peace Prize laureate Ales Bialiatski—just to name a few. But thousands more remain invisible and receive very little support. Repressions affected more than 1500 Belarusians who support Ukraine and oppose the war. The regime treats political prisoners as hostages, using them to cast fear inside the country and to bargain for international recognition. The regime maintains a high level of terror while changing the political system, ideology, and legislation into neo-Stalinism. The very concept of solidarity is outlawed in Belarus as the regime tries to break every horizontal connection in the society. Nevertheless, Belarusians have not given up fighting for a day. But now we must resolve two formidable tasks: liberate Belarus from tyranny and preserve its independence. The democratic forces of Belarus are not delegating this work—it is our duty and responsibility. But we need help of the world to win this fight.

There is no doubt that an independent, sovereign, democratic Belarus is in the interest of the entire international community. We, Belarusians, are the legitimate force to bring democracy to our own country and this by default cannot be seen as an interference in internal affairs. We have seen an unprecedented outpouring of support and solidarity since 2020. This energy should become the international strategy to realize the commitment to independent and sovereign Belarus. The most damaging factor to democratic hopes of Belarusians has been Russia's interference in our internal affairs. Without the Kremlin's help Lukashenka would have lost power even before 2020. To return the debt he makes illegal concessions to Russia. This includes agreements expanding Russian military presence and handing over economic and financial controls to Moscow. The Russian military is freely using Belarus territory, making our country a co-aggressor in the war against Ukraine. To please Moscow and make space for the Russian world, Lukashenka destroys Belarusian national identity, the core of the nation's soul and resilience before external threats. Finally, Putin just announced that Russia is deploying tactical nuclear weapons in Belarus by July 1 this year. This is his way to deter Western support for Ukraine but also portraying Lukashenka as Putin's puppet. Some call it occupation, some creeping annexation, but it is clear that Russia's actions damage Belarusian and global interests. As long as Belarus remains under Russian control it will be an outpost of its aggressive projects, and this is unacceptable for us and for the world.

It is time for a strong response to Russia's hostile, colonialist actions against Belarus. I urge the world to support our demand of full removal of the Russian military from Belarus and complete termination of its involvement in the war. We cannot postpone Belarus until after the war. As we see this, a democratic Belarus would drastically shorten the way to Ukraine's victory. Going further, we see sustainable peace as the result of a comprehensive approach to stabilizing the region. This should entail a Marshall Plan for Ukraine, Moldova, and Belarus since regional security and stability are only possible when all these nations are free of Moscow's control.

In the same vein, it must be guaranteed that the post-war arrangements have no place for Russia's special interests in Belarus. Such deals would lay the foundation for new instability. Discussions about peace must include the Belarusian democratic forces who have the legitimacy and think about national interests.

Russia denies to both Belarus and Ukraine their fundamental right to have a sovereign state. However, these two nations are not the final destination for Russia's ambitions, they are a stepping stone on the path to dismantling the Transatlantic partnership. Therefore, I urge the US and like-minded nations to continue supporting Ukraine, including with the most advanced military equipment, in its brave fight for the right to be themselves and decide on their future.

The war has made it clear to Belarusians that relations with hostile Russia must change. The United Transitional Cabinet has adopted an approach to revising ties with Russia. This includes leaving the military alliance and the Union State Treaty. Instead, we started working on the European perspective for Belarus. This will also include joining regional initiatives and broad partnerships with neighboring states. I ask the US Congress to support this strategic change for Belarus.

The US Congress has always been active on the Belarus agenda. In 2021, the Belarus caucus was officially launched in the House. Senator Shaheen and Senator Wicker founded the Free Belarus caucus in the Senate. The Congress adopted four iterations of the Belarus Democracy Act and resolutions assessing and highlighting the developments in Belarus. Now is the right moment to update the BDA to reflect the role of Lukashenka in the war and suggest policies for the US government. Lukashenka lost the mandate to represent the Belarusian people. Yet, he and Putin perceive the lack of full derecognition as a green light to realize their illegal ambitions and enjoy impunity along the way. I call the US to complete this effort and to fully de-recognize Lukashenka and his regime as being under full control of the foreign power to the detriment of the very statehood of Belarus. This process must be accompanied by a growing recognition extended to democratic forces. The US sanctions against the Lukashenka's regime have shown their impact. This leverage should be further strengthened by removing loopholes and enhancing coordination with the EU, UK, and Canada.

The regime is implicated in a series of crimes and must be held accountable for the crimes against humanity, the crime of aggression and for complicity in the war crimes in Ukraine. Lukashenka made the war against Ukraine possible. The attack on Kyiv and Bucha came from Belarus. He remains the only ally of Russia, fulfilling all requests of Putin to help him in this aggression while brutally repressing any forms of protest from Belarusians against the war. Lukashenka deserves to sit next to Putin at the tribunal for the crime of aggression. Finally, I want to reiterate the need of not just keeping Belarus in the agenda but to make this attention practical, to focus international efforts on taking away space and resources from the regime. Cooperation with the US in this sphere has proven to be impactful and this momentum can be further increased, especially when it comes to the UN and its Security Council. In conclusion, I would like to express my deepest gratitude to the United States, its people and government, for the decades of your principled and genuine support for democratic, sovereign, and independent Belarus. The US global leadership on these issues has always had a decisive role. We share the same values and aspirations, and we should stay in this fight together. Thank you. I am looking forward to your questions.

Source: Tsikhanouskaya, Sviatlana. 2023. Testimony to US Senate Foreign Relations Committee. March 28, 2023. https://www.foreign.senate.gov/imo/media/doc/45179b35-ff38-bb09-829a-641cb1d81a84/032823_Tsikhanouskaya_Testimony.pdf.

Testimony of Amy Spitalnick to the US House Homeland Security Subcommittee on Oversight, Investigations, and the Law (2023)

The following document focuses on the rise of white supremacy across the United States and the danger it poses. Testimony by Senior Advisor on Extremism at the international human rights organization Human Rights First provides examples of extremism and how it has been fueled by strategically designed misinformation campaigns. The testimony outlines recommendations for action to curb its growth.

Thank you, Chairman Bishop, Ranking Member Ivey, and members of the Committee. I'm grateful for the opportunity to be here today. My name is Amy Spitalnick and I am a Senior Advisor on Extremism at Human Rights First, a nonpartisan organization committed to ensuring that the United States is a global leader on human rights. I am also the incoming CEO of the Jewish Council for Public Affairs, a nearly 80-year old nonpartisan organization that serves as the national convener of Jewish coalitions to build a safe, just, and inclusive democracy. I previously led Integrity First for America, the nonpartisan nonprofit that held accountable the neo-Nazis, white supremacists, and hate groups responsible for the August 2017 violence in Charlottesville.

Many of us remember the visceral horror of watching neo-Nazis with torches storm the University of Virginia, chanting things like "Jews will not replace us" as they beat students and other community members. Or seeing the horrific images of violence the next day, culminating in the car attack that claimed Heather Heyer's life and injured so many others. That violence was no accident. Rather, it was planned meticulously in advance—on social media sites like Discord, via text, and on other channels—down to discussions of whether they could hit protesters with cars and claim self-defense. As the evidence in my organization's lawsuit made clear—and as the jury agreed, when they found every single defendant liable—these extremists planned violence; came to Charlottesville to engage in that violence; and then celebrated that violence.

This matters, not only because a young woman was murdered and so many others were grievously injured. It also matters because Unite the Right was a flashpoint in the rise of deadly white supremacist extremism—serving as a harbinger of a cycle of far-right violence that continues to claim lives around the country.

Charlottesville. Pittsburgh, where a white supremacist murdered 11 Jews praying in a synagogue. El Paso, where a white supremacist targeted a predominately Hispanic community, killing 23 people at a Walmart. January 6th, where extremists with Confederate flags, nooses, QAnon conspiracy theory propaganda, and even a "Camp Auschwitz" shirt attacked the seat of our government with the intent to harm members of Congress and law enforcement.

Buffalo, where a year ago Sunday a white supremacist drove hours in order to target a Black community, murdering 10 people at a grocery store. And earlier this month, in Allen, Texas, where a man who held neo-Nazi and white supremacist views, and sported a swastika tattoo and "Right Wing Death Squad" patch, murdered eight people shopping at an outlet mall. And these are just a handful of far too many examples I could cite. We are experiencing a tidal wave of white supremacist extremism in which individuals and communities are attacked based on who they are. It targets entire groups with the goal of making them feel unsafe, unwelcome, and unable to protect themselves. But I don't just want to share examples. I want to talk about data—the hard facts that are too often missing from these conversations.

According to data released earlier this year by the ADL, every single extremist-related murder in 2022 was committed by right-wing extremists. The vast majority of those were white supremacists. Over the past decade, 96 percent of the events in which extremists killed someone were committed by people with right-wing ideologies. In the same time period, three-quarters of the murders linked to extremism were committed by right-wing actors, while only 4 percent were linked to left-wing actors. A 2022 University of Maryland-led study specifically looked at disparities in violence among extremist groups, concluding radical acts perpetrated by individuals associated with left-wing causes are less likely to be violent. Research from the START Center at the

University of Maryland also tracks trends in mass casualty terrorist attacks and failed terrorist plots. Attacks are considered "mass casualty" when the perpetrator intended to kill or injure four or more people. Their data show that, over the last thirty years, far-right actors were responsible for 74 percent of these planned or successful terrorist attacks by domestic extremists. In comparison, far-left perpetrators were responsible for only 13 percent. It's not just NGOs and academic institutions that are tracking this disproportionate threat. In late 2020, former President Trump's Department of Homeland Security found that white supremacists were "the most persistent and lethal threat" in the United States.

This isn't to say that other forms of political violence don't exist. Of course they do. That includes left-wing or anarchist violence; Islamist violence; or violence that doesn't fit neatly into one particular ideology. There was a time when left-wing extremist violence was a bigger threat: nearly 50 years ago, during the 1970s. But since the 1990s, available data show that right-wing extremism has consistently been the most violent domestic terror threat. Unless we're clear-eyed about the facts, the data, and the reality of the current violent threat—which every indicator tells us is disproportionately emanating from the far right—we will never be able to intervene and break the cycle of violent extremism. It's all the more important to understand this reality because it's not happening in a vacuum. Rather, the rise in right-wing violence has gone hand-in-hand with an increasing normalization of right-wing extremism.

Human Rights First is particularly focused on the mainstreaming of hate. The ideology driving far-right extremism, and the broader anti-democratic movement, in the United States has become increasingly visible in our institutions, policies, and public discourse, and represents an existential threat to our democracy. This hate and bigotry is not new but it has been given new life through the rampant spread and normalization of racist, antisemitic, misogynistic, anti- LGBTQ+, and other bigoted conspiracies. Conspiracy theories that were once relegated to the dark corners of the internet—like the Great Replacement Theory—are espoused not just by mass murderers but by elected officials, political candidates, and pundits. Policies aimed at dehumanizing and stripping away the rights of certain communities are fueling attacks on those communities—such as the neo-Nazi organizations using anti-drag and anti-trans protests as recruitment opportunities.

Violent extremists take the normalization of conspiracy theories and bigotry as license for violence: for attacks on our democratic institutions and on vulnerable populations. It's not just a threat to our communities; it also directly threatens our democracy and our national security. The challenge ahead of us is great because this extremism is no longer relegated to fringe actors and violent groups, it is both mainstream and it is a movement. Therefore, mitigating this threat requires an approach that includes addressing the violent and most visible components of the movement, but also the mainstream networks that build support for the movement. It also means acknowledging the age-old bigotry this network has employed, addressing their attacks on civil and human rights across our country, and repairing and reconciling the harm it has caused.

So what can do we do about it? While we can and should invest in responsive measures like security, we also acknowledge that we can't simply sue, prosecute, or barricade our way out of this crisis. We need comprehensive solutions emphasizing protection of our democratic institutions, processes, and values. It also requires real accountability, supporting targeted communities, and building societal resilience to mitigate the further normalization of hate and extremism. This includes:

- **Defending Election Legitimacy:** Undermining the legitimacy of our elections, the cornerstone of our democracy, is a key goal of this extremist movement and is already
- **Protecting Democratic Institutions & Civil Rights:** Creating a concerted effort to protect our public education, healthcare, and voting systems—as well as communities' fundamental civil and human rights—against the antidemocratic attacks at the local, state, and federal levels.
- **Seeking Accountability:** Holding elected officials accountable for the impact of the extremist rhetoric they perpetuate, such as the harmful "invasion" narrative and "Great Replacement" conspiracy theory in furthering violence.
- **Confronting Extremism in the Military and Law Enforcement**: Recognizing and addressing the threat of extremism in the military and law enforcement.
- **Empowering Civil Society:** Empowering our society with tools to identify mis/disinformation and conspiracies and prevent radicalization: from media and digital literacy and other forms of education, to resources for parents, educators, and caregivers.
- **Combating Armed Extremism:** Making it harder for violent extremists to get their hands on the deadly weapons too often used in these acts of mass violence.

- **Building Cross-Community Coalitions**: Understanding that growing, mainstreamed extremism puts all of us at risk—and building cross-community coalitions rooted in the necessary idea that none of us are safe if one of us isn't safe.

The facts and the data are clear: we are grappling with a very real threat of right-wing extremism in this country. Every single statistic makes clear that the vast majority of extremist violence is perpetrated by those motivated by white supremacist and other right-wing ideologies. Acknowledging that doesn't take away from the fact that other forms of political violence exist. But this moment requires us to be clear-eyed about our reality if we're to do something about it. Again, I'm grateful for the opportunity to be here today, and I look forward to your questions. Thank you very much.

Source: Spitalnick, Amy. 2023. Testimony to the US House Homeland Security Subcommittee on Oversight, Investigations, and the Law. May 16, 2023. https://www.congress.gov/event/118th-congress/house-event/115946/text.

30

6

Resources

Many resources exist concerning human rights. This chapter includes resources that provide information and explore ideas central to the field. The material provided will assist the reader in continuing their human rights education.

Books

Abulhawa, Susan. 2006. *Mornings in Jenin.* Bloomsbury Publishing.

This is a novel that portrays a Palestinian family's history through several generations. It documents their struggle through the turbulent Israeli–Palestinian conflict in a way that tells the perspective of how they attempted to negotiate and survive oppression and uncertainty.

Akreyi, Widad. 2019. *The Daughter of Kurland: A Life Dedicated to Humankind.* Novo Reads.

In this book Akreyi tells her life story in what became an award-winning book. She describes her childhood in the Kurdistan region, her years as a university student, and highlights her phenomenal resilience in exile. She details her efforts to avoid persecution and document crimes against humanity. Her resilience is evident through her survival and inspiring journey.

Members of different tribes congregate in Brasilia, Brasil, to protest for Indigenous land rights in 2023. The rights of Indigenous peoples to their traditional lands and the resources found in those lands have been violated worldwide, often leading to environmental harm that exacerbates the impact on human rights. (Marcos Casiano/ Dreamstime.com)

Arendt, Hannah. 1973. *The Origins of Totalitarianism*. Harcourt, Brace, Jovanovich.

Totalitarianism is not a thing of the past, but an ever-present danger to democratic societies. Arendt's book reviews what totalitarian and authoritarian governments are, how their leaders manipulate the public to support them, and why we should be concerned about their revival across the world.

Atwood, Margaret. 1998. *The Handmaid's Tale*. Vintage.

This book has become a modern classic. A dystopian novel, it forecasts a future filled with the oppression of women as well as showcases how environmental disasters impact communities. The book examines the lives of fertile women who are enslaved in order to produce children for the leaders in a politically totalitarian regime. The main character, a woman, is deprived of her freedom, her family, and even her own name. The book has gained popularity because it describes a struggle that confronts women around the globe today.

Boggs, Grace Lee. 2012. *The Next American Revolution: Sustainable Action for the 21st Century*. University of California Press.

This book examines current world crises and recommends social changes that must occur for the country to be sustainable. The crises that Boggs considers are environmental, economic, social, and political. The author's persona experiences in social movements such as the civil rights movement, women's rights movement, worker and labor rights, lead her to encourage a new revolution of sorts for the twenty-first century. She argues that the next American revolution will rely upon creative, innovative, new forms of social institutions and relationships.

Brown, Dee. 1970. *Bury My Heart at Wounded Knee: An Indian History of the American West*. Holt, Rinehart & Winston.

This nonfiction book documents the impact of European colonization and westward expansion on Indigenous peoples from the 1850s to the 1890s. The book covers critical events depicting horrific crimes against Indigenous people, such as the Trail of Tears, the Sand Creek massacre, the Battle of Little Bighorn, and the massacre at Wounded Knee. It puts the reader into a position where they can see these events from the Native American point of view in a powerful description of real historical events.

Carson, Clayborn, Garrow, David, Gill, Gerald, Harding, Vincent, and Clark Hine, Darlene, 1991. *The Eyes on the Prize Civil Rights Reader*. Penguin.

This book is a collection of key documents and recollections of the 1960s civil rights movement. This time period was monumental in creating social change that transformed the narrative of America. The book contains descriptions of key events such as the US Supreme Courts decision of *Brown v. the Board of Education*. It includes writings such as Martin Luther King Jr.'s "Letter from the Birmingham City Jail," Ralph Abernathy's "And the Walls Came Tumbling Down," and selections by Malcolm X. Contributions by Rosa Parks, Bobby Seale, Herman Badillo, Jesse Jackson, Harold Washington, and Nelson Mandela are also contained in this book, which captures the struggles of that time.

Chakrabarti, Shami. 2024. *Human Rights: The Case for the Defence.* Allen Lane.

This book is a global overview of what human rights are and why they need to be defended. It provides a historical view of them, defines the different dimensions of rights, and uses a legal framework to examine their importance. It provides facts and arguments that can equip human rights defenders to make their case to an international audience about why it is essential to global society to embed and protect human rights for all.

Frank, Anne. 1947. *The Diary of a Young Girl.* Contact Publishing.

This book has become a classic. It is by Anne Frank, a Jewish teenager, during World War II, written while she was in hiding for her life. Her diary documents this young girl's life from 1942 to 1944 and provides a firsthand account of her experiences, thoughts, and emotions while hiding with her family in Amsterdam to escape Nazi persecution. Her family was eventually discovered, and Anne died in a concentration camp. Anne's diary was published by her father, fulfilling her wish to become a published author.

Friedlander, Saul. 2008. *Nazi Germany and the Jews, 1939–1945: The Years of Extermination.* Harper.

The World War II German government enacted extermination policies that murdered 6 million Jews. This action depended upon a variety of social factors, including the cooperation of the public, local authorities, the police, business, political, and spiritual leaders.

This book contains a vast array of documents, diary and letter accounts, and other memoir and historical information that gives us pause to consider what happened in the past—and whether something this horrid could happen again.

Furedi, Frank. 2011. *On Tolerance: A Defence of Moral Independence.* Continuum.

Furedi observes in this book that society is dominated by cultures that tolerate and even encourages the intolerance of others. This he finds true even in democratic societies. Intolerance is often aimed at people who refuse to accept norms, values, and lifestyles promoted by the dominant culture. People can be condemned for even minor things, such as what they eat, what they wear, how they do their hair, as well as for what they believe. He attempts to identify the real motives and drivers behind stigmatization and intolerance.

Gilio-Whitaker, Dina. 2020. *As Long as Grass Grows: The Indigenous Fight for Justice from Colonization to Standing Rock.* Beacon Press.

Researcher and social activist Dina Gilio-Whitaker analyzes the history of Indigenous people's resistance to corporate and government take-overs of their native lands. She examines the historical tension that exists between Indigenous peoples, politicians, and environmentalists in the struggle to protect both the rights of the Native American tribes and the consideration of environmental human rights.

Gourevitch, Philip. 1998. *We Wish to Inform You Tomorrow We Will Be Killed with Our Families.* Picador.

This book documents the government of Rwanda's call to everyone in the Hutu majority to kill the Tutsi minority, which resulted in the murder of 800,000 Tutsis. Gourevitch utilizes research and interviews with survivors, perpetrators, and firsthand witnesses to articulate the events leading up to, during, and after the Rwandan genocide.

Griffin, James. 2009. *On Human Rights.* Oxford University Press.

Griffen explores what human rights are and how people can use them to solve social and personal conflicts. He traces the idea of a natural right from its origin in the late Middle Ages through the seventeenth and eighteenth centuries and the Enlightenment. He argues that the language of human rights has become debased and that "human rights" has become a confusing term that needs to be better codified. Figuring out whose rights are more right is an important examination in contemporary society.

Hunt, Lynn. 2008. *Inventing Human Rights: A History*. Norton.

This book is a history of human rights from the Enlightenment to the current day. It also looks at the cultural, intellectual, humanities, and relational aspects of human rights, and why they are important.

Kaye, David. 2019. *Speech Police: The Global Struggle to Govern the Internet*. Columbia Global Reports.

Kaye notes that the internet was designed to be a kind of free-speech paradise but now is used to promote violence, untruth, intolerance, and hate. He examines options for what can be done about this problem. Kaye serves as the United Nations' special rapporteur on free expression, and his book asserts that the internet's original commitment is to free speech, free of any company's or government's absolute control, while finding ways to modulate its worst aspects.

Lee, Harper. 1960. *To Kill a Mockingbird*. J. B. Lippincott & Company.

Through the perspective of a young girl, Scout Finch, the novel explores themes of racial injustice, moral growth, and the loss of innocence. The book follows Scout as she navigates the racially divided South and how she copes with witnessing the injustices against Tom Robinson, a minority man who is negatively stereotyped by the community.

Lee, Min Jin. 2017. *Pachinko*. Grand Central Books.

Min Jin Lee follows four generations of Korean immigrants through struggles, trials, war, and death in a novel. She weaves human rights issues throughout it, especially in her description of identity, belongingness, and what it means to be a member of a community. Poverty, inhumane treatment, discrimination, and marginalization are other human rights themes present in this book. Her work begs for the reader to consider the similarities between how the Japanese treated Korean immigrants and the challenges that other immigrants face today in the United States.

Leitao, S., and Vissing, Y. 2023. *Child and Youth Refugee Resettlement and Community Formation Issues.* Vernon Press.

Children around the world are on the move, either with their families or as unaccompanied youth. As refugees, young people's human rights are at risk as they try to establish residence in a new community or country. How well communities greet these strangers and help put into place the structures and processes they need in order for them to survive and thrive may vary dramatically. This edited book by international scholars examines what communities can do to help resettle young refugees.

Liefaard, Ton, and Sloth-Nielsen, Julia. (Eds.). 2017. *The United Nations Convention on the Rights of the Child: Taking Stock after 25 Years and Looking Ahead.* Leiden: Brill/Nijhoff.

This edited volume provides essays from scholars around the world that examine the history of the creation of the United Nations CRC and its impact improving the lives of children around the globe.

Lim, Louisa. 2014. *The People's Republic of Amnesia.* Oxford University Press.

This book on Tiananmen Square in China was a finalist for the Helen Bernstein Book Award for Excellence in Journalism and listed for the Lionel Gelber Award for the Best Nonfiction book on foreign affairs. Lim charts how the 1989 killing of unarmed civilians in China has been buried and expunged from the public's understanding of the past. Lim uncovers details of a brutal crackdown in what has been a near-perfect case study in the state's power and ability to rewrite history and excising the a country's painful episode of the past.

Miller, Arthur. 2003. *The Crucible.* Penguin.

Miller's classic book on real-life historical events has been turned into plays and movies as it continues to provide relevance to thinking about contemporary life and the stigmatization of others. It is based on the Salem Witch Trials in Massachusetts, which unleashed the destructive power of socially sanctioned violence against those who were labeled to be witches. It provides a powerful parable about McCarthyism and other current trends that are designed to disparage and dehumanize others.

Mulley, Clare. 2020. *The Woman Who Saved the Children: A Biography of Eglantyne Jebb Founder of Save the Children.* Oneworld Books.

Human rights treaties are often inspired by a charismatic leader, and this book by Mulley describes how Eglantyne Jebb motivated an international community to view children as entitled rights holders. While this is a biography, it is also a historical document that points out how our histories shape what we do, and how we need partners in order to move any human rights endeavor forward.

Nickel, James. 2007. *Making Sense of Human Rights.* Wiley-Blackwell.

Nickel discusses the fundamental rights covered in the UDHR and why they remain important in contemporary society. He also discusses due process rights, social rights, civic rights, minority rights, and terrorism's attack on human rights. He integrates law, politics, and theory in his examination of the historical relevance of the treaty.

Northup, Solomon. 1853. *12 Years a Slave.* Graymalkin Media.

This book chronicles the life of Northup, his kidnapping in 1841, years of being in the slave trade, and rescue in 1853. Over his twelve years of enslavement Northrup is forced to endure and witness mental and physical suffering. He documents these experiences, his resiliency, and his resourcefulness, which eventually leads to his rescue.

Orwell, George. 1949. *1984.* Secker & Warburg.

Set in a dystopian world, *1984* explores themes of government oppression, surveillance, propaganda, and the erosion of individual freedom. The novel follows Winston Smith who decides to rebel against the Party and joins a resistance movement.

Orwell, George. 1945. *Animal Farm.* Secker & Warburg.

Animal Farm utilizes a group of farm animals to create a political allegory representing the events leading up to the Russian Revolution of 1917. Through the farm animals, themes of power, corruption, propaganda, and the betrayal of revolutionary ideals are displayed. The novel depicts the slow corruption of the farm animal leaders and their descent into violence, manipulation, and oppression.

Rawls, John. 2007. *The Law of Peoples: With the Idea of Public Reason Revisited.* Harvard University Press.

Rawls' book examines what social contracts are, and he identifies standards that both liberal and non-liberal societies should consider in how they set policies, practices, and interactions with each other. What should be the law of the people is explored from different vantage points. Political and economic conditions influence perceptions of morality and the rights of individuals.

Rowling, J. K. 2015. *Harry Potter and the Order of the Phoenix.* Bloomsbury Publishing.

The Harry Potter books have become popularized around the world and have become beloved for their presentation of youth activism and agency. Young people attempt to protect the world from harms unseen by the general public, as those in power seek to oppress them and the goodness of magic in the world. The Order of the Phoenix has been identified to be a veiled discussion of terrorism and the importance of fighting for human rights.

Serres, Alain, and Fronty, Aurelia. 2023. *I Have a Right to Be a Child.* Groundwood Books.

This is a beautiful picture book about what human rights are that is written for a younger audience but one that can be appreciated by older ones as well. It shows what the basic rights are that all children everywhere have in a readable and positive way. The book embraces the idea that "I have a right to be a child" is important to a child's social, emotional, physical, and personal development.

Snyder, Timothy. 2021. *On Tyranny.* Ten Speed Graphic.

Snyder's book, *On Tyranny*, has been a *New York Times* best seller in its examination of the history of tyranny and its re-emergence in contemporary society. He has a narrative version and a graphic version; the graphic version is an enticing read that makes a very heavy topic more understandable and enjoyable to digest. Snyder points out how the founding fathers of the United States tried to put into place safeguards to protect the nation from tyranny. However, he notes that just as Europeans saw democracy fall to fascism and Nazism, societies today are at that same kind of risk, perhaps oblivious to the danger and threats of totalitarianism that confront contemporary society today.

Ung, Loung. 2005. *Lucky Child: A Daughter of Cambodia Reunites with the Sister She Left Behind.* Harper Perennial.

This book documents Loung's recollections of fleeing the Khmer Rouge regime in Cambodia to her new life in the United States. The theme of family bond is shown through the focus on Loung's efforts to reunite with her sister from whom she was separated from during the chaos of the Cambodian genocide. Loung's story displays the complexities of survivor's guilt, determination, resiliency, love, and hope.

United Nations. 2015.*The Universal Declaration of Human Rights.* Aegitas

The UDHR was established in 1948 with the support of Eleanor Roosevelt. It is the major human rights treaty in the world that has been the foundation for the creation of other United Nations human rights treaties. This book gives an overview of the treaty and details of what it contains and why it is important.

Vissing, Y. 2023. *Children's Human Rights in the USA: Challenges and Opportunities.* Springer.

This 700+ page book provides an overview of what children's rights are and why they are important. While it has a decidedly United States focus, as the US is the only UN nation not to ratify the CRC, it contains foundational and theoretical information that is relevant to the study of child rights everywhere in the world. The book examines issues of provision (education, healthcare, food, housing, etc.), protection (from violence and all forms of abuse), and children's right for participation. It views children as a minority group that is entitled to the same rights as any other minority group. It argues that changing the narrative of children away from a property or object perspective to having agency as a human rights holder will be in the best interests of the child.

Wiesel, Elie. 1956. *Night.* Les Éditions de Minuit.

This book follows Wiesel's experiences as a teenager during the Holocaust, particularly his time in Nazi concentration camps, including Auschwitz and Buchenwald. Wiesel documented the horrors committed by Nazis and its impact on his faith, outlook on humanity, and his identity. In his suffering Wiesel grapples with questions about God and the world while finding moments of hope and resilience.

Yousafza, Malala. 2013. *I Am Malala.* Little, Brown and Company.

This book provides Yousafza's personal account of growing up as a girl in Pakistan. She reveals how restriction on girls' education, enforced by the Taliban, inspired her to advocate for women's rights. She details how her activism for girls' education led to her being shot by the Taliban and her remarkable recovery in which she continued her advocacy.

Journals

Childhood

The journal publishes theoretical and empirical articles, reviews, and scholarly comments on children's social relations and culture from international authors. The journal covers a variety of children's human rights issues, such as child poverty, nutrition, mental health, education, and child labor.

Health and Human Rights

The journal is dedicated to analyzing connections between human rights and health outcomes worldwide. The mission of the journal is to amplify voices of marginalized communities, challenge systemic injustices, and advocate for policy change and promote the right to health for all individuals.

Human Rights Education Review

The journal provides a platform for discussion on research and scholarship on human rights and diversity in education. The target audience of the journal are scholars, students, policy-makers, and human rights educators. In 2021 the journal won the first Amnesty International's UCCHRE *Human Rights in Higher Education Award* for contributions to human rights education worldwide.

Human Rights Law Review

Launched in 2001, this journal promotes awareness and knowledge of human rights through publishing governmental, and non-governmental spheres, concerned with law, policy, and fieldwork.

Human Rights Review

This journal provides a theoretical and philosophical perspective of human rights to be explored. The journal welcomes submissions across areas of study including diverse methodologies, case studies, quantitative analysis, legal scholarship, and philosophical discourse. The aim of the journal is to create social change through dialogue that advances the understanding and protection of human rights.

International Human Rights Law Review

The review is published bi-annually with the target audience of academics, students, government officials, human rights practitioners, and lawyers. The journal aims to provide a platform to human rights scholars, practitioners, and activists in the field to express their experiences in the field or discuss cases and practices that are generally inaccessible to European and North American audiences.

International Journal of Children's Rights

The journal centers on publishing articles documenting leadership and practical policy development regarding children's rights and development during childhood. The journal gathers work from all disciplines, including political theory, psychology, psychiatry, educational theory, sociology, social work, health, social anthropology, economics, theology, and history.

International Journal of Human Rights

This is an international journal publishing material addressing a variety of human rights issues, including human rights and the law, race, religion, gender, children, class, refugees, and immigration. This journal also provides articles and reports regarding genocide, torture, capital punishment, and the laws of war and war crimes.

International Journal of Human Rights Education

This journal presents an examination of theory, philosophy, and research that are central to the field of human rights education. The journal covers a wide variety of topics, including empowering youth, diversity, equity, and inclusion, and integrating human rights into education.

Journal of Human Rights Practice

This is an online-only academic journal that highlights the activism and practice of human rights. The journal addresses the issues relating to activism, the barriers to achieving it, social impacts, and political effects. The journal is intended to be useful for professional practice and across geographical boundaries. The journal welcomes feedback, reflection, and analysis from its readers to promote discussion and ensure the active application of human rights issues internationally. The journal's aim is to advance research, gather documentation, and investigate methodologies and ethics of human rights.

Journal of Human Rights and Social Work

The journal combines human rights in practice, research, policy, and advocacy from around the world from the fields of psychology, sociology, social policy, social welfare, and social development. The journal addresses topics such as LGBTQ+ rights, refugee rights, disability rights, and human trafficking. The journal is intended to be a resource for educators, practitioners, and administrators in the field of social work.

Articles

Abreu, R. L., Sostre, J. P., Gonzalez, K. A., Matsuno, E., and Mosley, D. V. (2022, March 24). Impact of Gender-Affirming Care Bans on Transgender and Gender Diverse Youth: Parental Figures' Perspective. *Journal of Family Psychology*. doi: 10.1037/fam0000987.

This article explores human rights issues pertaining to gender affirming care bans on transgender and gender diverse youth. The article documents and investigates gender affirming care bans against hormone replacement therapy, gender affirmation surgeries, and puberty blockers. The article exposes the systematic nature of transphobia across economic, political, and social spheres. The study utilized an open response online survey completed by 134 parental figures of transgender and gender diverse youth. The results of the study identified six themes as a result of gender affirming care bans: depression and suicidal ideation, anxiety, increased gender dysphoria, decreased safety, increased stigma, and lack of access to medical care. Parents provided insight that gender affirming care bans result in criminalizing transgender and gender diverse youth, medical professionals, and parents who support gender affirming care.

Alonso, E. B., Cockx, L., and Swinnen, J. (2018, March 23). Culture and Food Security *Global Food Security*, 17: 113-127. https://www.sciencedirect.com/science/article/pii/S2211912417300676?casa_token=6h6noShmO00AAAAA%3AmnSb1mAshd_pmw-os6ImNl5W5xLh3Rdtq4Vj6JkSGqLF9x83qc1nBdKfuTeTZDS9rGXJJy7TdQ.

This article discusses the relationship of food and culture as a human rights issue. Access to food is essential in people's ability to participate in their culture by sharing meals, creating cultural dishes, and honoring traditions. The article explores how past interventions to increase access to food failed due to the lack of consideration of culture. The foundation of food security includes the availability, access, utilization, and stability of food. This foundation encompasses the ability of people to travel to food sources, purchase food, prepare food, and the likelihood of food being available in the future. Considering culture is critical in ensuring that these foundations of food security are adequately fulfilled.

Baez, Narciso Leandro Xavier, and Mezzaroba, Orides. (2012). Fundamental Human Rights and Controversial Cultural Practices: A New Reading of the Concept of Human Dignity. *Filosofia Unisinos*, 13 (1): 2-14. doi: 10.4013/fsu.2012.131.01.

This article proposes benefits of examining human rights through the concept of human dignity developed by Immanuel Kant. Two views of human rights exist: one is opposed to the universality of rights, while the other advocates for the unconditional support of rights in all cultures. The authors argue that a compromise between these two views can occur. Using Kant's framework of understanding human rights, it is possible to maintain human dignity while protecting people against their objectification or demeaning them as rights holders. This philosophical article explores the moral peculiarities of culture and how to move past the objectification of individuals so their dignity as rights holders can be respected.

Erdman, J., and Cook, R. (2020). Decriminalization of Abortion: A Human Rights Imperative. *Best Practice & Research Clinical Obstetrics and Gynaecology*, 62: 1-24. https://www.sciencedirect.com/science/article/pii/S1521693419300471?casa_token=haXQwINnAOIAAAAA:b6UCyMzCugEq6YTO25-iRVjY0ucT8lZHulmSlEXC0who4U4hwmXAsN9bmyA-KQPZmeOiysMVhg.

This article discusses the importance of decriminalizing abortion as a fundamental human rights issue. The authors articulate the public safety risk and human rights violation that banning abortion causes. A history is provided about the protection of abortion rights, criminalization of abortion, legislation for and against abortion, and calls to action to policy makers. The World Health Organization incorporated safe abortion practices for healthcare providers and policy makers to improve the health and lives of people. Statistics of abortion laws are reported globally and compared to other nations.

Sobantu, M., Zulu, N., and Maphosa, N. (2019). Housing as a Basic Human Right: A Reflection on South Africa. *Southern African Journal of Social Work and Social Development*, 31 (1). doi: 10.25159/2415-5829/4177.

This paper discusses how access to housing is a human right in the context of post-apartheid South Africa. The government of South Africa has set forth numerous laws that state affordable housing as a priority. Despite this statement there is a housing gap of 2.1 million, and more than 7 million people have resorted to informal settlements. The writers emphasize how access to housing is a critical aspect for social and economic development. They note how lack of affordable housing harms people in poverty and unhoused people. The paper argues that housing is a human right as it provides safety, stability, and security, which allows people to participate in society.

Treaties, Acts, and Declarations

The Code of Hammurabi

The Code of Hammurabi is a set of laws and regulations inscribed on a stone monument, and it is one of the earliest examples of written legal codes. It was set forth by Babylonian king Hammurabi, who reigned from 1792 to 1750 BCE.

The Code of Hammurabi established standards for commercial interactions and set fines and punishments to meet the requirements of justice. The Code contains harsh punishments and inequalities, particularly in its treatment of women, slaves, and individuals of lower social status, which reflect society's social hierarchy at the time.

The Magna Carta

The Magna Carta was enacted in 1215 during the reign of King John of England. It was written in response to grievances between the king and his barons, who sought to limit the monarch's power and protect their own rights and privileges. The purpose of the Magna Carta was to standardize principles of government, individual rights, and the rule of law.

The Declaration of the Rights of Man and of the Citizen

The Declaration of the Rights of Man and of the Citizen is a document of the French Revolution, adopted by the National Constituent Assembly on August 26, 1789. The key points of the declaration are the guarantee of freedom of speech, religion, and assembly; the right to equality under the law; the right to property as a human right; and the sovereignty of the people as the basis of political authority. It guarantees the rights of individuals accused of crimes, including the presumption of innocence, the right to a fair trial, and protection against arbitrary punishment.

The Universal Declaration of Human Rights

The UDHR was adopted by the United Nations General Assembly on December 10, 1948. It is regarded as the foundation of international human rights law and represents a landmark achievement in the quest for global peace, justice, and dignity for all. The declaration contains thirty articles that cover the rights of all people, ensuring equality across the justice system, healthcare, adequate living conditions, freedom of speech, and freedom of movement. Full details of each article can be read at: https://www.un.org/en/about-us/universal-declaration-of-human-rights

The Civil Rights Act of 1964

The Civil Rights Act of 1964 was enacted on July 2, 1964 by the United States Supreme Court. It outlaws discrimination based on race, color, religion, sex, or national origin. The key features of the act include desegregation, banning of employment discrimination, prohibited discrimination in public accommodations, and prohibited discrimination in programs receiving federal financial assistance.

The Voting Rights Act of 1965

The Voting Rights Act was enacted in 1965 by the United States Congress. The act provided legislation that aimed to overcome legal barriers at the state and local levels that prevented African Americans from exercising their right to vote. Key features of the act include prohibiting any voting practices or procedures that discriminate on the basis of race, color, or language minority status and establishing a formula to identify jurisdictions with a history of voter discrimination. It requires covered jurisdictions to obtain federal approval, or preclearance, before making any changes to their voting laws or procedures, and requires jurisdictions with language minority populations to provide bilingual election materials.

The International Convention on the Elimination of All Forms of Racial Discrimination

The ICERD is a human rights treaty adopted by the United Nations General Assembly in 1965 that enforces an international effort to combat racial discrimination and promote equality and non-discrimination on the basis of race, ethnicity, or national origin. ICERD is one of the core international human rights treaties and is considered a foundational document in the fight against racial discrimination.

The International Covenant on Civil and Political Rights

The ICCPR is a fundamental international human rights treaty adopted by the United Nations General Assembly on December 16, 1966. The Covenant sets forth civil and political rights that are universally recognized, including the right to life, right to liberty and security of person, right to a fair trial, freedom of expression, freedom of assembly and association, and prohibition of discrimination.

The International Covenant on Economic, Social and Cultural Rights

The 1966 International Covenant on Economic, Social and Cultural Rights outlines a comprehensive framework for the protection and promotion of economic, social, and cultural rights, including the rights to work, social security, health, education, adequate standard of living, and cultural rights.

Roe v. Wade

Roe v. Wade is a landmark legal case in the United States that dealt with the constitutionality of laws restricting access to abortion. The case began when Norma McCorvey (aka Jane Roe) filed a lawsuit challenging the state's abortion laws. At the time, under Texas law, abortion was illegal except to save the life of the mother. McCorvey argued that the law violated her constitutional rights, including her right to privacy. On January 22, 1973, the Court upheld that the right to privacy was guaranteed by the Fourteenth Amendment, which includes a woman's right to choose whether to terminate her pregnancy. In 2022, *Roe v. Wade* was overturned by the US The Supreme Court; however, individual states are allowed to assign their own regulations regarding abortion restrictions. Some states in the US have placed bans on abortion entirely, not at all, or based on the trimester of pregnancy. Prior to the ruling being overturned, it was upheld in *Planned Parenthood v. Casey*, *Whole Woman's Health v. Herllerstedt*, and *June Medical Services v. Gee.*

The Declaration on the Elimination of Discrimination Against Women

The Declaration on the Elimination of All Forms of Discrimination against Women (CEDAW) was adopted in 1979 by the UN General Assembly. The declaration provides eleven articles that outline the UN's protection of women's rights. Equal access to education, employment, public office, voting, participation, and control over their bodies are essential. Safety from domestic abuse and freedom from discrimination are part of this declaration.

Convention against Torture and Other Cruel, Inhuman or Degrading Treatment or Punishment

In 1984 the Convention against Torture and Other Cruel, Inhuman or Degrading Treatment or Punishment (CAT) was created so there would be international agreement that torture, cruel, inhuman, and degrading treatment will not be used as a form of punishment against any person, anywhere, of any age, or for any reason.

The Convention on the Rights of the Child

The CRC was adopted by the United Nations General Assembly on November 20, 1989. The CRC is a human rights treaty that sets out the civil, political, economic, social, and cultural rights of children. The CRC is based on the principle that every child, regardless of race, ethnicity, religion, or social status, is entitled to enjoy a full range of human rights and freedoms. It recognizes children as individuals with their own rights and interests, deserving of special protection and care.

International Convention on the Protection of the Rights of All Migrant Workers and Members of Their Families

The 1990 International Convention on the Protection of the Rights of All Migrant Workers and Members of Their Families (ICMW) aims to protect migrant workers and members of their families. It serves as a guide for a moral standard for the treatment of migrant workers and their rights. Migrant issues are a global issue and the ICMW seeks to protect them no matter where they work and live.

International Convention for the Protection of All Persons from Enforced Disappearance

The 2006 ICCPED is an international human rights instrument that is designed to prevent the forced disappearance of individuals, which is defined by the United Nations and international law as one of the crimes against humanity. The disappearance is most commonly found in women, especially those who are of minority designation.

Convention on the Rights of Persons with Disabilities

The 2006 Convention on the Rights of Persons with Disabilities is designed to protect the rights and dignity of individuals with disabilities, and to promote and protect their dignity so they can enjoy the full enjoyment of rights that all people, including people without disabilities.

Online Resources

American Jewish World Service, https://ajws.org

American Jewish World Service (AJWS) is founded on the Jewish value of justice and seeks to promote and protect human rights and end poverty in Africa, Asia, Latin America, and the Caribbean. AJWS addresses issues of sexual health, sexual rights, humanitarian disaster response, climate justice, and civil rights.

Americans for Democracy and Human Rights in Bahrain, https://www.adhrb.org

Americans for Democracy and Human Rights in Bahrain was founded in 2002 for the purpose of awareness of and support for democracy and human rights in Bahrain and the rest of the Middle East and North Africa (MENA) region. The organization creates public awareness of human rights violations in the MENA in the media and government.

Amnesty International, https://www.amnesty.org/en

The mission of Amnesty International is to expose human rights violations, uncover the truth, and use the community of people around the world to create positive change. Amnesty International fights injustices through involvement in a variety of human rights areas, including protecting people involved in torture, gun violence, war crimes, the death penalty, detainment, indigenous people's rights, police brutality, elder's rights, and reproductive rights.

Changemakers, https://www.power-humanrights-education.org/multimedia/changemakers-stories-of-young-human-rights-educators

The Human Rights Council, in support of the fourth phase (2020–4) of the World Programme for Human Rights Education adopted an action plan and filmed young human rights changemakers around the world. These films celebrate the positive contributions that they are making to help others in their communities to promote and protect human rights. It is a multimedia educational tool that is available in Arabic, English, French, and Spanish. This film project builds upon the documentary movie A Path to Dignity: The Power of Human Rights Education, which a series of partners produced with the Office of the High Commissioner for Human Rights.

Child Fund Alliance, https://childfundalliance.org

Child Fund Alliance is a global network of eleven child-focused development organizations that assist 23 million children and their families in seventy countries to work to protect children's rights and to help them to reach their highest potential. They work with community partners to end violence and exploitation against children and to overcome poverty and the underlying conditions that prevent children from having their best lives.

Conflict Dynamics International, https://www.cdint.org

Conflict Dynamics International was founded in 2004 and is an international organization that seeks to address root causes foundational to the creation of conflicts. Its approach to peace and humanitarian action is regarded to be unique and innovative because while it addresses immediate human suffering, its approach is sustainable, neutral, and impartial, and uses dialogue to help create long-term outcomes that will make peace possible. It builds upon the interplay between meeting humanitarian needs, peace, human rights, and international law as essential to creating sustainable human development.

Coordination des Associations et des Particuliers pour la Liberté de Conscience (CAP Freedom of Conscience), https://freedomofconscience.eu

CAP Freedom of Conscience was established in 1995 to protect the right to freedom of beliefs and religion. The organization uses testimonials to raise awareness of violation of religious rights and advocate for religious freedom for any religion or spiritual group.

Equality and Human Rights Commission, https://www.equalityhumanrights.com

The Equality and Human Rights Commission (EHRC) was founded to promote equality and diversity, eliminate unlawful discrimination, and protect and promote the human rights of everyone in Britain. The EHRC is responsible for being a catalyst for change, providing information on laws and rights, promoting legislative protection for human rights, evaluating the effectiveness of laws, and enforcing laws and ensuring compliance to standards of human rights.

Equitas, https://equitas.org

The Equitas organization promotes human rights education not just in Canada but also around the world in their International Training Program in Human Rights. They have a summer training program to teach people how to become human rights defenders, and their website contains many different types of human rights educational materials that are ready to use.

First Focus, https://firstfocus.org

First Focus is a US advocacy organization dedicated to prioritizing children and families in the development of federal policy and budgets. A bipartisan organization, it implements a broad advocacy strategy to bring about policy solutions with real-world impacts for children and families.

Forum Asia, https://forum-asia.org

The Asian Forum for Human Rights and Development was founded in 1991 to strengthen the human rights movement in Asia by empowering civil society and marginalized communities. Forum Asia works across twenty-three countries through research, evidence-based advocacy, and the protection of marginalized communities.

Freedom of the Press Foundation, https://freedom.press

The Freedom of the Press Foundation works to preserve and strengthen First and Fourth Amendment rights in the US. The organization lives out its mission through a platform to exchange services, SecureDrop, digital security training, US freedom tracker, encryption tools, news, and advocacy.

Front Line Defenders, https://www.frontlinedefenders.org/en/who-we-are

Front Line Defenders was founded in Dublin in 2001 with the aim of protecting human rights defenders at risk around the world. Human rights defenders may be in situations where they require rapid and practical support. This organization provides emergency to defenders who are in danger, to train them and others about security and protection strategies, and to network with others to protect human rights defenders at risk.

Hope for Children CRC Policy Center, https://www.uncrcpc.org.cy/en/about-us

This is a group of international scholars who work to advance children's human rights and the CRC. They conduct research, make presentations, and do human rights advocacy to promote children's rights. The Hope for Children organization also provides a series of services to abused children, refugee and immigrant youth, delinquents, and supports to help them to live successful lives.

Human Rights Action Center, https://www.humanrightsactioncenter.com

Human Rights Action Center (HRAC) views access to arts, music, theatre, film, and literature to be key elements that need to be defended in a human rights-oriented society. HRAC works with organizations around the world to support the creative arts, culture, and humanity.

Human Rights Careers, https://www.humanrightscareers.com

Human Rights Careers was founded in 2015. The website is designed to support students, alumni, graduates, and professionals to locate human rights jobs and opportunities.

Human Rights Educators USA, https://hreusa.org

Human Rights Educators (HRE) USA is a network founded on the basic human rights principles of human dignity, equality, and non-discrimination. HRE USA values diversity, inclusiveness, transparency in its mission to learn, teach, organize, advocate, and innovate human rights education in the United States. The organization supports a national movement for human rights education, promoting policies that advance human rights education at national, state, and organizational levels. HRE USA advocates for the inclusion of human rights education in national and state education standards, curricula, and pedagogy, and teacher training.

Human Rights Campaign, https://www.hrc.org

The Human Rights Campaign (HRC) strives to protect the rights of LGBTQ+ individuals. HRC has gained power in political spheres through grassroots movements, volunteers, and petitions. HRC raises awareness about oppressive legislation, government officials promoting discriminatory policies, discrimination, and murders of LGBTQ+ people and the community to action against injustice. HRC organizes ways for people to get involved in their mission of equality through singing petitions, a directory of local events, and fundraising.

Human Rights Foundation, https://hrf.org

The Human Rights Foundation promotes liberal democracy in countries ruled by authoritarian regimes and by supporting activists and providing them with the resources, skills, contacts, and attention they need to make a difference in their countries. It holds that liberal democratic values are best expressed through the rights outlined in the ICCPR.

Human Rights Measurement Initiative, https://rightstracker.org

This is a fascinating data tool that allows for searchers to go into specific countries and regions to identify what their position is on human rights and how they compare with other areas.

Human Rights Now, https://hrn.or.jp/eng

Human Rights Now is an international human rights non-government organization that is based in Tokyo, Japan, and has a special consultative status with the UN. Founded in 2006, it was the first human rights nongovernment organization in Japan. Today is has over 700 members that include lawyers, social service providers, scholars, and journalists.

Human Rights Watch, https://www.hrw.org

Human Rights Watch investigates and reports about human rights violations around the world. The documentation of abuses and exposure of abuses is critical to the goal of creating change. The advocacy work done by Human Rights Watch is focused toward governments, armed groups, and businesses, pushing them to change or enforce their laws, policies, and practices.

Human Rights Watch Student Task Force, https://www.hrwstf.org/wordpress

The Human Rights Watch Student Task Force is a special unit within the Human Rights Watch organization. It is based in California and works with high school and college students to promote educational and advocacy endeavors that will support the dissemination of human rights. It works on regional issues such as challenges that face farm workers, climate change, education, and juvenile justice. Its work has inspired other youth focused human rights groups as well.

Humanity in Action, https://www.humanityinaction.org

Humanity in Action is an international organization that reports having over 3,000 members around the world who are fighting for social justice. It is a non-partisan, nongovernment organization. Their goal is to increase understanding about the crises that face democratic societies and to promote respect for diverse peoples.

International Federation for Human Rights, https://www.fidh.org/en

The International Federation for Human Rights (FIDH) is an international human rights nongovernmment organization with 188 partner organizations from 116 countries. Founded in 1922, FIDH defends civil, political, economic, social, and cultural rights as set out in the UDHR.

International Society for Human Rights, https://ishr.org

The International Society for Human Rights and its national branches are independent non-governmental human rights organizations that base their work on the UDHR to promote international understanding and tolerance in all areas of culture and society. It is independent of all political parties, governments, or religious groups and believes that improvement of social conditions must be obtained through human rights and cannot be pursued through use of force or violence. It supports human rights education, humanitarian aid, and people who are persecuted, imprisoned, and/or discriminated against because of their affiliations.

Journalists for Human Rights, https://jhr.ca/about

Journalists for Human Rights works to educate, train, and engage local journalists and organizations to encourage coverage of human rights news in local contexts. The mission of Journalists for Human Rights is to promote objective media and empower local voices.

KidsRights, https://www.kidsrights.org

This international nongovernment organization views children as changemakers who have ideas that deserve to be listened to. KidsRights works with young people to create a world in which their rights are guaranteed. It seeks to empower children to realize their great potential through providing them greater opportunities for social action.

Leading for Kids, https://www.leadingforkids.org

This organization, started by pediatrician David Alexander, focuses on how to work with organizations to support the wellbeing of children in every aspect of their life. It provides tools for working with organizations, assessment tools, educational resources, and networking information.

Learning for Justice, https://www.learningforjustice.org

Learning for Justice, founded as Teaching Tolerance in 1991, supports the mission of the Southern Poverty Law Center to be a catalyst for racial justice and advance the human rights of all people. It provides free educational resources that include articles, guides, lessons, webinars, conferences, and workshops to help communities engage in positive and just relationships.

Muhammad Ali Center, https://alicenter.org

Boxer Muhammad Ali was a human rights advocate and his center revolves around six core principles: believing in oneself, one's ability and one's future; the conviction to stand behind that belief; to devote oneself to betterment; to give without expecting something in return; to respect the worth of oneself and others; and to have a sense of awe, reverence, and peace in our connection with all of creation. The Center's "Creating Our Future" curriculum consists of six modules, each focusing on a single core principle embodied in the life and work of Muhammad Ali, inspiring the development of a "life plan" that reflects a positive sense of self, a commitment to community, and preparation for the future.

Odhikar, https://odhikar.org

Odhikar, established in 1994, is a human rights organization in Bangladesh. The purpose of the organization is to raise awareness of human rights violations and enact change through training human rights defenders across Bangladesh.

Oxford Human Rights Hub, https://ohrh.law.ox.ac.uk

The Oxford Human Rights Hub provides a platform for academics, practitioners, and policymakers from across the globe to collaborate and advance the understanding and protection of human rights and equality around the world. The Oxford Human Rights Hub uses videos, podcasts, blog posts, and a journal to expand research tools for students, teachers, academics, and advocates of human rights both in Oxford and beyond.

Rights.com, https://www.rightscon.org

Rights.com is an international conference that explores human rights in the digital world, with an expansive set of free and fascinating set of workshops. It has a decidedly youth, creative, and innovative focus.

Robert Kennedy Center for Justice and Human Rights, https://rfkhumanrights.org

The Robert Kennedy Center seeks to expose injustice, educate others about the importance of human rights, and encourage civic engagement and activism that will promote democracy and justice for all. It has a set of programs, resources, networks, and awards.

Southern Poverty Law Center, https://www.splcenter.org

The SPLC is a nonprofit organization that monitors and exposes hate groups and advocates for civil rights and social justice. The website provides a series of education resources and is cutting-edge in its advocacy for marginalized individuals.

***The Guardian*, https://www.theguardian.com/us**

The Guardian uses investigative journalism to report on American and international news. *The Guardian* is proud of its independent ownership to ensure freedom from political and commercial influence.

United Nations High Commissioner for Human Rights, https://www.ohchr.org/en/ohchr_homepage

The United Nations High Commissioner for Human Rights has a responsibility to promote and protect all human rights, empower people, assist governments to prevent abuses, and ensure a human rights perspective in all United Nations Programs.

United Nations International Children's Emergency Fund, https://www.unicef.org

UNICEF was established in 1946 in the aftermath of World War II. UNICEF is dedicated to serving children everywhere through emergency services intervention, research, innovative technology, social policy, education, child survival, and child protection. UNICEF serves over 190 countries and territories; it is the world's largest provider of vaccines, and it supports child health and nutrition, safe water and sanitation, quality education, and HIV prevention and treatment for mothers and babies.

University of Alabama Birmingham Institute for Human Rights Blog, https://sites.uab.edu/humanrights

The mission of University of Alabama Human Rights Blog is to support the global human rights movement by creating innovative educational programs, research initiatives, and outreach solutions. The blog allows for collaboration of scholars, educators, students, practitioners to discuss advocacy, educate others, raise awareness, and design plans of action to support human rights.

Voice of Salam, https://voiceofsalam.com

Voice of Salam (Peace) was founded in 2015 for the purpose of raising awareness of global infractions against human rights. Voice of Salam is dedicated to exposing injustice, protecting human rights, and understanding interfaith, social, and cultural issues.

Videos

UNICEF, https://www.unicef.ca/en/teachers/article/global-classroom-videos

The Universal Declaration of Human Rights, https://www.youtube.com/watch?v=5RR4VXNX3jA

What Are the Universal Human Rights Ted Talk, https://www.youtube.com/watch?v=nDgIVseTkuE

Eleanor Roosevelt Speech on Human Rights, https://www.youtube.com/watch?v=sPVWmmVKVk0
Kofi Annan: The Courage to Change, https://youtu.be/t8__8wxUVKQ
The History of Basic Human Rights, https://youtu.be/6XXGF_V8_7M
Open Society Video on the International Human Rights Movement, https://www.youtube.com/watch?v=IhUnj1sAwLI
The Story of Human Rights, https://www.youtube.com/watch?v=6XXGF_V8_7M&t=322s
Shami Chakrabarti: Human Rights in the 21st Century Ted Talk, https://www.youtube.com/watch?v=21hYFWDGdhI
Andora Svitak, What Adults Can Learn from Young People, https://www.youtube.com/watch?v=V-bjOJzB7LY

TRANS RIGHTS
PROTECT TRANS LIVES
LET TRANS KIDS THRIVE
LOVE
Brunswick

7

Chronology

Human rights have existed as an important underlying foundation for human relationships since before the Common Era. This timeline provides details about persons and events that have contributed to the evolution of human rights around the world.

1754 BCE: The Code of Hammurabi is written by Hammurabi, the sixth king of the first dynasty of Babylon. It is a lengthy, well-organized legal text that addresses fair treatment, protection of property rights, and principles of justice.

1440 BCE: The Torah of Moses is created, giving the tribes of Israel the ten commandments, including "Thou shalt not kill."

539 BCE: The armies of Cyrus the Great, the first king of ancient Persia, conquer the city of Babylon. The Cyrus Cylinder chronicles the fair treatment of peoples who are conquered and is considered the world's first charter of human rights.

528 BCE–486 BCE: In India, a prince named Gautama Buddha advocates morality, reverence for life, non-violence, and right conduct. His premises become the foundation for Buddhism.

500 BCE: Chinese scholar Confucius puts forward teaching based on "jen," or benevolence and respect for other people, which becomes the basis for Confucianism.

Supporters march during Transgender Day of Visibility in Melbourne, Australia, 2023. Human rights movements around the world attempt to address the problem of discrimination based on gender identity and sexual orientation. (Matt Hrkac via Flickr, Creative Commons license CC-BY-2.0)

27 BCE–476 CE: Concepts of natural law and the rights of citizens are promoted in the Roman Empire.

26–33 CE: In Palestine, Jesus Christ preaches morality, tolerance, justice, forgiveness and love, which becomes the basis for Christianity.

613–632: In Saudi Arabia, Prophet Mohammed teaches the principles of equality, justice, and compassion revealed in the Qur'ān, which becomes central to the founding of the Muslim faith.

930: The Althing is founded in Iceland, the oldest parliamentary institution in the world.

1215: The Magna Carta document is created in England. It acknowledges that free men are entitled to judgment by their peers and that even a King is not above the law.

1583–1645: Hugo Grotius, a Dutch jurist credited with the birth of international law, promotes the idea that there is a brotherhood of humankind and that all people need to be treated fairly.

1628: The English Petition of Right is created, a document that identifies protections of individuals against the state, including no taxation without the consent of Parliament, no imprisonment without cause, no quartering of soldiers on subjects, and no martial law in peacetime.

1679: The Habeas Corpus Act is created. It ensures the right for individuals to have a fair trial.

1689: In England, Parliament adopts the Bill of Rights, which curtails the power of the monarch and includes freedom from torture and from punishment without trial.

1690: John Locke develops the idea of natural rights in Second Treatise of Government.

1776: In the newly formed United States, a Declaration of Independence is created by a group of leaders, which proclaims that "all men are created equal" and endowed with certain inalienable rights.

1787: The United States Constitution is signed.

1789: In France the National Assembly adopts the Declaration of the Rights of Man and of the Citizen, which guarantees the rights to liberty, equality, property, security, and resistance to oppression.

1790: The United States Naturalization Act of 1790 bans Native Americans, African Americans, Asian Americans, indentured servants, slaves, and women from becoming citizens.

1791: The United States Congress adopts its Bill of Rights, amending the US Constitution to include rights to trial by jury and freedoms of expression, speech, belief, and assembly.

1815: Slave revolts take place in Latin America and in France.

1833: The British Parliament abolishes slavery through the Slavery Abolition Act.

1840: In Ireland the Chartist Movement demands universal suffrage and rights for workers and poor people.

1847: Liberian Declaration of Independence from the American Colonization Society is adopted and signed.

1859: In Italy the Battle of Solferino inspires Henry Dunant to mobilize volunteers to help provide medical care to soldiers and those in need.

1862: The Anti-Coolie Act imposes a tax on Asian Americans who attempt to work in manufacturing factories and employers who hire Asian Americans.

1863 The work of Henry Dunant leads to the creation of the International Committee of the Red Cross.

1863–9: Over 10,000 Chinese laborers work to complete the US transcontinental railroad.

1864: The first Geneva Convention establishes rules for the protection of people wounded and sick in armed conflicts. It was initiated by Henry Dunant and the International Committee of the Red Cross.

1868: A Gun Control Act regulates imported guns, expands the gun-dealer licensing and record-keeping requirements, and places specific limitations on the sale of handguns in the United States.

1870: The Naturalization Act of 1870 allows naturalized citizenship for African Americans while denying naturalization to any other non-white person.

1871: The National Rifle Association is assembled in the United States.

1875: The Page Act of 1875 makes it illegal to transfer people from China into the United States.

1878: Individuals from Asia are ineligible for naturalized citizenship according to the Ah Yup rules.

1879: The California Constitution of 1879 forbids employers from hiring Chinese immigrants.

1882: The Chinese Exclusion Act of 1882 law bans immigration of Chinese laborers.

1885: The Rocks Spring Massacre takes place in Wyoming, when white miners attack Chinese miners, set fire to their homes, and kill twenty-eight people.

1885: The Tacoma (Washington) Riots take place; white businessmen, police, and political leaders descend upon the city's Chinese community, violently expel them, and burn down Chinatown.

1889: The Treaty of Paris ends the Spanish-American War.

1893: New Zealand is the first country in the world to give women the right to vote.

1897: First Zionist Congress takes place in Basel, Switzerland, and the first Zionist organization is founded.

1899: The first Hague Convention is signed, which forms the basis for International Humanitarian Law.

1918: The Representation of the People Act gives women in the United Kingdom over age thirty the right to vote.

1919: One of the most important treaties of World War I, the Treaty of Versailles is signed and ends the state of war between Germany and most of the Allied Powers.

1919: The International Labor Organization is established as part of the Versailles Peace Treaty to improve working conditions and promote social justice.

1920: The 19th Amendment to the Constitution is established, allowing women in the United States the right to vote.

1923: In *United States v. Bhagat Singh Thind*, the US Supreme Court rules that Indians are ineligible for US citizenship.

1924: The Johnson Reed Act limits the number of immigrants allowed entry into the United States through a national origins quota system.

1924: US Congress approves the Snyder Act, granting all Native Americans full citizenship.

1926: The Geneva Conference adopts the Slavery Convention.

1933: The League of Nations adopts the International Convention for the Suppression of the Traffic in Women of Full Age.

1936-1939: A Palestinian rebellion occurs against the British Mandate and Jewish immigration.

1938: A Fair Labor Standards Act establishes a minimum wage and working conditions for people in the United States.

1939: The United Kingdom issues a White Paper document that limits Jewish immigration.

1941: President Franklin Delano Roosevelt's State of the Union Address introduces a model of global human rights based on four essential freedoms: freedom of speech and religion and freedom from want and fear.

1942: The US government interns over 120,000 Japanese-Americans during the Second World War.

1942: US Zionists meet in New York and adopt the "Biltmore Programme," which calls for establishment of Palestine as a Jewish Commonwealth and for unlimited immigration.

1942–5: President Franklin Roosevelt issues executive Order 9066 authorizing the evacuation of all persons deemed a threat to national security from the West Coast to relocation centers.

1945: End of World War II and of the Holocaust.

1945: The United Nations is created. The United Nations Charter sets forth the organization's goals, functions, and responsibilities.

1947: The UN General Assembly passes Resolution 181, which calls for Palestinian territories to be divided into two states, one Jewish and one Arab.

1948: The Universal Declaration of Human Rights is adopted by the United Nations.

1948: The Convention on the Prevention and Punishment of the Crime of Genocide is adopted by the United Nations.

1948: Israel declares independence.

1948: The United Nations General Assembly passes Resolution 194, calling for the repatriation of Palestinian refugees.

1948: President Harry Truman issues Executive Order 9981 to end segregation in the Armed Services.

1950–3: The Korean War occurs.

1950: The European Convention on Human Rights is adopted by the Council of Europe.

1951: The Convention Relating to the Status of Refugees protects the rights of people who are forced to flee their home for fear of persecution on specific grounds.

1954: Following *Brown v. Board of Education*, the US Supreme Court makes segregation illegal in public schools.

1954: The Convention Relating to Stateless Persons is created.

1954–75: The Vietnam War occurs.

1955: Emmett Till, a fourteen-year-old from Chicago, is brutally murdered in Mississippi for allegedly flirting with a white woman.

1955: Rosa Parks refuses to give up her bus seat to a white man, which begins the Montgomery bus boycott.

1956: Convention on the Abolition of Slavery, the Slave Trade, and Institutions and Practices of Slavery.

1957: Convention on the Abolition of Forced Labour.

1957: US President Dwight Eisenhower signs the Civil Rights Act of 1957 into law to protect voter rights.

1959: The Declaration of the Right of the Child is created.

1960: African Americans Joseph McNeil, Ezell Blair, Franklin McCain, and David Richmond refuse to leave a Woolworth's "whites only" lunch counter without being served.

1960: Ruby Bridges becomes the first Black student to integrate into William Frantz Elementary School in New Orleans.

1960: Seventeen Sub-Saharan African nations regain their independence from their former European colonists in what is known as the "Year of Africa."

1960: Sirimavo Bandaranaike of Sri Lanka becomes the first woman in the world to be elected head of government.

1960: The US Discrimination Employment and Occupational Convention prohibits discrimination at work on many grounds, including race, sex, religion, political opinion, and social origin.

1961: US President John Kennedy signs an executive order establishing the Peace Corps.

1961: Amnesty International is created, as a result of a campaign to free two Portuguese students imprisoned for seven years for making a toast to freedom.

1963: US civil rights leader, the Reverend Martin Luther King Jr., delivers his "I Have a Dream" speech.

1963: Declaration on the Elimination of All Forms of Racial Discrimination is enacted.

1964: The Civil Rights Act of 1964 ends lawful segregation in the United States.

1964: US President Lyndon B. Johnson signs the Civil Rights Act of 1964 into law, preventing employment discrimination due to race, color, sex, religion, or national origin.

1964: The Palestine Liberation Organization is founded in Cairo.

1965: The Voting Rights Act of 1965 in the United States outlaws voter discrimination on the basis of race.

1965: The International Convention on the Elimination of All Forms of Racial Discrimination obliges states to take steps to prohibit racial discrimination and promote understanding among all races.

1965: Southern US states adopt "Black codes" that forbid Black persons from possessing firearms.

1965: Malcolm X is assassinated during a rally by members of the Nation of Islam.

1965: US President Lyndon Johnson signs the Voting Rights Act of 1965 to prevent the use of literacy tests as a voting requirement.

1966: The International Covenant on Economic, Social and Cultural Rights protects rights like the right to an adequate standard of living, education, work, healthcare, and social security.

1966: The ICCPR includes the right to vote, the right to freedom of association, the right to a fair trial, right to privacy, and the right to freedom of religion.

1966: The First Optional Protocol to the ICCPR creates a mechanism for individuals to make complaints about breaches of their rights. The Second Optional Protocol concerns abolition of the death penalty.

1966: In San Francisco, the Compton's Cafeteria riot takes place in response to violent and constant harassment of drag queens and transgender people.

1967: Declaration of the Elimination of Discrimination Against Women is enacted.

1967: Proclamation of the Tehran International conference on human rights.

1967: The Six-Day War breaks out between Israel and its Arab neighbors.

1967: The United Nations Security Council Resolution Calls for Israeli Withdrawal of Palestinian lands.

1968: Martin Luther King Jr. is assassinated.

1968: The Convention on the Non-Applicability of Statutory Limitations to War Crimes Against Humanity takes place in New York.

1969: The Stonewall Riots targeting LGBTQIA+ individuals take place in New York.

1969: The International Convention on the Elimination of All Forms of Racial Discrimination is drafted.

1969: The American Convention on Human Rights for the Americas is held.

1970: First gay pride parades takes place on the one-year anniversary of the Stonewall Riots.

1971: The Declaration of the Rights of the Elderly is established.

1971: Declaration of the Mentally Retarded Persons is enacted.

1971: Doctors Without Borders is founded in France.

1972: Sweden is the first country that allows transgender individuals to legally change their gender.

1972: In the United States, Title IX is enacted as part of the Education Amendments of 1972: to prohibit discrimination against students on the basis of sex/gender in federally funded education programs and activities.

1973: *Roe v. Wade* gives American women the right to have an abortion.

1973: International Convention on the Suppression and Punishment of the Crime of Apartheid is held in New York.

1973: The Yom Kippur War ensues when Egypt and Syria attempt to retake the Israeli-occupied Sinai Peninsula and Golan Heights.

1975: Declaration on the Rights of Disabled Persons protects all persons from being subjected to torture and other cruel inhuman or degrading treatment or punishment.

1976: The Soweto uprising takes place and represents the turning point in the liberation struggle in South Africa.

1978: A United Nations Convention concerning the rights of migrants and the promotion of equality of opportunity and treatment of migrant workers is held.

1979: The Convention of the Elimination of All forms of Discrimination against Women is created to ensure that states must take steps to eliminate discrimination against women and to ensure that women enjoy human rights to the same degree as men in a range of areas, including education, employment, healthcare, and family life.

1979: Israel withdraws from the Sinai Peninsula.

1980: The Refugee Act of 1980 is signed into law by US President Jimmy Carter. It provides a clear national policy for regulating asylum for refugees.

1981: The African Charter on Human and Peoples' Rights is created.

1981: Declaration on the Elimination of All Intolerance and Discrimination Based on Religion or Belief is enacted.

1984: The Convention against Torture and Other Cruel, Inhuman or other Degrading Treatment of Punishment aims to prevent torture around the world. It requires states to take steps to eliminate torture within their borders.

1984: The Convention Against Torture and Other Cruel, Inhuman or Degrading Treatment or Punishment is held.

1985: The first memorial to the Nazis' gay victims is unveiled at the Neuengamme concentration camp, a pink granite stone monument inscribed, "Dedicated to the Homosexual victims of National Socialism."

1985: The Committee on Economic, Social and Cultural Rights is established to monitor international convention on economic, social, and cultural rights.

1986: The Declaration on the Right to Development is created.

1987: ACT UP is founded in the LGBT Community Center in New York City to bring attention to AIDS-related issues using civil disobedience.

1987: The First Intifada is incited when an Israeli driver kills four Palestinians in a car accident.

1988: The Civil Liberties Act is signed by US President Ronald Reagan to compensate former internees of Japanese internment camps with $20,000 each.

1989: The CRC is created to outline the human rights protections to which all children are entitled.

1989: The International Labour Organisation Indigenous and Tribal People Convention (No. 169) aims to protect the rights of Indigenous and tribal peoples around the world.

1989: The Second Optional Protocol to the ICCPR, aimed at the abolition of the death penalty, is constructed.

1989: Denmark becomes the first country to legally recognize same-sex unions.

1990: The International Convention on the Protection of the Rights of All Migrant Workers and Members of Their Families is created to ensure that migrant workers enjoy full protection of their human rights, regardless of their legal status.

1990: The Cairo Declaration of Human Rights in Islam is produced.

1990: The Basic Principles for the Treatment of Prisoners is established.

1991: The Madrid Peace Conference begins.

1992: The United Nations Conference on Environment and Development is held.

1992: The Declaration on the Protection of All Persons from Enforced Disappearances is adopted.

1993: The Declaration on the Elimination of Violence against Women is issued by the UN General Assembly.

1994: Apartheid ends in South Africa.

1994: The Declaration of the Arab Charter on Human Rights is created.

1994: The Israelis and the Palestinians sign the Gaza-Jericho Agreement, which begins implementation of the Oslo Accords.

1994: Israel and Jordan sign a peace treaty, settling their territorial dispute and agreeing to future cooperation in sectors such as trade and tourism.

1995: World Conference on Women's Rights is held in Beijing.

1998: The United Nations adopts the International Criminal Court Statute that states that individuals can be tried on four charges: genocide, crimes against humanity, war crimes, and crimes of aggression.

1999: The Columbine High School in Colorado is the site of a mass shooting.

2001: The World Conference Against Racism, Xenophobia and All Forms of Discrimination is held in Durban, South Africa.

2001: Four coordinated terrorist attacks are carried out by al-Qaeda in the United States.

2002: The New York Human Rights Law expands the definition of "gender" to include protections for transgender and gender non-conforming people in employment, housing, and public accommodations.

2002: A terrorist attack kills thirty people at a Passover celebration at a hotel in the Israeli city of Netanya.

2002: Israel begins building a security barrier in the West Bank to protect Israeli cities and towns from terrorist attacks.

2004: Massachusetts becomes the first US state to legally recognize same-sex marriage.

2004: The Arab League adopts the Arab Charter on Human Rights, which defends the right of national self-determination and the "sovereignty of the law and its contribution to the protection of universal and interrelated human rights."

2006: The Convention on the Rights of Persons with Disabilities is created to promote, protect, and ensure the full and equal enjoyment of all human rights by persons with disabilities including the right to health, education, employment, accessibility, and non-discrimination.

2007: The Declaration on the Rights of Indigenous Peoples is adopted by the United Nations. The declaration addresses the human rights of Indigenous Peoples around the globe.

2007: The Rights of Person with Disabilities treaty requires a sufficient standard of living, social protection, and eliminating discriminations dealing with marriage, family, and personal relations for disabled people.

2007: Israel imposes a blockade on the Gaza Strip after an armed takeover of Gaza by Hamas.

2007: Hamas occupies the Gaza Strip.

2008: Israel broadens its sanctions and completely seals off the Gaza Strip.

2008: The OIC established its Independent Permanent Human Rights Commission with the goal of promoting human rights in member states and upholding the fundamental freedoms for all people without distinction as to race, sex, or religion.

2009: President Barack Obama signs the Matthew Shepard and James Byrd, Jr. Hate Crimes and Prevention Act, which expands the 1969: U.S. federal hate-crime law to include crimes motivated by a victim's actual or perceived sexual orientation, gender identity, or disability, and it becomes the first federal law to include legal protections for transgender people.

2011: The "Don't Ask, Don't Tell" policy is repealed in the US military. Its repeal does not lift regulations barring transgender people from serving.

2012: The Sandy Hook Elementary School shooting occurs in Connecticut.

2012: In November, Israel launches "Pillar of Defense" an eight-day military operation against the Gaza Strip.

2013: The United States federally recognizes same-sex marriages, extending federal benefits to couples in states that allow same-sex marriage.

2013: Alicia Garza, Patrisse Cullors, and Opal Tometi create the Black Lives Matter movement.

2014: The Department of Education states that transgender students are protected from discrimination under Title IX.

2015: The US Department of Health and Human Services issues an official revision that shortens the deferral period for blood donation from men who have sex with men.

2015: The Supreme Court rules that states are constitutionally required to issue marriage licenses to same-sex couples, legalizing marriage equality in all fifty states.

2016: Pulse Nightclub Shooting occurs in Florida targeting gay individuals.

2016: US President Obama again calls on Congress to enact or renew a law prohibiting the sale and possession of assault-style weapons and high-capacity ammunition magazines.

2017: US President Donald Trump announces that the United States will recognize Jerusalem as the capital of Israel.

2017: US President Donald Trump signs an executive order that discriminates against Muslims and bans refugees.

2017: US President Donald Trump signs a revised executive order restricting travel to the United States by citizens of Iran, Libya, Somalia, Sudan, Syria, and Yemen and drastically cutting back refugee admissions.

2018: The Genetic Non-Discrimination Act makes it a criminal offense for a service provider or anyone entering into a contract with a person to require or compel that person to take, or disclose the results of, a genetic test in Canada.

2019: Shirley Raines officially registers Beauty 2 the Streets as a nonprofit organization serving unhoused individuals living in Skid Row.

2019: The Trump administration recognizes Israeli sovereignty over the Golan Heights.

2019: In Canada, The Final Report of the National Inquiry into Missing and Murdered Indigenous Women and Girls shares the truths of more than 2,380 family members, survivors of violence, experts and Knowledge Keepers collected during two years of cross-country public hearings and evidence gathering.

2019: The Parliament of Canada passes the National Housing Strategy Act, which recognizes housing as a human right and commits organizations and governments to reform housing laws, policies, and programs from a human rights perspective and to involve communities in meaningful ways.

2020: The Centers for Disease Control and Prevention and the World Health Organization declare a global health emergency due to the COVID-19 virus.

2020: The First Nations Act is enacted in Canada and creates minimum national standards for the delivery of child and family services to Indigenous people and establishes a clear pathway for Indigenous nations to enact their own child and family laws.

2022: Florida Governor Ron DeSantis signs the "Don't Say Gay Bill," which prohibits classroom discussion about sexual orientation or gender identity in certain grade levels or in a specified manner.

2022: US President Joseph Biden signs the Bipartisan Safer Communities Act, which provides more funding for mental health services and school security, expands criminal background checks for some gun buyers, bars a larger group of domestic-violence offenders from purchasing firearms, and funds Red Flag programs that allow police to seize guns from troubled individuals.

2023: The 2023 Anti-Homosexuality Act restricts the ability of LGBTQ+ Ugandans to participate in public life and engage in advocacy.

2023: US President Joseph Biden announces the "Asylum Ban," which blocks asylum seekers at the border from entering the United States for five years unless they obtain an appointment through the cellphone application "CBP One."

2023: Hamas launches a surprise attack on Israel.

2023: Israel launches "Operation Swords of Iron" against Gaza following Hamas attack.

2024: United States Senator Ben Cardin and Representative James McGovern introduce the *Human Rights Defenders Protection Act of 2024*, a bill that seeks to protect human rights defenders facing retaliation globally for defending human rights and democracy.

2024: The Human Rights Defenders Protection Act of 2024 enhances the United States' ability to protect individuals abroad who are attacked for peacefully defending human rights and democracy.

2024: Greece becomes the first Christian Orthodox-majority country to legalize same-sex marriage.

Glossary

Ableism: treatment of individuals according to their abilities or challenges, often used to describe maltreatment of people who have disabilities

Ageism: treatment of individuals in stereotyped ways according to their age; people at the extremes of the age spectrum are most likely to be negatively viewed or treated poorly

Arbitrary arrest: individuals who are arrested by authorities for questionable or no violations

Assembly: groups of people who get together for a common purpose

Authoritarianism: a form of government that is led by an individual or group with a special interest; citizens have a bit more participation than in an autocracy

Autocracy: a form of government that is totally controlled by a single person or group

BIPOC: Black, Indigenous, and people of color

Capital punishment: the death penalty

CEDAW: Convention on the Elimination of all Forms of Discrimination Against Women

Corporal punishment: use of violence to punish people or force their compliance

CRC: Convention on the Rights of the Child

DEI: diversity, equity, and inclusion

Disinformation: intentional lying about facts that are made to seem true

ERA: Equal Rights Amendment

ESCR: Economic, social, and cultural rights declaration

Human rights: human rights are the collective rights of everyone because everyone is a human being and member of the human family. They include civil rights, political rights, economic rights, social rights, cultural rights, and environmental rights that are inherent to all human beings, regardless of their sex, race, nationality, religion, ethnicity, language, ability, social class, or other factors.

ICCPR: International Covenant on Civil and Political Rights

ICPPED: International Convention for the Protection of All Persons from Enforced Disappearance

Inalienable: people cannot take the rights away from others

Indivisible: all rights are interconnected and cannot be divided since one impacts the other

LGBTQ+: lesbian, gay, bisexual, trans, questioning/queer, and other types of sexual or gender orientation

LPWP: life in prison without parole

Misinformation: inaccurate or skewed information that is presented as true but is not

Natural law: a fundamental premise of human rights that assumes that God is the giver of rights or natural law, and that human rights are universal, inalienable, and indivisible and cannot be taken away by anyone

Oligarchy: a form of leadership that is run by wealthy individuals or groups

Racism: maltreatment of individuals because of the color of their skin or other physical attributes

Sexism: treatment of individuals in a negative manner because of their perceived sex or gender

Terrorism: acts of political brutality or violence that are designed to provoke fear so that people can be manipulated, injured, or killed

UDHR: Universal Declaration of Human Rights

UNCAT: Convention Against Torture and Other Cruel, Inhuman or Degrading Treatment or Punishment is often referred to as the UN Convention Against Torture

Universal: rights belong to everyone, everywhere, no matter who you are

Values: broad ideas about how people believe they should live their best lives that inform ethics, morals, politics, and laws

Index

About the Author

Yvonne Vissing, PhD, is a sociologist, Professor of Healthcare Studies, and director of the Center for Childhood & Youth Studies at Salem State University. She is the author of twenty-five books, including titles on homelessness (*Changing the Paradigm of Homelessness* and *Out of Sight, Out of Mind*), unaccompanied and refugee youth (*Child and Youth Refugee Resettlement and Community Formation Issues* and *The Rights of Unaccompanied Minors: Perspectives and Case Studies*), globalization and social justice (*Discourses of Globalisation, Ideology and Social Justice* and *Globalisation, Ideology and Human Rights*), sports, and children's wellbeing. Her book on *Children's Human Rights: Challenges and Opportunities* is the primary book on children's rights. She is the US policy chair for the United Nation's Hope for Children Convention on the Rights of the Child Policy Center and a member of the Universities Network for Children in Armed Conflict. She is on the Human Rights Council for the American Association for the Advancement of Science, Steering Committee and Regional Representative for Human Rights Educators USA and is a consultant for the American Sociological Association. She a National Institute of Mental Health Post-Doctoral Research Fellow, Whiting Foundation fellow, UCONN democracy fellow, and a clinical sociologist.